D0779076

If You Hear the Message
Three Times, Listen

If You Hear the Message Three Times,

LISTEN

PATRICIA HELLER

HAMPTON ROADS
PUBLISHING COMPANY, INC.

Copyright © 2004
by Patricia Heller
All rights reserved, including the right to reproduce this
work in any form whatsoever, without permission
in writing from the publisher, except for brief passages
in connection with a review.

The Way We Were
from the motion picture THE WAY WE WERE
Words by Alan and Marilyn Bergman
Music by Marvin Hamlisch
©1973 (renewed 2001) COLGEMS–EMI MUSIC INC.
All rights reserved. International Copyright Secured.
Used by Permission.

Alfie
Theme from the Paramount Picture ALFIE
Words by Hal David
Music by Burt Bacharach
Copyright © 1966 (Renewed 1994) by Famous
Music Corporation
Internaional Copyright Secured. All Rights Reserved.

Blow Gabriel Blow by Cole Porter
©1934 (Renewed) WB Music Corp.
All rights reserved. Used by permission.
Warner Bros. Publications U.S. Inc., Miami Florida
33014

Bridge Over Troubled Water
Copyright © 1969 Paul Simon
Used by permission of the publisher: Paul Simon
Music

I Don't Know How to Love Him
by Andrew Lloyd Webber, Tim Rice
Copyright © 1971, renewed 1999 by Universal-
MCA Music Publ., on behalf of MCA Music Ltd.
[ASCAP] Used by permission. International copy-
right secured. All rights reserved.

Cover photograph and design by Steve Amarillo
Author photograph by East End Photography

Hampton Roads Publishing Company, Inc.
1125 Stoney Ridge Road
Charlottesville, VA 22902
434-296-2772
fax: 434-296-5096
e-mail: hrpc@hrpub.com
www.hrpub.com

1-800-766-8009 (orders only)

Library of Congress Cataloging-in-Publication Data

Heller, Patricia, 1947-
 If you hear the message three times, listen / Patricia Heller.
  p. cm.
 ISBN 1-57174-419-3 (alk. paper)
 1. Heller, Patricia, 1947---Health. 2. Chronic fatigue
syndrome--Patients--United States--Biography. 3. Healing. I. Title.
 RB150.F37H454 2004
 362.196'0478'0092--dc22

2004013414

10 9 8 7 6 5 4 3 2 1

Printed on acid-free paper in the United States

For

Dougie Lazer

My son.

My love.

My life.

He lives an extraordinary life in an ordinary way.

Being fearless he's taught me no fear.

*By watching him never falter to take a step forward
I've learned to step up.*

*Living with joy, compassion, and gratitude
he personifies heart-center.*

And with that said,

Don't forget, Dougie, I want a granddaughter.

Acknowledgements

My thanks to the many people who believed all along that I could write this book. While I never doubted I'd finish, many times I thought I was dragging it out.

Jody Stump jump-started this project when I mentioned I was thinking about taking a writing course or going back to college. She nonchalantly said, "Why don't you go to Yale, I hear they have a good program," like it was a fait accompli. Me at Yale? I went, life changed.

Thanks to Peggy and Winkie Kaufman and Wayne Viera for their support and the surprise party they gave a 50-year-old kid going off to university.

To the Nantucket writer's group and my first reader, June Meyer, goes much appreciation. I thank Susan Cole for her suggestions. Much love to my New York surrogate family who believe I make magic—Laura, Bill, and Danny Hagan, and our very special daughter, Diana.

My thanks to my first editor, writing teacher, and muse to the gods, Valery Pine Behr, who nudged this fledgling out to fly and write on her own. Our "chance" meeting in Hawaii was no coincidence.

Gary Kelly encouraged while I read aloud a first draft. To my believers in New Mexico, they, all successful in their own creative endeavors, never had a doubt about me and mine—Gabriella Lopez-Waterman, Linda Durham, Florence Sohn, Liz Rose, and Amy Lynn.

Many thanks to my other readers, Carolyn Conger, and the Colorado Springs Writing and Editing Group, whose insights and advice made my editing an easy job. To my sister Kat Tansey and sister-in-law Barbara Kimbell, my gratitude.

To Bill Gladstone for efforts on my behalf, and Bob Friedman, my publisher, thanks guys for liking what I had to say.

I'd be remiss not to thank all the teachers, instructors, and trainers who entered my life bringing their own brand of illumination to self-discovery, self-healing, and enlightenment—sometimes it was fun, sometimes bumpy—always clarifying. In particular—cups up to you, Brugh Joy.

Last, to all authors who have gone before me, you light the way.

Table of Contents

Part II. Healer

Part III. And Beyond

INTRODUCTION
Ordinary People—Extraordinary Experiences

I was always the child who required more sleep. When I was 30, I took this trait to the extreme. At the time, I was an active young mother with a budding career as a singer and actress. In the afternoon at four o'clock, I'd pick up Dougie, my six-year-old son, who because of dyslexia, went to the Lab School in Washington, D.C. Then, after dinner and getting everyone settled in, I'd run out to rehearsals for an 1890s music hall show at the British Embassy. Being so very American, I was introduced as "the guest from the colonies." I'd sing my heart out, return home between eleven and one, sleep, and be up and ready to go at 7 A.M. Following getting Doug off to school and my husband off to work, I'd put on my contractor's hat, go downstairs, and tell my subs what to do on the renovation of our Victorian town house in Dupont Circle. It was during this busy time that my life took an unexpected turn.

I became ill and couldn't get well. I began experiencing constant flu-like symptoms and overwhelming fatigue and slept all the time.

Doctors found nothing in their tests to confirm that anything was physically or psychologically wrong. Finally, several years later, after hundreds of thousands of others voiced the same complaints, my illness got a name. Atlanta's Centers for Disease Control called it chronic fatigue syndrome. They also reported that it was an autoimmune deficiency and that there was no cure.

I decided I was *not*, as the doctors recommended, going to learn to live with it. While I've always had an innate feeling we can heal ourselves from any illness, this illness certainly tested my theory. To this day, some people don't believe CFS is real, and those doctors who do still deem it incurable.

After 12 long years of exhausting every treatment in conventional, homeopathic, holistic, experimental, and even illegal medicine, I gave up and got on a plane to Arizona to go study something called heart-centered transformation, self-discovery, and spiritual enlightenment.

My fellow students at the conference were a mixed bag—everything from doctors of psychology, to former hippies, to people with strong religious upbringings—all of whom seemed to know more than I did about this sort of thing. I wasn't raised religious, nor did I have a conventional higher education, and as far as a flower-power/love-is-all-you-need philosophy from the sixties, I wasn't aware of Woodstock until it was over.

It didn't dawn on me that these people's backgrounds must not have been all that satisfying if they were there with me looking for something more.

So, why did I, in my mid-forties, play catch-up and pretend I fitted in?

I persevered because from the very beginning, what I learned, worked.

During the first week into the conference, I discovered how to heal myself. After 12 years of looking outside for answers, I found the answer inside in minutes. Sounds fantastic? It is. While it took time to integrate this knowledge into my life, I literally became well instantly. I also learned that I was able to facilitate healing in others by using energy radiating from my hands and by guiding them into their own self-discovery. *I had healing hands!* I didn't know what to do with them, but it was great incentive to keep going to find out.

During my years of study with various teachers and lots of books, I found answers to questions I'd had all my life. "How do I stay healthy? Are our lives guided?" And, "Is there a God?" Other questions like, "Why do I always win at drawings?" "How is it that I know what people are thinking before they do?" "Why can I call dice?" found answers, too.

Eventually I got to the point on my journey when a natural transition occurred and the need for teachers and books waned. I, as many others on this path, found my own individual connections to Source and universal messages were as clear as any minister, teacher, or psychic I admired.

When I'd be drawn to tell a friend or stranger a certain tale from my new life, I'd see an "aha" in their eyes. It was as if they were waiting for a message and I was the carrier. They were learning lessons without having to experience illness, intensive workshops, or pilgrimages to faraway places. The stories behind my various experiences seemed to have incredible healing powers.

It was time to write a book.

If You Hear the Message Three Times, Listen contains many messages that had to come to me in threes before I could hear and understand them. From those, I gleaned three major messages I share in this book.

First, there is no right or wrong way to make a transformational journey to self-healing, higher consciousness, and spiritual enlightenment. My story is certainly a testament to that fact. It didn't take me long to realize that transformation doesn't always mimic the images we see in films or read about in books. Most times it was quite the opposite. You will laugh at some of the irreverent circumstances surrounding many of my biggest breakthroughs.

The second message is that we can heal ourselves from any illness. I believe anyone can achieve health the way I did. By sharing the history of the treatments I tried, I hope to save you time and money. Don't think I reject conventional medicine. Conventional medicine can be very beneficial and has a valuable place in the healing process. It saves lives. What I learned is that we must tune in and listen to our own innate healing messages if we want a lasting cure.

The third message is to affirm that gifts of healing, intuition, and manifestation are available to anyone willing to open to them. I'll tell you how amazing things surfaced during my heart-centered transformational journey—everything from heightened intuition to the manifestation of healing powers, money, and love. And, I'll show you how the big jump in my learning curve happened when I accepted that *there are no coincidences.*

So, please, read on with a beginner's mind. Allow yourself to be a clean slate, *tabula rasa.* If an idea or story I present resonates, sit with it. If something I say strikes you as inconceivable, consider the possibility. If I make you question, reconsider, or open your heart, I've fulfilled my intention.

My love to you,

Patricia Heller, New Mexico

PART I

healing

I

RUNNING ON WATER: Transformation, Enlightenment, Passion, and Purpose

On an island in Hawaii, an ancient cave leads down to a beautiful, large underground lake. It's hard to find. Hawaiians protect their spiritual places by not marking them. The islanders say that Pélé, the Goddess of Fire, formed the underground cavern as she prodded the area with a stick in search of an appropriate home site. Instead of striking fire, she struck water. Thus Pélé moved on, eventually making her home in the fiery crater of the Kilauea volcano.

Climbing up to the entrance of the Waikapala cave, one immediately senses the spirit of this serene yet rugged area of Kauai, a feeling the old Hawaiians call *mana*, which translates into "a power that emanates from sacred places." Once inside the cavern, it's about 40 or 50 feet down to the lake, lit only by the opening to daylight. A handful of the participants in the Sacred Space Conference I was attending used the *mana* of this deep, dark lake as a kind of spiritual bath. Swimming together, they made their way across the water, held their breath, dove under a ledge, and surfaced in a small blue lagoon. There they felt as honored as if it were a *heiaus*, a place of worship.

Although I was wearing my swimsuit, I came up with an excuse not to join them. I'd always been a water baby. I was a life-guard, a synchronized swimmer, and a certified scuba diver. I knew the importance of swimming with a buddy. But at this point in the sensual, heart-pounding, altered space of Kauai, I felt I could do anything and be just fine. I wanted to experience this sacred place alone.

Several days later, I returned to the cave unaccompanied. Our conference teacher told us with a smile that to find the cave entrance, all one had to do was turn left and cross the street at the two egrets. A joke, to be sure. Yet, as I walked across the one-lane bridge over the Wainiha River on the road that ends at beautiful Ke'e beach, there they were, two stately white birds standing in the field directly across from the footpath that led up the hill to the cave.

Because it was a gray, dismal day, I had the cavern to myself. I quickly took off all my clothes, placed them neatly on a clean, large rock, and touched my toe in the water. It was comfortably warm. I dove in.

In my mind's eye, I had imagined how it would be: my long, naked body gliding gracefully to the spot where I would dive under a rock wall and magically surface on the other side in a mystical blue lagoon, a sacred place where questions would be answered and lives transformed. I thought with a smile, *Perfect.*

As I hit the water, I was mortified to find I was gripped with such cold, I thought I was going to drown from the shock. I felt as if I was being sucked down into a black abyss. What happened to the warm water?! Panicked, I struggled to find a way out of the imaginary vortex swirling around me to get back to the safety of the land. Although I'd made a shallow dive, it seemed like hours before I broke the surface, gasping for air. The cold hit my body so hard, it pushed the air out of my lungs. It was only 20 feet back to land, and though I swam as fast as I could, the journey seemed endless. I remember thinking, *What the heck is going on? The water wasn't cold when I tested it. Why is this happening?*

When I got back on dry land, I dressed and sat on the rocks for a while, more curious than shaken or disappointed. The last lines from "I Don't Know How to Love Him" from the rock Broadway hit *Jesus Christ Superstar* came to my mind. They poured from my heart as I sang in this acoustically perfect place.

He's a man, he's just a man
and I've had so many men before in very many ways.
He's just one more.
Should I bring him down? Should I scream and shout?
Should I speak of love? Let my feelings out?
I never thought I'd come to this.
What's it all about?
Yet, if he said he loved me, I'd be lost, I'd be frightened,
I couldn't cope, just couldn't cope. I'd turn my head, I'd back
    away,
I wouldn't want to know.
He's scares me so, I love him so, I want him so.

At first, after spontaneously singing this, I was afraid I was falling for the conference teacher. I got embarrassed about this for a moment and then let it go. Becoming a groupie for anyone certainly wasn't my style. So what was going on? The obvious, that I was afraid of surrendering to something higher than myself, never occurred to me. I kept asking, *Who was I singing to? And what fear was so intense that it could have caused this bizarre reaction? What would turn warm water freezing cold?*

I slowly walked back alongside Makana Mountain to our beach houses, enmeshed in thought. I considered the metaphor of "diving" into my own subconscious to understand why I couldn't make the cave dive. That only confused me more. I walked on. Even my roommate, who wasn't a great swimmer, had gone to the cave and had successfully made the dive alone.

I was glad I hadn't broadcast my intentions to anyone at the conference. I didn't want my ego bruised a second time. I'd felt enough embarrassment at dinner the night before when I'd mentioned I was writing a book. Inevitably, I was asked, "What's the title?" I hemmed and hawed, uncomfortable that I had to dance around the fact I didn't have one. Trudging on, I continued to think about my book, a book on my own self-healing.

Now, that had been a long journey.

Twelve years spent going to endless doctors, accepting any treatment that offered even a modicum of relief for my "incurable" illness. Twelve long years before I could accept what I'd always known in my heart, that we all have the ability to heal ourselves. I smiled when I thought how stubborn I'd been about letting go of the search for answers outside myself. When I finally was able to grasp the possibility that we have more responsibility for what happens to us in our lives than I'd thought, I still had to hear the message on how to get well *three times* in *three different ways* before I could accept and understand it.

As I walked on, I continued to muse over that for a while. Letting go of old beliefs is hard. I had to hear the answer three times, *three* times. Maybe that was another metaphor for my life. I needed to listen more closely. Then it hit me, *Wait a minute,* I realized. *What was I saying? That's it! If You Hear the Message Three Times, Listen!*

That's the name of my book!

I had gone to the cave to be transformed in a blue lagoon. I had some vague notion of a Hollywood-type production with me, as Esther Williams, swimming off into the water to receive the meaning of life. *Bring up the blue lagoon lights, boys, Patricia's on her way.* Transformation would have included golden white light exploding everywhere and me with a sainted, beatific look on my face, hands in prayer position, dressed in gossamer white, levitating back to shore to live the rest of my life in a serene holy state of grace.

I did get answers and had my life transformed that day, just not in the style I'd foreseen. Instead of the sacred vision I imagined, I starred as more of a cartoon character, shooting up out of the icy pond, legs spinning around at the knees as I raced across the water leaving puffs of clouds behind in my frantic attempt to get back to shore.

When I left the cave without making my sacred dive, I walked home deflated. Gone was any ego about being a great swimmer and going it alone. Gone, too, were my expectations of coming out changed and enlightened. I was humbled, vulnerable, and open.

My cave experience taught me that in order for me to hear the messages coming through to me, my ego has to be put aside in one way or another. Tough order. I don't want to count how many times my ego has had to be distracted so a message could be heard.

While I was motivated by ego to begin a transformational journey (ego took me to the cave), it wasn't until after the black needle came out (the illusion of cold water) and punctured my ego-inflated balloon that lasting changes or insights took place (the name of my book).

I started my dive that day with an attitude that I could walk on water. Learning happened only after my bubble burst and I found myself in the water, up to my neck in humility.

My path was sealed that day. With a name, my book would become a reality. Could I quiet, distract, or surrender my ego enough times to hear all the messages I needed? And, was there a right way to go about this?

2

THERE'S NO RIGHT OR WRONG WAY:
The Individual Path to higher Consciousness

One day in March 1997, I called my friend Duane and suggested we go for a walk. We both, as it happened, were following new paths to careers we always wanted. While we loved what we were doing, there were times when feelings of scarcity and fear attached themselves to our processes of starting new lives at 50. We decided a walk on Nantucket's moors would be the perfect antidote.

Duane, a native of this small, faraway island, has an intimate bond with its secrets and treasures, along with a noticeably heightened sense of sight and hearing. These facts were never clearer to me than on that spring day.

Not long after we began our walk, he pointed out the scratchings on trees made by deer shedding their antlers. As we continued, I told him about an artist friend in Vancouver who creates powerful art out of the death and regeneration of animals in nature. Two seconds later, he reached down and picked up the left side of a buck's four-point horn lying on the ground, one tip broken from a wound long ago. He was excited. Never, in the countless times he'd been through the moors, had he come upon a buck's antlers. I was awarded this prize to send to my artist friend.

Duane was leading us on our usual route. We left my house in Polpis, cut through my neighbor's yard on top of a small hill to get to a winding deer path that would eventually take us to the dirt road that runs through the moors. From there, the road allows an easier, faster walk.

On that day, however, when he pointed to the dirt road, I said it seemed more adventuresome to stay in the moors. Turning back, he chose a deer's path we'd never traveled before. Winding through the long way with mattress grass brushing against our pant legs and stickers attaching to shoelaces, we branched off onto a path that led through a small pine grove the dreaded bark beetles hadn't yet found. After a while, we turned onto a different trail that skirted around bayberry bushes. Finally, path after path, we came to a halt at a spot surrounded by what seemed to be an impenetrable thicket of scrub oak. When we stopped to look around, the sounds of our crashing through the thick underbrush subsided, and the clearing became calm and quiet.

Simultaneously we noticed two seldom-used paths leading through the brambles. I suggested that the right one seemed less dense, but Duane had already headed purposefully off to the left. Bending down to deer height, we made our way under the scrub oaks and into the deep thicket. By this time, we'd traveled at least an hour and several winding miles into unknown territory. Duane, ahead of me by about ten feet, let out a whoop. When I caught up to him, he was standing with an incredulous look of wonder on his face. In his hands, he held the perfect right side of the buck's four-point antlers.

There are no accidents. What seem to be coincidences in our lives are actually messages and guides. If we quiet ourselves, we are able to hear them.

That night as I fell off to sleep, I asked, "Please, what is the message behind finding the deer's horns?"

This is what I heard.

"You can't go home again"—Thomas Wolfe. *Follow the deer's path. Let go the past and shed things that hold back, for while old broken ways seem a safe link back in time, in reality they restrict. Shed even more. Shed ways that seem strong, perfect, and unbroken, for they now unbalance and catch in the inevitable thickets of life's path, forever looping the path back to the old. Allow the dizzying freedom of no restrictions to prevail. Then, gently, move without restraint into the clearing of true self—neither masculine nor feminine. Feel safe. Points of light emanating from you are already forming into a more radiant crown.*

Just as Duane and I hadn't set out to find the treasures we discovered on our circuitous route, I didn't just stop and say to myself in 1993, "I think I'll embark on a path of self-discovery to higher consciousness." I had no idea that was what I was doing, much less what path I would take. I was simply trying to get well, and the only option left to me was to go outside conventional medicine to recover my health.

I had much to shed from the way I was living my life. Illness being the way for me to learn to lead a more enlightened life was one. Like the deer's antlers, my old ways had to be cast off one after another.

I did learn tenacity and surrender through chronic fatigue syndrome. Not only did I feel terrible, I had to fight for my right to feel that way. I learned to stand up for what I feel. CFS taught me to be selfish about what I need and selfless when things are bigger than me.

I had many of CFS's companion illnesses: environmental illness (poisoned by twentieth-century man-made chemicals), candidiasis (an imbalance of yeast), and low levels of metal toxicity. My thyroid was attacking my own body, and my immune system was always "on," continuously fighting off everything, good or bad, exhausting the rest of my system. Last, I was found to be a universal allergic reactor to everything I inhaled, ingested, or put on my skin. I was allergic to the world.

I was told the only thing I could do was to clean up my environment and learn to live with it. Here is an example of what "living with it" would have meant.

Imagine someone has given you a big bottle of liquid lead to drink. As you swallow, it goes into your bloodstream and turns your blood into slow-moving lead. In every artery and every vein, thick, heavy, slushy lead flows, weighting you down and making your movements inordinately slow and difficult.

And because the lead is toxic to your system, as it moves through your bloodstream, it poisons every muscle, every tendon, making them tender and sore and not quite able to function properly. As the liquid continues moving, the poison makes your brain hurt. Cognitive functions are so fuzzy, it feels like your brain is wrapped in layers upon layers of gauze. Thinking hurts. Remembering? Not possible.

Next, your lungs ache, just a little, slightly congested. A day later, that symptom's gone, but now your heart feels bruised. You have palpitations, anxieties, just a little, not for long.

On the day the poison hits your throat, it strips a layer of skin and makes it a little raw, a little sore, a little raspy, but only on some days.

On different days, you could go through your entire body feeling every organ, sometimes, not quite functioning up to par. Everything hurts from the lead, but not always, and not always that bad, and the symptoms keep moving.

You continually feel like you are getting the flu, but you never do. Actually, you'd love to get the flu, so you could get sick and get well. But, no such luck. Instead, you just drag around complaining, and every now and then you begin to think you are going crazy.

Eventually it all comes down to the fact that even the thought of doing anything mundane and routine becomes overwhelming.

Like a Shower

As I peered out from my hiding place
deep inside my bed
I noticed someone had moved the bathroom miles away.
After taking what seemed like hours to cover the distance
I sat down exhausted on the side of the bathtub.

11

Hauling myself up, I opened the shower door,
turned on the water,
tested the water, and wondered if I was allergic to water.
Pulling my nightgown over my head
I climbed in.

As I lifted the hypoallergenic shampoo
I thought, "Why is this little bottle so heavy?"
When I slowly lifted my leaden hands up
to massage in the shampoo
I noticed even my hair hurt.

Going through the same, slow motion
with the conditioner,
I left it on and washed,
then rinsed the rest of my body.
Finally, dragging myself out of the shower
I crept back to bed.
Before passing out,
I lay wrapped in a wet towel
and groaned at the realization that . . .

I'd forgotten to brush my teeth.

This is an example of what doctors wanted me to learn to live with.

Not acceptable.

I was totally unconscious at the time about the possibility that there might be a connection between my mind, my body, and my spirit. As it turned out, at the time most of the doctors and health practitioners I went to were unconscious about it, too.

So began my 12-year quest for health through conventional, homeopathic, holistic, experimental, and illegal practices. I started with a conventional doctor, an internist, who, when all my tests came back negative, patted me on the derriere and told me to see a psychiatrist. I did. I went to the foremost psychiatrist in Washington, D.C. He pronounced me very intuitive and self-analytical, said I didn't need him, and wished me luck on my quest for health. I went on to a chiropractor, who told me about Dr. Crook's book, *The Yeast Connection*. I tried an anti-yeast diet of only meat, fish, chicken, eggs, and vegetables. I got skinny but not well. Niacin, and then nystatin were prescribed to kill yeast. Nothing changed.

When the next doctor found I was allergic to everything for which I was tested, it mattered not whether I was breathing the substance, eating, or touching it, I was called a "universal reactor." I did self-injected allergy shots and sublingual drops. On an elimination diet, I ate tubers from South America and bear meat from Canada, the theory being if I hadn't eaten it before, I couldn't be allergic to it. My husband and I had our new home stripped of anything that might cause allergies—brand new wall-to-wall carpeting was taken up because it out-gassed formaldehyde; all plants except spider plants were given away because of mold. I had all the mercury fillings in my teeth replaced with porcelain so the mercury wouldn't leak into my system. While my smile looked really good, I still felt lousy.

In Pennsylvania, I had about a pint of my blood removed, mixed with ozone and vitamins, and put back into my body via an intravenous drip three times a week for months. Then, I was allergic to the B vitamins in the drip.

In Manhattan, I tried megadoses of intravenous vitamin C (100,000 cc three times a week). I had a treatment in California for two months—low-heat/fresh-air saunas for three to four hours a day to sweat out the low levels of chemical poisoning. At the Pritikin Institute in Florida, I learned that a CFS patient couldn't function on a low-salt diet. Without salt even the slightest bit of exercise caused me to collapse. (Johns Hopkins now has a study that confirms this need for salt.)

In Houston, I tried a drug called Kudipressian that had been used for years in Europe for victims of chemical warfare, but my major virus turned out to be cytomegalovirus, not Epstein-Barr, and this treatment had only been successful with EBV. At Hippocrates Health Institute in West Palm Beach, I ate organic raw vegetables, drank liquefied wheat grass (yuck), and gave myself enemas twice a day. Yes, I did say enemas.

I traveled to a doctor in North Carolina who had become well known for treating CFS. His approach was to "get 'em in, get 'em all on antidepressant drug treatment, strict diets, multitudes of vitamins and herbs, and get 'em out. Call in six months." Next, I tried a therapy written up on the cover of *Newsweek* that alternated exercise and rest with hot and cold treatments to raise and lower the heart rate. The theory here was if all the organs could be "tricked" into working in unison, the immune system could heal itself.

After that, there was an intravenous treatment in Florida and the Bahamas—an herbal concoction of enzymes, thymus from a calf's embryo, vitamins, and the illegal part—DMSO, dimethyl sulfoxide. The DMSO was used as a ferrying agent for the herbs. A friend of mine who races horses in Florida came to see me during this treatment and instantly recognized I was using DMSO because of the horrible garlic smell I gave off. He said he had been using it on his horses forever to enhance delivery of anti-inflammatory drugs to swelling. Apparently I smelled just like his horses. Nice. Along with this treatment, I also had colonics (more thorough enemas) every day and took 20-minute ozone baths daily in a steam cabinet with ozonated water shooting onto my body. It was alleged to cleanse in 20 minutes what it would take the liver three days to accomplish. I also put ozone in all the orifices of my body daily—every single one.

I tried reflexology—pressure points on the nerve endings in the feet to facilitate healing. Finally, my last attempt to find a cure was acupuncture and a horrible-tasting expensive muddy-looking herbal mixture administered by a very strange Chinese doctor.

Twelve years, twenty-one treatments, and hundreds of thousands of dollars. I met some very dedicated people and others possibly not so dedicated. For me, it all was necessary. All the detoxing I did for my allergic-to-the-world immune system must have helped. However, sustained wellness still eluded me. Before I could learn the way to lasting health, I had to go through another major jolt that would literally knock me from my present way of living.

3

Tbe Deatb of Denial: Love and Friendship—Grief, Sorrow, and Loss

It was seven o'clock on Wednesday morning, April 10, 1991, at the Park Hotel in Charlotte, North Carolina. The phone ringing brought me out of the few minutes of restless sleep I'd had during a night filled with anxiety and sadness.

I'd been in and out of bed all night on the phone with the nurse in intensive care at the Charlotte Memorial Hospital trying to make sure Alfred's wishes were going to be honored. It had started at three, when I awakened feeling a need to call and ask how he was doing. Alfred, my big, handsome, loving husband, had been in intensive care for three weeks after his second cardiac arrest in four months.

Kay, the young, blond nurse on duty, had taken a special interest in us, becoming a friend over the weeks. Tonight she told me about a conversation she'd had with Alfred in which he told her he was now ready to die. I gasped, and a lump formed in my throat. Sadly, I told her that that day I, too, had decided to let him go, and had made sure his hospital chart reflected that no extraordinary lifesaving measures were to be used any longer.

She quietly said, "No, Patricia, his chart still says full stat."

I was horrified. Alfred was ready to go, I was willing to let him go, and because of some miscommunication, he was going to have to suffer more indignities by living only through machines? I told her to change the chart. She replied that she couldn't, only a doctor could.

I almost yelled, "I'm his wife. If he wants to die, then he is going to die." I calmed down and told her to call Francis. Dr. Francis Robicsek was a noted heart surgeon and the chief of staff of the hospital. More important to us, he was Alfred's best friend and had been the best man at our wedding. Eight years before, when Francis had performed Alfred's quadruple bypass, they'd become close, fast friends. Francis is a commanding presence, tall, and lean in stature, with thinning hair and a craggy face, and he likes the word "cats."

"Call Francis and get him to change it now," I insisted. She called back to say he wasn't answering his page. It was now about three-thirty. I said, "I'm on my way. If Alfred wants to die, they will have to go through me to stop him." I threw on a long skirt and was pulling a light, loose sweater over my head when Francis called to say he had changed the chart to state that no extraordinary lifesaving measures were to be taken. Kindly, he mentioned nothing about the fact he'd suggested I change the chart and even pull the plug on the dialysis machine and intravenous feedings two weeks before. At the time, I wouldn't even consider it. I was following Alfred's lead. Even though he was connected to all sorts of machines, Alfred never once considered he was dying, so neither did I. We were still talking, smiling, and loving each other as we had for seven years.

The crisis had only been going on for three weeks. Just a few days before, I'd mentioned to Alfred I might leave his sickbed and fly up to New York for the day to attend the closing on a house we were selling. He'd said, "Wait until next week, and I'll go with you." We were in such denial. Death wasn't talked about or even considered. In my numb state I followed his lead, and played our game magnificently.

16

Earlier that week, I'd asked Francis why he didn't get Alfred a new heart. Francis was as well known in the medical community as famed heart surgeon Michael DeBakey, and if anyone had pull, he did. He tried to explain, "Patricia, with his overall health condition he would be sixteenth on the list for a heart. They are given to people who have the greatest chance of benefiting from them." I was way beyond caring about anyone else. I greedily wanted Alfred to have a chance, any chance. Francis added, "Besides, he'd also need a liver, lungs, and kidneys." I said, "Then get them." Francis gave me a hug and walked away.

I'd met Alfred in the fall of 1984, when my neighbor in Dupont Circle decided to be a matchmaker. He was her New York boyfriend's best friend. When Alfred and I met, it was love at first sight. Shortly into our first phone call, Alfred asked me to join him for brunch. He said by the time I got to the airport there would be a ticket for me at the Washington National/La Guardia shuttle and he'd be at the airport in New York to greet me. He was there. Dark hair, dark tan—all big and tall, with his chest puffed out. He was wearing a blue suede sports jacket, white shirt, gray slacks, and black loafers with tassels, and was almost beside himself with delight when he saw me.

I looked good. I was trim, wearing a red Anne Klein pantsuit and three-inch red heels that made me six-foot-one, and my shoulder-length blond hair was topped off with a red fedora.

While there were a couple of rocky times in our two-year courtship, we were pretty much inseparable for the next seven years.

Now at the hospital, all I thought about was that I didn't want Alfred to suffer any more. Three days earlier, he had asked to be allowed to sit up in a chair. Francis agreed, and two strong male attendants in white T-shirts and white pants carried Alfred out of bed and put him into a wheelchair. He had no strength to help at all. He was emaciated and slumped over. As they were tying him to the chair with a sheet, I kept getting in the way, trying to pull up the pastel printed hospital gown that continually fell off his left shoulder. The room became stuffy and close with antiseptic smells that were sickly sweet. There were so many people, everyone in the intensive care unit who wanted to help Alfred in his wish to live was there to support him. His room was filled to overflowing with attendants, nurses, doctors, and well-wishers.

I had to bend down so Alfred could peer at me from his sagging head, seemingly too heavy to hold up. His eyes were still so alive. No fear showed in them, just a kind of resigned recognition. After a few moments, he motioned to go back to bed.

Looking back, I realize that was the turning point. The look of recognition in his eyes was surrender. He realized his body had deserted him, leaving no life-sustaining system. His mind was as clear as the day I met him, but his body was spent. Back in bed, he slipped into a coma from the exhaustion of sitting up. I sat by him, laid my head on his arm looking at his handsome face with his soft flawless skin. I kissed him gently and whispered, "Thank you, my darling, for fighting so hard to stay and not leave me. Please know that if it is too hard, I will understand if you don't want to fight any longer."

The three weeks had been surreal. At that moment I wasn't thinking of consequences, I was thinking only how horrible it was to see Alfred totally depleted when he'd always been so vibrant. At that point, I had no idea I was the reason he was still alive, yet something inside me knew he wouldn't leave without my permission. He knew how much I counted on him. He so loved taking care of everyone—everyone, and especially me. He was the only man in my life who lived up to my expectations of making me feel safe and secure. Anything I wanted, he gave me. Anywhere I wanted to go, he got me there. Everything I wanted to do, he made sure I could. His wish for me was always to be happy and well. Happy, I was; wellness, with his loving support, I was constantly chasing.

In the hospital I fluctuated between reality and disbelief that he could ever leave me. The day before he died, he said to me, "Tell everyone good-bye for me. Don't forget anyone."

And, "Patricia, I love you so much you have no idea."

If I'd only realized. At that point I was in such denial, I didn't understand that these were his carefully chosen last words.

Looking back, I see there were other signs he might have known what was happening. He asked me to arrange for my son, Doug, to fly down from boarding school on Long Island so he could see him, I now realize, one last time.

At seven that morning, the phone continued to ring until I pulled myself out of a groggy sleep to answer it. It was Dr. Robicsek saying, "Patricia, Alfred's gone into cardiac arrest. We will not resuscitate."

I said, "I'm on my way."

His reply was, "Don't hurry. You won't make it."

I told him I was still dressed from my aborted trip at 3 A.M. and I'd be right over.

As I rounded the corner of the long, sterile, white hall to Alfred's room, I could see him through the window in the door. There he was. My Alfred. Oh, he looked so good, so peaceful, and I was oh, so happy to see him. The tubes were gone. All the hideous tubes that had been poking into him everywhere had been taken away. For an instant my heart sang, "He's back. Alfred's back with me as he was before he got sick."

Then it hit me. No. He's not back. The missing tubes meant just one thing.

As I crossed over to his bed, I could see the nurses dressed in white at their workstation through the glass in the interior door. I was glad they didn't see me. I slid my arm under Alfred's back, laid my head down on his chest, held him, and cried. I could still feel his warmth and, when I snuggled my face into his chest, I could smell his familiar musky scent.

"Oh, my, God," I moaned. "What made me think it would be okay for him to die?"

I thought I'd be relieved when his pain and suffering ended.

Now all I selfishly wanted was Alfred alive and back with me, no matter what the circumstances or his pain.

He was gone, my best friend and most ardent supporter was gone.

When Alfred passed away, I didn't know what I thought about death. Before his passing, the only feeling I'd had when someone close died was a kind of nebulous anger. At what? I wasn't sure.

I suppose it was an irrational anger that we had no choice but to live an existence in which people leave those who love them. It made no sense to me, but I had no support system or beliefs to see me through, so anger was what I felt.

I had an innocence surrounding what should and shouldn't happen when a person passed on. Was there an afterlife? If so, just what was it comprised of? I liked the idea of friendly ghosts and spirits, but I didn't have much faith in stories surrounding them.

My only supernatural experience with the deceased had happened ten years before, when my 34-year-old best girlfriend was in the hospital with a cerebral hemorrhage after a diet of mostly stress (her husband had gone bankrupt), Dexatrim, coffee, cigarettes, light beers, and small amounts of food to lose weight. She came to me in a dream and said very calmly, "Patricia, I'm dead." I found out at her funeral that several other people had had similar experiences at the time of her death.

After Alfred died, I felt as though he still watched over me. One night in 1992, about a year after his death and during an exceptionally bad week in the estate battle his family was waging, I had a dream Alfred visited me. The dream was so vivid, I could feel his warmth and even smell the Aramis cologne he'd reluctantly stopped using because I was allergic to it.

In the dream, we were sitting in the corner of a plush green L-shaped sofa talking about various things. I said, "If we're going to sit around and talk like this, can I ask you about the estate mess?"

Alfred's answer was, "Yes." And that was the end of the dream.

Over the next few weeks, I tried in vain to reconnect with him in my dreams, hoping he could give me some indication of his wishes for the estate. I had been locked into a bitter battle since the week after his death. His brother, David, who had also been his business partner, and Alfred's son, Peter, contested his will. Not only did I have to deal with the death of the love of my life, I had the added shock of no resources but my own to fall back on. And, I was still ill.

Alfred's brother had been furious with him for marrying me, presumably because I wasn't Jewish. He hadn't attended our wedding, which infuriated Alfred. Because Alfred was so upset, David harbored his ill feelings until after his brother's death five years later, and then produced a never-before-seen, inequitable partnership agreement that purported to have been signed by Alfred three months before I met him in 1984 and three months after his quadruple bypass surgery.

This "*agreement*" stated that if David died, everything went to David's family, and if Alfred died, everything went to David. There was never an explanation as to why anything so unbalanced would have been written, and never any validation that Alfred actually signed it.

David and his attorneys did all sorts of nasty things geared to grinding me down. In deposition, David actually called our marriage "religious genocide." He astounded me time and again with his level of malevolence. There was one incident that backfired on him. He had his lawyers demand all the pictures Alfred and I'd taken during our seven years together. I get a smirk of satisfaction to this day when I remember the look on the courier's face when he realized he would have to go back to get a handtruck. He had to make two trips to handle the eight large book boxes filled with thousands of photos. It must have cost a fortune to have people at the law office paw through all the pictures of Alfred and me smiling, kissing, hugging, and laughing our way through our marriage and vacations.

In all my attempts to connect to Alfred again through my dreams, nothing happened. I couldn't get back to that place of safety and security I had felt the night he visited. I shared my dream with my yoga teacher and asked if she knew anything about meditation and, "Could I possibly reach Alfred that way?" This was the first time the old saying, "When the student is ready the teacher appears," applied to me.

Short, perfectly shaped Meredith with reddish-brown hair framing her sweet face wouldn't promise she could connect me to Alfred. She did say she would lead me in meditations to inner guidance. Having never meditated before, I had no idea what she was talking about.

When we started, I was lying on the carpeted floor in the exercise room. She told me to close my eyes. In a soft voice, she guided me through relaxing my body with liquid golden light that flowed from my head and moved through every organ and body part to my feet. Then she said, "I want you to visualize a sacred room." Next she told me to request a guide to come forth to answer questions for my highest and greatest good. Most times, my guide was a kind of nameless faceless entity who had comforting, but no earth-shattering, messages for me.

One day, however, when I was directed to ask my guide to enter my sacred room, completely unexpectedly, in walked Alfred.

He was perfect.

He shuffled into the sacred room with his proud way of walking, shoulders back, chest out, and feet barely off the ground, leading with his heart. He was dressed, not in my favorite outfit, but his, the red, paisley short-sleeved silk Gucci shirt, and red suspenders holding up his Lee jeans. He was wearing his gray sneakers with the Velcro closings (he didn't like messing with laces) instead of the tasseled brown Jordan loafers I had always liked.

I sighed with happiness.

My Alfred.

I asked my long-awaited question again, "Alfred, can you help me with the estate mess?"

This time he replied, "Don't worry about it, Patricia. It's all taken care of."

This simple statement was what I needed to hear. It instantly brought me peace. I didn't have to wonder what he meant. I knew. It was the beginning of my realization that it's how you view things, not how they turn out that shapes your life.

I knew that no matter what happened with the estate, win or lose, I'd be just fine.

Alfred's shared wisdom that day started me on a new path to healing.

And, that was not his only visit.

On another day when Meredith was guiding Vita, my assistant, and me, I was aware I wasn't very deep in meditation. I could feel myself lying on the exercise room floor carpet and was conscious of everything going on around me. I was miffed at myself. While I didn't have anything specific to ask, I wanted to be in Alfred's presence again and didn't feel I was "doing" this session right.

I was also thinking Vita would get to see Alfred, and I wouldn't, since I wasn't in a deep meditative state. The year before, on the night Alfred died, tiny four-foot-ten-inch Vita, with her short raven hair, had been on vacation at her parents in the Philippines. In the middle of the night, her sister saw a man going up the stairs to Vita's room. Vita saw Alfred in her dream. He said to her, "Vita, please take care of Mrs. Heller for me."

She replied, "I will, Mr. Heller."

I just knew she was going to see him, and I wasn't.

With envious thoughts toward Vita in my heart and my conscious awareness of my surroundings, I was certain this session was a loss. Then, at the same time all the chatter was going on in my head, I felt a presence around me. Slowly, yet suddenly, a heaviness descended upon my body from above. Someone or something had lain down on top of me. Shaken and curious, I stayed with it, feeling the pressure of a body on my body and sensing a now familiar presence.

It was Alfred.

He went to hold me and put his arms around me in a compassionate embrace. While I was amazed and frightened, I was also exhilarated and ecstatic to have the familiar feeling of his loving arms around me.

Then he started to make love to me.

I actually felt sexual pressure and movement, and silently freaked. Without making a noise so I wouldn't disrupt Vita and Meredith, I jerked myself out of whatever was happening.

When I asked my meditation teacher about the episode, she said, "Oh that happens all the time when people have died too soon or have left something undone. They come back to comfort the one they love."

Over the next three years, Alfred came back two more times to make love to me. I wasn't even trying to summon him but I was very relaxed and open. Those times were once in meditation when I was alone sitting upright on the floor of my New York apartment and the other after I'd moved to Nantucket while I was resting on a massage table in my home after an extremely relaxing, meditative massage. When I felt his presence, I stayed very centered and balanced and had what I can only describe as full body orgasms. Starting at my heart, it was as if thousands of light beams were radiating out to every part of my body. An explosion of ecstasy, like fireworks, filled my heart, my head, and my sexual being with a blissful feeling of oneness with everything in the universe.

Alfred's brother's vendetta went on for seven years. David never weakened in his resolve that he deserved his brother's money or that he had any obligation to honor his brother's wishes. At one point in the battle, my lawyers and their wildly exorbitant fees became the biggest threat to my security. In midstream, I learned about a contingency plan they hadn't mentioned and switched to it. Now instead of an hourly rate, they would receive one-third of what they won or 25 percent of their bill, whichever was larger.

Throughout it all, I kept hearing Alfred saying, "Don't worry, Patricia. It's all taken care of," and hung on to the fact there was a bigger picture.

Finally, I let it all go. David had strung the fight out past the Internal Revenue Service statute of limitations, so not only would he receive the money Alfred intended for me, he wouldn't pay the inheritance tax of two million dollars he owed. It just didn't matter to me anymore. I gave David Alfred's share of Perfect Manufacturing Company. I would have paid all the money I lost to learn what I had in those seven years. One, money is only a tool—inner peace can't be bought, nor health; and two, there is always more money. Without even trying, I was making a fortune buying and selling homes for myself.

Although the pain of losing Alfred was great, his passing was

a turning point for me. After death, Alfred found a way
me the most precious gift of all—death of denial and a tran
mation to higher consciousness. Now my real journey was abou
to begin.

4

IF YOU hEAR ThE MESSAGE ThREE TIMES, LISTEN: healing from Illness

Wings spread wide, the red-tailed hawk made three large circles in the sky as he watched the black Cadillac sedan approaching from miles away. Perfectly timed just before the car turned off the paved road, the hawk soared down and landed on a mound of dirt next to the entrance of the Wildflower Lodge Conference Center in Paulden, Arizona. Behind him were miles of dry, flat, dusty land all the way to Black Mountain where the car was headed. Only a few scrubby cacti, sprigs of sage, scrawny tumbleweed, and great spiny yucca plants shooting out six-foot flowers broke up the terrain. The regal hawk stood on his knoll welcoming us to this land of high desert as if he were an elegantly dressed doorman at a Park Avenue apartment building. My driver voiced his surprise at this unusual sight.

That was July of 1993. Major changes had occurred since Alfred's death two years before. I'd just moved into New York City after selling our house in Long Island. Through women in a course I'd been taking in the city called "Overcoming Overwhelm," I'd found a meditation teacher, Barbara Biziou, who has authored two beautiful books on rituals, *The Joy of Rituals* and *The Joy of Family Rituals*. When Barbara first came to my apartment, she said she thought we'd met. Noticing Doug's school newsletter on my entry table, she cried out, "I've got it! Our sons went to the same school in Connecticut. I saw you and your husband win the Mercedes at the drawing on parents' weekend!"

Nine million people live in New York. What are the odds I'd be provided with someone with whom I felt I had a connection? Barbara had not only been witness to my best win yet, she'd also seen Alfred and my son.

After we worked together for several months, she suggested I study with W. Brugh Joy at his conference center in Arizona. While I had no idea at the time, I was putting out all the right vibrations. I was in what I call the "fluidity zone"—on my path and the speed was picking up. Everything I wanted and needed, things, people, places, were falling at my feet.

I called Brugh Joy's offices and found that the conference I wanted to attend, his Foundational Heart-centering Initiation Conference, was in five days, fully booked with a 50-person waiting list. I was on the phone with the lodge receptionist, talking about the coincidence of her son and me having birthdays on April 25, when a cancellation came in on another line. She came back on the phone and asked if I wanted to take the space. Shocked at how easy this was, I told her, "Let me call you right back." I hung up the phone and sat stunned for a few minutes. Now I was having second thoughts, but if what had just happened, happened—that I was being invited to take the newly empty slot despite all the people on the waiting list—it seemed like a sign I was supposed to go. I shivered, took a deep breath, called back, and said, "I'll be there."

In the papers faxed to me, it was suggested we read Joy's two books, his first, *Joy's Way: A Map for the Transformational Journey*, and a second, *Avalanche: Heretical Reflections on the Dark and the Light*, before attending. These are wonderful books, books that need to be read, contemplated, and savored. Trying to speed-read them in three days? Well, I did my best.

W. Brugh Joy, M.D. is a tall, slim man with pale skin and a wonderful shock of white hair. Twenty-five years before, he had been a conventional medical doctor with a thriving practice and impeccable credentials that included being Phi Beta Kappa at the University of Southern California, a Johns Hopkins internship, and residency at the Mayo Clinic. His transformation from practicing conventional medicine occurred when he contracted a life-threatening disease. Abruptly giving up his medical practice, he traveled the world studying new realms of healing through body energies and meditation, and by reaching other levels of consciousness. Within six weeks of leaving his old life, he was well. He continued his travels, and in places such as Tibet, Egypt, Scotland, and England, found people not only getting well from these "new" ways of healing but staying well. He came back to the United States to teach what he had learned.

I look back now and wonder why I didn't feel even more trepidation about going off to study something so foreign to me. I'd only been dabbling in yoga (and didn't love it) and had been studying guided meditation with the help of a teacher or tape for about six months. The papers faxed to me suggested we let go of any expectations about the content of the conference. Okay, I guessed I could do that. It went on to say that "in order to fully open yourselves to the experience and assimilate the new ideas presented, you are asked to take care of personal and business affairs before you arrive so the 12 days can be spent with no outside contact. You will not be allowed to use the telephone unless there is a life or death emergency. Mail will be held until the end of the conference."

Uh-oh. This did nothing to alleviate my slight touch of foreboding. As I hurriedly prepared for the trip, my feelings were fluctuating between wonderment about what lay ahead and dread of what was to come.

In a separate cover letter, we were told that the conference was to be oriented to "Self-Realization" and therefore life renovating, and we were asked to prepare to be shifted significantly from the perspectives we were currently exploring. In other words, we were told to prepare ourselves to have our sense of reality radically changed. *Huge, huge understatement.*

I decided that if I was going to do this, I was going to do it all the way. Still ill, I hoped this might finally be the end of my quest and I would find my way to good health. I promised myself I would try not to buck the system too much. I had to give myself a little leeway. In conventional medicine, I'd always considered myself to be what Bernie Siegel, in his book *Love, Medicine and Miracles*, called an exceptional patient.

An exceptional patient is one that makes a doctor's life miserable by questioning everything. While it hadn't gotten me very far, that was me all the way for 12 years. This time I decided I'd try to do everything asked of me and not question too much and, as Brugh said in his book, "delete my *need* to understand." As far as I was concerned there was nothing else left for me to try. If I jumped into this with both feet and it didn't work, whatever "it" was, it wouldn't be because of my lack of participation.

Self-Realization, the letter said, with a capital "S" and a capital "R." Interesting. What could I possibly find out about myself I didn't already know? Then there was the thought, "What things could I find out about myself I didn't *want* to know?"

While I was committed to fully participating, I was still anxious. It was all so new. During the entire two-hour car trip from the Phoenix airport, in the grip of this anxiety, I kept repeating to myself, "No expectations, no expectations, no expectations."

After passing the hawk, the car slowed as the terrain across the last few dusty miles of the wide-open chaparral got rougher. The dirt road became winding and rutted as we approached the mountain. This was horse—or jeep—country. My driver was muttering to himself, probably worried the car might drop an axle. As far as my eyes could see, there were long, flat, dusty expanses of dry broken earth and scrubby plants that adapted to the monsoon summers and long dry winters. When we reached Black Mountain, we were in the Prescott National Forest, the largest juniper forest in Arizona. This wasn't like forests back home in the East, thick with tall pines and strong oaks; this was just more concentration of the few big juniper bushes I'd seen here and there on the chaparral. The car began to climb, making twists and turns up the mountain.

As we rounded the last curve at the top, there nestled in the mountainside was Wildflower Lodge. Even as a rank beginner, I felt something shift for me just seeing this place. There were three duplex cottages with big front porches and a lodge with a big stone chimney and guest quarters down halls off the main room. Higher up on the mountain was an octagonal conference center with a large fireplace, big plate glass windows, and a long, wide deck wrapping it on three sides. I could see that the view from there would be a thousand feet down the mountain to the distant plains that stretched out for 70 or so miles before reaching Granite Mountain, the next range. A separate building off to the left housed the cafeteria, kitchen, and offices. Situated below all the buildings was a stone waterfall cascading into a kidney-shaped swimming pool. A large Jacuzzi and pergola stood nearby.

It was a Wild West Shangri-La.

I was happy to be the first one to arrive so I could unpack, put my things away, and hide my luggage. I didn't want my cabin mates to see that I'd brought one medium and two large suitcases filled to overflowing with clothes, shoes, books, and toiletries. I always pack like I'm never going home.

When I finished, I hiked up a winding path that meandered back and forth across the mountain behind the conference center. Some areas were fairly steep with loose rocks. Usually, though, there was a place to get a foothold on an embedded larger rock so I didn't have to climb with my hands as well as my feet. Now and then, at a treacherous shift in the trail, there'd be a helpful branch of a juniper worn smooth by the grasps of all who'd gone before. At the crest was the prize. An old Indian stone ruin stood guarding the top of the mountain.

The panoramic view was well worth the somewhat strenuous hike. In every direction, there were miles and miles of long, flat, sandy-colored plains that in the far distance touched another mountain range. I could actually see the curve of the

Earth on the horizon. Having lived at sea level all my life, I felt on top of the world at 5,000 feet. The sunsets and sunrises had to be magnificent. I made a mental note to come up for them as often as possible.

Our first session began after dinner. At seven, we gathered in the octagonal room in the conference center. With a 50-foot diameter, it had plenty of space for the 44 of us to comfortably cluster in a large circle. We sat on maroon backjacks laid out on the plush mauve wall-to-wall carpeting.

Everything seemed to have been thought of for our comfort. Our beds were made with 100 percent white cotton Bill Blass sheets. There was a community laundry room that didn't require quarters. Afghans were provided in the conference center in case the air conditioning got too cold. The cost of the conference was so reasonable, I was surprised they didn't skimp on amenities. This was good for me to see. A spiritual path filled with good feelings of abundance.

In the conference room the first night, one by one we introduced ourselves to the other 43 fellow conferees and told where we were from and why we had come. The next day, it became apparent that while some things were scheduled, we weren't going to be told what to expect at the different sessions. No time was wasted in beginning the change in our perception of reality.

Our scheduled events included 6 A.M. yoga or aerobics in the conference center, and at six-thirty, a heart-centering meditation. Next came an early-morning dream-work session. That hour and a half was spent introducing us to aspects within ourselves that could help interpret images. Anyone who had a dream they wanted to work on put their name in a basket. A name was then drawn at random. By totally concentrating on the person telling their dream, we'd help them go beneath the obvious interpretation to understand the messages and information the unconscious brought forth via symbolism.

Our days were full. We were being introduced to many new life tools that I will explain later. Tools like the heart-center. We learned about divination—using different types of oracles from ancient traditions to access our subconscious and higher consciousness. We explored meditation, individual and collective rituals, inner and outer teachers, and the realization of the Gift of Life. So much was being given to us, I was afraid I wouldn't take it all in.

Yet, with all that was going on, or perhaps because of it, I began to become conscious of a message coming my way.

The first time I heard the message was during a session when we were being told the plans for the next three days. They were mostly about quieting our inner and outer chatter to see what would present itself.

I'm not sure why, but one woman participant raised her hand and asked, "What if I get a sexual urge during the three days?"

While the rest of us giggled like kindergartners, our teacher answered her question without cracking a smile. "Well, you could relieve it, or you could move it from your regenerative chakra to your heart chakra and let it go."

That brought me out of my embarrassed giggle.

What?? I thought.

I felt like I'd started geometry two weeks late.

What was he talking about? I looked around at the others. Was I the only one who didn't have a clue as to what was going on?

Move *what* to *where?*

Let go of what?

And *how?*

Now, by this time in my studies, I had heard of chakras. I knew our bodies have seven major energy points starting at the base of the spine running up through the body to the crown at the top of our head. I also knew these points had been recognized in the East and used in healing for thousands of years. The Chinese call them acupressure points. In India they're called *chakras*, an ancient Sanskrit word meaning "wheel" or "disk." In the Orient, they are believed to be as important in balancing good health as the vascular, muscular, nervous, and skeletal systems. I'd learned to use them in some of my meditations. I understood all that, but moving something from one chakra to another and letting it go? This was new. What was he talking about? Was he suggesting she move her sexual energy?

Not wanting to seem stupid if everyone else had "gotten it," I didn't ask for clarification. I was, after all, trying to practice what I'd just learned about "deleting my need to understand," and to let things unfold.

However, by the second time in the conference I heard the message about "let it go," I wasn't any more enlightened. We had taken a day trip to the Grand Canyon. From our vantage point standing on the South Rim where the driver had let us off, the Grand Canyon dropped down 5,000 feet to the Colorado River. Rock formations looked like temples balanced on top of mountains. Then mountains plunged as far as a mile into yet another deep canyon. Massive boulders seemed held up by ancient carved Greek columns, only it was nature's hand at work, not the ancient Greeks. Something this breathtaking, a grand vista of miles and miles of canyons and mountains and mountains and canyons, made it impossible not to feel that something bigger than ourselves was happening—a grandeur of which we all are a part.

Danny Glover, in his role in the movie *Grand Canyon*, put very succinctly how he felt viewing the Grand Canyon for the first time. He told Kevin Kline's character, "Sitting right on the edge of that big old thing, cliff rocks so old, it took so long to look like that. I realized what a joke we people are. What big heads we got thinking what we do is gonna matter all that much. Thinking our time means diddley to all those rocks. A split second we've been here, the whole lot of us, and one of us? That's a piece of time too small to give a name. Those rocks were laughing at me, I could tell. Me and my worries is real humorous to the Grand Canyon. I felt like a gnat that lands on a cow's ass that's chewing its cud next to a road on which you're going seventy miles an hour. . . . Small."

After our tour, we went to see the Grand Canyon IMAX movie. In it, I felt I was flying over the great panoramic vistas of the Grand Canyon. Seated next to the conference teacher, I put my hands over my heart, leaned over, and whispered, "This is so beautiful, it hurts my heart."

He whispered back, "Let it go."

That's two.

I sat there for a moment, with my brain once again going, "What??" Surreptitiously, from the corner of my eye, I glanced over at him and wondered if I would recognize an alien or pod person if I was sitting next to one.

What the heck did he mean, "Let it go?"

Let go of what?

What was he talking about?

The third time I heard the message, I got it.

I struggled with it, but I got it.

It happened the next week in an afternoon conference. I shared with the group that I was very angry with my father for keeping my mother alive through intravenous feedings and antibiotics an extra two years after she was pronounced brain-dead from Alzheimer's. The conference teacher's reply to me in front of the group was, "If you don't let go of that anger, you will never get well."

Up until this point, I had been feeling pretty healthy at the conference. Occasionally I did my CFS thing and slept a lot during the sessions, but I was beginning to recognize that I'd pass out about the time somebody was going into something very personal and deep about himself that I didn't want to face about myself. I wasn't too concerned. We had been told not to worry about napping or even skipping a session; we'd "get it" anyway.

Good thing in my case.

Over the years, I'd also recognized a pattern with my illness. When I'd leave behind the pressures of my regular life and lighten up, like on a vacation, I found I felt almost normal. Here at the conference, except for my bouts of sleeping in the sessions, I felt good enough to climb a different mountain every day with Bill, a new friend I'd met.

Now, though, a trigger had been struck. *If you don't let go of that anger, you'll never get well.* It felt like a personal attack, and again, the chatter in my head began working overtime.

What did he mean?

How dare he say I need to let go of anger toward my father or I'll never get well? The situation with Dad has only been going on for two years. I've been sick for 12. It doesn't compute.

I decided that one couldn't have anything to do with the other.

This guy doesn't know what he's talking about. He doesn't make any sense.

So angry I skipped lunch and, with my wounded "inner child," crawled under a juniper bush to hide and nurse my hurts. From this vantage point, I watched everyone coming and going from lunch and felt left-out and alone.

And, then I started to feel ill.

I became so sick, I couldn't move. A woman leaving lunch stopped at the end of the footbridge to play with the lodge dogs and spotted me in my hiding place. She told my friend Bill where to find me. He walked up the path, crawled into my secret hideout, and asked if I was ready to go climb another mountain.

By then I was in a full-blown Chronic Fatigue attack. I was so tired, achy, and weak, I wasn't sure I could make it back to my bed, much less up a mountain. Bill helped me back to my room, and I fell into a deep Chronic Fatigue nap for three hours. It was one of those coma-like naps from which you have to fight your way back to consciousness. When I finally awakened, I was so groggy, my brain felt it was wrapped in five layers of gauze. I couldn't see properly, I couldn't think straight, I couldn't move right, and everything hurt. I dragged myself down to the swimming pool and dove three times into the icy cold water. Nothing. I emerged just as dazed as before.

I decided to sit on my towel, face the Sun, and meditate. Since I was fairly new at meditation, this was one of the first times I'd tried it on my own without a teacher or guided tape. I decided to do a short version of things I'd learned.

Breathing deeply and slowly, in and out four times, I envisioned sending a grounding root down from my body to the center of the Earth. Gradually, I began to feel my body solidly connecting. I imagined vibrant swirling Earth energy coming up through the root, filling my body from my toes all the way to my head. I had been taught how to check my chakras, those seven major energy points, just to observe what was going on, whether it be a color, a feeling, or any other sensation. Not do anything, just observe.

I focused my attention at each center, starting at the top of my head at the seventh chakra, or crown chakra, located about where a baby's soft spot is on the top of the head. It was fine. I noticed nothing out of the ordinary. The next, the sixth chakra, also known as the third eye, at the middle of the forehead just above the line of the eyebrows, seemed okay, too. The fifth, at the throat, the point of communication, felt a little tight, but it usually felt that way. The fourth chakra at my heart, midchest a little above and between the breasts, felt nice and open. But when I got down to the third chakra at my solar plexus, about two inches below the middle of the rib cage, I noticed, a little off to the right, a burning sensation like indigestion or heartburn. Like a chime, a soft inner voice went off in my head and said, "Anger."

I was taken aback. This was the first time I'd ever heard my inner voice, my inner teacher, my body's wisdom or whatever you want to call it. It said, "Anger." *Anger?* I thought. *Okay—so what?*

Curious, but since I didn't know what to do about it, I decided to continue checking my last two chakras. The second or regenerative chakra, about three inches below the belly button, also known as the creative and sexual center, was fine. And the Kundalini, life force or first chakra, at the base of the spine, was free of any feelings of constraints and seemed open and functioning.

I brought my focus back to my solar plexus and sat concentrating on the burning sensation. My thoughts were that maybe this was not just anger from the teacher's comments about my feelings toward my father. Maybe this was a bigger, older, all-encompassing anger, a much deeper emotion.

The same old chatter started in my head, *So, now what?* and *I haven't a clue what to do.* Things I'd just heard popped into my mind, *Delete the need to know, make no judgments, have no comparisons.* More words, the words we focused on when heart-centering, were flying around, *compassion, innate harmony, healing presence, and unconditional love.* And, *Okay, sooo?*

I wanted someone to tell me what to do. I wanted to manifest my teacher walking by so he could exactly instruct me in the proper procedure for handling what an inner voice tells you. A book on the subject would have been nice, or a cell phone to call my meditation teacher. But no, I was on my own.

My mind raced on. I thought about our conference teacher telling the woman to move "it" to her heart and "let it go." Obviously now, "it" must have been sexual energy from the regenerative chakra. Okay, okay, I rationalized, moving energy from one chakra to another seemed to be possible and, in her case, might be quite pleasant. But what if I tried to move anger energy from my solar plexus chakra to my heart chakra and "let it go"? Would my heart ache? Or even break? About then I was thinking, *I wonder if I can die messing around with this stuff without an instruction book or someone to tell me what to do?*

My thoughts went back to the IMAX movie and the second time I'd heard the idea of moving energy. But that was only about letting go of feelings of beauty and joy that were stuck and hurting my heart. While I was becoming comfortable that the heart-center was an amazing resource, I had no idea whether moving anger energy from the solar plexus to the heart would work. It seemed like a whole other ball game. It might just be another repressed emotion, but it seemed to me a rather dark, bigger one. I decided to open my eye a fraction, peek out, and see if I'd materialized anyone to help me out with this major concern.

Nope. No one.

I was on my own.

To my way of thinking, I had two choices. Either experiment with something I felt I knew nothing about or pull myself out of the meditation and ask someone's opinion.

I thought, *What the heck, I said I would go all the way, I'm going to experiment with this, and if I die, I die, ha, ha.* Even though I was half joking, I was so new at all this, I had no idea what might happen when moving an emotion as big as anger to my heart to "let it go." Maybe death was a possibility? Or a heart attack?

I didn't know.

I now knew this "anger" I was experiencing as a burning feeling was anger from forever. It was every hurt and slight and words I hadn't spoken throughout my life, while struggling to keep up the illusion that my life was always full of joy and light.

The moment I decided to "go for it" was the first time I consciously "surrendered." I was jumping into the void and had to trust my own inner wisdom that something bigger than myself was happening.

With 12 years of illness behind me and no other visible paths in front of me, I went ahead and took the leap.

"What the heck, if I die, I die," I'd said. Surrender with a capital S.

Focusing my attention on the burning sensation at my solar plexus chakra, I visualized moving it to my heart. I placed my hands over my heart, right under left, as we had learned to do in morning heart-centering meditations. When I "felt" the anger energy come to my heart, I visualized letting it go out through my heart chakra. I even waved my hands away in a motion of release.

I finished the meditation by becoming fully present in my body and knowing I was sitting poolside in Paulden, Arizona. After wiggling my fingers and toes, I opened my eyes.

I couldn't believe what had happened.

I felt completely well!

It had worked!

My mind was sharp, my sight so crystal clear, the trees looked etched on the horizon.

My body was totally free from aches and pains!

I felt vibrant and better than I had for years.

All this from hearing a message three times, stopping to listen and consider what it might be saying to me?

Let go? Let go? Let go?

After 12 long years of looking everywhere for answers to good health, *this* was it? Identify repressed or denied emotions and let them go? This was the secret to radiant health? It seemed too simple. But it had happened. I had heard the message to "let go" three times, and when I finally listened and did as instructed—let go of my repressed emotions of anger—the rewards were phenomenal.

That day, I learned to trust a larger process. When I finally had recognized and let go of anger, I had had no idea of the possible consequences. I wasn't thinking, *Will I get well if I move anger energy to my heart?* I just knew I didn't want or need the anger I'd discovered, and that in some way it was blocking me. I surrendered, let it go, and allowed myself to trust that something greater than myself was at work.

I was well. I felt great. However, I had trouble immediately accepting that I had discovered an incredible path to good health and that I should probably back off and process all that had happened. Instead, during the rest of the conference, I had almost an obsession to be the best at everything asked of us.

During one of the first sessions, we were told to get out into the stark landscape of the high Arizona desert and find something in nature that talked to us. A totem—something that would help guide us on our paths.

Out I went, diligently trudging over one mountain after another looking for my teacher, totem, or sign. After being told that everything that happens has significance, accidentally kicking a rock would overwhelm me with the possibility that the rock might be fraught with meaning. While everything around me seemed to be speaking to me, nothing monumental presented itself with a message to help me on my path to good health, greater awareness, and higher consciousness.

By the end of the conference, I started getting a little concerned. I was determined on my last hike to find my totem. I headed back up to the old ruin to say good-bye. I left the meandering trail and climbed straight up the mountain. Scrambling over loose rocks with both hands and feet, I was careful not to crush any cacti or sage as I continued off the beaten path. When I came to a large, flat, slanted wall of rock, I immediately tried to scale it. As soon as I got my fingers gripped over the top, I lost my footing. *Just great,* I thought, *what am I doing, hanging by my fingertips, body flattened out, spread-eagled on a slab with no foothold?*

I started to chuckle. I wondered what my friends, lawyers,

and others back in Manhattan would think if they could see me now.

I could just hear them. "Is that Patricia in khakis and hiking boots hanging on for dear life onto the side of a mountain?"

"It can't be . . . isn't she having lunch with her lawyers at the Russian Tea Room?"

"I'm not sure. Squint your eyes and in your mind take away her jewelry, designer clothes, and stiletto heels. Now look closely at that French manicure on those extended nails. I swear that's her."

I didn't have long to think about this scenario before my fingers, thwarted by my acrylic nails, gave out. With adrenaline pounding in my head, I slid down five feet to a small foot hole at the bottom of the rock. At that point, if there'd been room, I would have been on my knees kissing the ground. If I had landed wrong, it would have been a long, long tumble to the bottom of the mountain. My pulse still pounding in my temples, I gingerly bent over with my hands (nails intact) on my knees to catch my breath and laughed aloud, excited at my success and failure.

The conversation I'd had with my roommate that morning when I'd voiced my concern over not yet finding my totem came back to me. She'd admonished me saying, "Patricia, a spiritual quest is like climbing a mountain. One meanders up and slowly reaches his or her destination at the top of the mountain." I told her I climb mountains by heading straight up, moving fast, until I reached the top. Then I celebrate my victory by stripping off all my clothes and doing a little, "Yippee, I did it, I did it" song and dance. After dressing, sitting, and meditating, then I would meander—slowly making my way down the mountain, processing all that had happened on the way up.

Back at the slab, my breath finally becoming regular, I carefully made my way around the large, flat rock. Then, using both hands and feet, I quickly crawled the rest of the way straight up the mountain on all fours. I was back to worrying that I wouldn't find my messenger. Even though I'd already had so many incredible experiences, I didn't want to flunk "Finding Totems in Nature 101."

Reaching the top of the mountain, I inched around the less precarious side of the rock ruin, which still had a steep drop-off. I sat down in a safe place on the ruin wall and dangled my legs over the side. Thoughts of my near mishap intermingled with others about the incredible healing meditation in which I identified anger, released it, and became well. Now and then I would come back to the present and turn my attention to the panoramic view of the chaparral and the distant mountain range, and let the chatter in my head grow silent.

I almost missed the red-tailed hawk circling far out in front of me. I'd forgotten about the hawk's greeting on my arrival. Now though, as he circled, I remembered it and thought about another time I'd noticed him. I'd seen him four days before when I was hiking up the riverbed. That day he seemed to be guiding me in the right direction. My eyes and thoughts drifted off the distant hawk and back to the more expansive view.

All of a sudden, I heard a loud, shrill cry. Jerking my head up to see where the sound was coming from, I saw the hawk right overhead.

Then it hit me.

This was the hawk's third visit!

I laughed out loud.

Once again, I had to hear a message three times.

"Okay, Hawk," I thought as I stood up on the rock wall and waved both hands at him in recognition, "I get it. You are my messenger. Thank you. I understand."

As I walked slowly back down the mountain, I recalled things I'd read that resonated with me about the spirit of the hawk as a power ally in Jamie Sams' and David Carson's book, *Medicine Cards—The Discovery of Power Through the Ways of Animals.* "When the hawk comes into your life, he represents your ability to be an emotionally detached observer. Flying high he gets an overview of all that is and survives by never shutting down his powers of observation on any level."

Was this how I was going to survive with vibrant health? During the meditation in which I came out well, I made a connection between my emotions and body I had never been able to make before. I was able to see a bigger picture, then focus and go inside to the answer. And the reverse, just as the hawk so gracefully soars above the Earth, I got to glimpse the grand scope that is so difficult to see when we are only focusing on the problem at hand. Was Hawk telling me "to go to the place of the observer and never again be afraid to examine what had become too painful to feel, too unbelievable to hear, or too dark to see?"

I think so now, but so many times I refused to believe this true.

5

how does your illness serve you?
Illness as a helpmate and a Messenger

Silence and fasting? For three days?!? Are they nuts?

These were my thoughts when it was being explained that we would be observing silence and fasting for the next three days of the conference.

Again my brain began spinning into overdrive.

During the preceding 12 years when I'd been ill, I had done a lot of fasting so I could be tested for food allergies. Every single time, I had severe withdrawal reactions from foods to which I was allergic and/or addicted: coffee, wheat, eggs, dairy, corn, whatever.

It seemed to me that directing people to fast without telling them they could get severe migraine headaches, diarrhea, stomach trouble, depression, and a plethora of other symptoms was irresponsible.

I could just visualize all the cranky, silent people dragging around the property the next few days. Oh, joy!

Though my inner chatter continued, another part of my brain picked up on a story being told by the conference leader about a woman in Florence, Italy, who had been fasting for 21 years. Drinking only water, she tapped into another source of energy. While I had some trouble believing this, I still thought, *Aha! That must be what people were talking about when they talked of the pleasures of fasting.* Obviously, I'd never been there.

I had decided earlier in the week that sometime during the conference I wanted to spend a night alone in the juniper forest. Still under the impression I might get weak and die from fasting for three days, I left early the first morning while I had enough strength to carry a sleeping bag and backpack filled with two gallons of water and juices. Hiking around the side of the lodge property and up the dry riverbed, I continued back two mountains into the national forest. We had been given some guidelines on exploring. We were told to watch where we put our hands and feet, so we wouldn't get stung, stabbed, or bitten, and to go east if we got lost and we'd find a highway. I could do that.

I felt pretty comfortable trekking around; after all, I had been raised on the mountainous island of Kodiak, Alaska, with the world's largest bears. Kodiak bears grow to 11 feet tall. Not that I ever saw one, though I do remember *not* seeing one. My family and I were coming back from the ski lodge up in the mountains where we went tobogganing, not skiing. Everyone in the car yelled, "Look, Patty, look; there's one way over there." That's the one I never saw but said I did.

Growing up on Kodiak, I survived snowdrifts three to four times my childhood height that could cover the doors to our naval base duplex house. I also survived swimming in icy water at white sandy coves during the one or two days in the summer it was deemed warm enough to go in.

As far as I was concerned, hiking up mountains in Arizona would be a breeze. I had Alaskan frontierswoman blood in me.

After a couple of hours in the dry riverbed, I looked up and saw a hawk circling the sky overhead. Deciding it was my sign I'd gone far enough, I climbed up the side of Black Mountain. When I got to the top, I quickly found what had to be the best campsite in all of Arizona. Out on a small point high above the riverbed, a rock ledge jutted out. It was one of the few places that didn't have a million little ragged pebbles that would thwart my sleep. A large juniper protected the west side of my ideal camp-site, groups of prickly cactus were to the south, and some old dead scrub oaks secured the north. The east side, from which I'd be able to view the sunrise, was the open ledge high above the canyon floor. Breaking off a piece of juniper to use as a broom, I swept the area clean to set up my campsite. Sleeping bag laid out, I left the three layers of 100 percent cotton white clothes in my backpack that I'd decided to wear not only to honor the fast but for warmth. I'd been sleeping outside in the hammocks around the conference center and had found my first night out that it gets quite cold in the high desert.

I felt I was the first female Davy Crockett and quite the expe-rienced camper. The fact that I hadn't ever been camping in my life didn't cross my mind; after all, I was raised on that wild Alaska navy base. And I had occasionally slept outside with my comforter on a chaise longue on the second-floor deck off our master bedroom when Alfred and I lived in Atlantic Beach, New York. I'd watch the lights of the town of Lawrence across the channel until I'd fall asleep.

I'd left at dawn and walked for a couple hours, so after I'd set up my campsite, I still had the whole day before nightfall. I decided to kill time by investigating the top of my mountain. Once again, wanting to be one with nature, I struck off to explore the surrounding area as a bare-skin native with only my socks, hiking boots, and an umbrella to keep off the relentless sun.

On this first day of our observing silence and fasting, I soon discovered silence was not something I did well. If my footing slipped, I'd say, "Darn you, rock." When I realized I'd goofed, I'd apologize to the police of silence, saying, "Sorry." There was a, "Hi to you, Mr. Rabbit," when a bunny scurried off. This was upset-ting. I was really disappointed at my inability to be silent. I decided to double my efforts.

Being a singer, I also found it hard not to break into song. It was so beautiful on the top of my mountain, it really called for a stirring rendition of "The Hills Are Alive with the Sound of

Music." Good thing no one was around to see me. I must have looked like a demented Mary Poppins, dancing around to my inner songs, nude, in my combat boots, swinging an open black umbrella.

Outer and inner silence never did get very quiet for me this trip.

It took about an hour and a half to explore the mountaintop. Delighted to find there were no signs of civilization in any direction, and feeling I was truly the first woman explorer, I scouted out the best place to watch the sunset that would come in seven hours. It was going to be a long day until nightfall, when I thought my real adventure would begin. I decided to make my way back to my campsite, put on some clothes, and find a juniper to read under to get out of the sun and kill time. Going back to camp, I practiced my "I am a quiet Indian" step. Walking so softly without noise, at one turn I practically bumped into an elk's rear end. I'm not sure who jumped higher. Once again, in my best nonsilent behavior I shouted out, "Sorry, Mr. Elk," as he darted off.

Wow. Elks, rabbits, birds—cool!

I couldn't find my camp.

Anywhere.

Ten o'clock in the morning, no clothes on, and I'd lost my campsite.

I searched for another hour and a half, retracing my steps all along the rim of the mountain. I was so grateful Bill had told me to take an umbrella, I would have been a crispy critter after three hours in the sun. Gratitude aside, where was my camp? Options, like hiking back nude to the lodge, didn't enter my mind. Finally, two passes later, I found it. I decided before venturing out again, it might be clever to look for landmarks.

After dressing, I took a couple of treks out to find shade and a place to read, and soon realized there wasn't any place as comfortable as my campsite, so I stayed put. Lodging the umbrella over my shoulder, I leaned back against a rock softened by my backpack and read, napped, meditated, drank water and juices, and waited excitedly for nightfall. During one of my meditations,

I asked what my future was. I saw a picture in my mind of a high desert scene, much like where I was but flatter, different.

I'd brought the book *Inner Knowing*, edited by Helen Palmer. *Inner Knowing* contained essays by renowned psychologists, writers, and scientists on the hidden powers of the mind. Instead of reading this book cover to cover, I decided to practice my newly taught skill of bibliomancy. I opened the book at random to receive wisdom particularly meaningful to me. The essay I opened to was "Experiential Knowing" by Abraham H. Maslow, about getting "utterly lost in the present." No past or future exists for that time; one is totally in the here-now experience. All there, immersed, concentrated, fascinated.

That pretty much summed up how I was all day on my mountain, lost in time, even though I was anxiously awaiting nightfall.

Finally, it happened.

It got dark.

Fast.

The Sun

dropped

like a rock.

Boom . . . gone.

I hadn't considered a fire because there'd been a drought, and everyone had been warned against starting a brush fire.

Boy, it got really dark, really fast.

Really, really dark.

I quickly got into my sleeping bag. It began to dawn on me that I hadn't looked around my campsite for signs of things that could come creeping out and about in the night. I poked out my head to look around. The dead scrubs sticking up behind me gave no comfort. Their stark, almost luminous limbs reached up like bones into the foreboding black void behind and above them. I glanced at the big juniper that bordered my camp to the west and sensed more than saw many crags and rocks under it. I considered what might have been hiding there during the day. Scorpions, rattlers, tarantulas—were they coming out of their holes scurrying around in the dark with one thought in their tiny little brains, that of sharing the warmth in my sleeping bag? I took inventory of what I'd seen during my day. An elk, rabbits, and birds. Why couldn't there also be mountain lions, bears, cougars, buffalo, wild boars, and packs of marauding wolves?

It was then the awful truth hit me. Spending seven years from the ages of three to ten in a duplex on a naval base in Kodiak, Alaska, did not qualify me to spend the night alone in the woods!

Within seconds I was up, packed, and walking down the front of the mountain, which I imagined to be the shortest distance back to the conference center. I realized that the small, six-by-half-inch flashlight, which Vita had bought for me along with my camping equipment at Eddie Bauer's in New York, that we'd thought was so cool, had just a tiny—no, make that a minuscule—beam that shone no more than two feet out and no wider than six inches. My left brain went into action. *Patricia, how are you going to walk down the front of two mountains you've never been on, in pitch black with a flashlight that would barely get you down a familiar hall at home?* My right brain whined, *I don't care, I want outta here, I'm afraid.* After I had gone about 40 steps, my left brain took control. *Stop! You couldn't find your campsite this morning in daylight, and you know there isn't another decent place to camp on the mountain. Go back before you get really lost.*

As I trudged back, dejected I'd lost the argument, I made a pact with myself. I promised me I could stay awake all night.

Luckily, I found my site right away, again set up camp, and crawled back into my sleeping bag. I began to realize that sleeping on a rock ledge that had been soaking up the hot sun all day was going to be quite different from sleeping in the open-air hammocks back at the lodge. It wasn't cold up here. I was burning up. I took off one layer of clothes. I took off another layer of clothes. Finally I was down to my last layer of 100 percent white cotton clothes and I was still dying of the heat. There was no way I was lying nude in my sleeping bag. Running around naked all day in daylight was one thing, sleeping with nothing on to protect me from all the boogey things out there in the dark was quite another.

Finally I decided to call on all the meditations and everything I'd ever learned about gathering inner strength. With my eyes closed, I envisioned a circle of all the inner aspects of myself I'd been introduced to over the year. I called on my feminine consciousness, my masculine consciousness, my wise woman, my child within, my warrior, my council of elders, and checked in with each one. They all had very settling messages for me. All promised to stand guard in a big safe circle if I decided I wanted to go to sleep. Feeling much, much better with this crowd around me, I lay down and watched the stars and satellites.

During my nights out in the hammocks, I'd check my watch to see what time the stars moved overhead, but I'd taken it off when we started our fasting and silence. Now I realized I could approximate the time by the position of the stars. Mostly by where the Milky Way was as it moved across the sky, but I could now track satellites and knew some went over about every 30 minutes. I'd learned where the Pleiades, a constellation known as the Seven Sisters, was. I knew Orion's Belt, and of course, I took comfort in the always available Big and Little Dippers and bright North Star. Looking at the sky, I knew it was about midnight.

Now that my heart was beating at less than heart attack rate, and satisfied that all was well within my world, I soon fell off to sleep. Every so often I'd awaken, open my eyes, check out the stars, and think I was the bravest, luckiest girl in the world. I was at peace. The last time I woke up, there was a beautiful sunrise and a gentle morning breeze picking up. I had survived the night!

With my newfound resolve, I packed up my belongings, had my morning juice, and walked toward the lodge down the front of the mountain. This was not the gentle slope I'd envisioned. I never would have gotten back that way the previous night. I had to climb down one mountain, up another, then over to, and down from, the ruin that was near the lodge. Boy, was I glad to get back. After I had conquered the wilds, the next two days of fasting and silence back at the conference center were a breeze. Never once did I get weak or tired. In fact, I would have turned cartwheels if I'd known how. Instead, I did little happy dances up and down the dirt road leading to the lodge—heel, toe, skip, heel, toe, turn—dah, dah, dah, da. I just kept feeling better and better. So this was what tapping into another source of energy felt like—euphoric.

Because of my experience of going "blindly off into the night" and conquering my fears of being ill-prepared and alone, I found inner resources I never knew were available to me to use in daily life situations. It was after this conference I confronted my "Madison Avenue" attorneys about their fees for Alfred's estate case. I went home and negotiated a contingency basis. While the lawyers still made more money than I did (actually I figured it out—what I paid them could keep one person at minimum wage for 40 years), if I'd stayed scared and done nothing, I would have had to pay them five times the settlement I accepted.

That quiet night in Arizona, I left the safety of the known, the lodge, and walked off into the wilds with a childlike innocence and an unconscious anticipation that a greater knowing would be provided to me on my adventure. It had been. My journey into the woods reminded me that my search for inner peace, fortitude, kindness, and trust would be resolved inside myself. To learn that, I had had to go really, really outside. Outside with no protection, totally exposed, to learn once again how truly safe and protected I am.

After the three days of silence and fasting, I was exhilarated when we started back into the conference. I couldn't wait to report (brag) about my adventure to the group. We sat in our circle leaning on our backjacks, waiting for the session to start. I had positioned myself across from our conference leader so he could see how absolutely vibrant I was from my yet-to-be-revealed experiences.

Rather than starting, as he usually did, with sharing, he instead posed a question. Unhurriedly, he looked around the room, acknowledging with his eyes those of us who had come with an illness to heal. Very slowly, he asked, "How," pausing for an instant, "does your illness serve you?"

At first, I wasn't sure I'd heard him right. His question disoriented me. Weren't we going to talk about our three days of silence and fasting? Then what he said hit me. *How does my ill-ness SERVE me? NO! Wait a minute! My illness does NOT serve me.*

Once again I'd had my bubble burst. I wanted to talk about my great and heroic adventure. I completely rejected any idea that my illnesses might be some form of self-manipulation. Being ill didn't serve me. I wanted to be well more than anyone. Hadn't I proven it by the dozen years I spent looking for a cure? I felt sorry for the few people who were attending the conference with immediate life-threatening health problems. If I felt upset, how did that question make them feel? Cancer, heart disease, and dia-betes were *serving* them?

Even as I fought against it, something inside me was trig-gered. This conference had given me so many incredible tools I could use to make my life easier and more conscious. Tools like letting go of expectations, comparisons, and judgments. So, maybe there was something behind this question, "How does your illness serve you?" I didn't want to think my being ill was anything other than a random hit in the dark. If my illness served me in any way, wouldn't that tie me in to having some responsibility for contracting it in the first place?

I was not ready to accept that one for a single second.

My strong reaction to the posed question was another tool I was learning to use the hard way. A strong reaction usually equals a nerve being hit because there's truth there. We were now getting into the little-known fact that we attract whatever we choose to give our attention to—whether wanted or unwanted. Slowly it began to make sense. All I'd thought about for 12 years was being ill and how to get over it. I hadn't thought about being well.

No wonder I wasn't healthy.

During this conference, everything to which I'd tightly clung was being challenged, every belief that I held was shaken to its core. This was my wake-up call. That was funny, considering my illness was sleeping all the time. However, I was really having trouble with accepting lessons such as *nothing happens at random in our lives*, and *we draw to us what we need to learn and grow*.

So, did this mean I could actually learn why things happened in my life, to my body, and with my relationships? Things that heretofore had seemed out of my control or simply accidental? I was beginning to realize that as soon as I recognized my participation in events that seemed to guide my life, I could actually change them.

I was also awakening to the fact that there is no such thing as a "victim." What victims really are, are persons who only know how to draw bad things to themselves. It's insidious. If something bad happens and it isn't a wake-up call to someone, more and more bad things will be drawn until, hopefully, they get tired of being victimized and awaken. The more violent and menacing the experience, the more asleep a person has been to the changes they need to make, that we are all capable of making.

So, could that mean if what I am feeling and vibrating is fear, then illness, accidents, and even natural disasters will be my life mates? But if I feel and vibrate joy, I'm connecting to my inner higher spirit and, from that place, whatever I wish for will be mine? I was learning the Law of Attraction.

Until I started on a path of self-discovery, I never would have guessed I was getting sick to avoid life. But when I really thought back, I realized my whole life was about playing small and pulling back from who I am and all I could be. I didn't want Dad to feel eclipsed by a daughter's accomplishments. I didn't want to prove Mom wrong about her feelings that the music business was too hard and that a woman's place was behind the man's. I didn't want my sister to feel I might be more intelligent, I didn't want my brother to have a moment's worry about being the long-awaited golden child. So, unconsciously I'd slide into a shell of illness, so I wouldn't hurt or anger people and have them not like me. How had this happened to *me*?

Could this be true? That somehow we use illness, any illness, all illnesses, to keep from seeing or dealing with something we feel is more painful or frightening than being ill? When the teacher at the conference said if I didn't let go of my anger toward my father I'd never get well, what did I do? Rather than consider the possibility, I got ill. By quickly getting very, very tired and sick and going to sleep, I didn't have to think about how hurt and angry the teacher had made me with his comment. I put out the thought, *How dare he when I'm so sick. . . .* And I got "so sick."

Now there seemed to be two choices. I could die, which is hard for a Chronic Fatigue Syndrome sufferer who just kind of limps along feeling near death, to do unless, like the two CFS women who did use him, one knows Dr. Kevorkian. The second choice was to wake up to what I was doing *and change it!*

Several months later, I got to see how deeply unconscious my pattern of slipping into "not feeling well" was for me. I slowly began to comprehend that my *"and change it!"* plan might take a little more time and diligence than I had realized.

It happened a couple months after returning home from the conference in the fall of 1993, when my son was driving us from New York to Delaware to have our new car titled there. Out of nowhere, I started feeling groggy, fatigued, and sick. I asked Doug to turn down the radio so I could meditate to see if I could find out what was happening. I had hardly done the beginning deep breathing when I heard my inner chatter. A lot of voices started going off at once but all were saying the same thing. *I'm angry with Alfred for dying and leaving me to deal with cars.*

Now, that may seem a little irrational until you know that I learned at my daddy's knee that the care and maintenance of cars was a man's job. With Alfred, I'd finally had a husband who took on this responsibility almost to the extreme. On Saturday mornings he hired the Cadillac dealership's mechanic and body men to come and work on cars at the factory. I'd nicknamed it the "Saturday Morning Boys Club" because everyone, from off-duty policemen to Frankie, the owner of Rao's, the legendary Italian restaurant in Manhattan, would drop by and "play cars."

Alfred served breakfast pastries and coffee and great deli sandwiches for lunch. I started planting shrubs and flowers around the factory on Saturdays so I'd have an excuse to hang out and be a part of this tradition. Alfred loved having me around. He'd come out to see what I was up to and then would send someone out to help me plant. I missed the Saturday Morning Boy's Club. I missed Alfred.

That day in the car, while I thought I was focusing on the joy of being with my son, the beautiful weather, and the fun time we'd have together in Rehoboth, I had instead become maudlin about what used to be. I was unconscious of the fact that my longing for Alfred had started low energies vibrating inside me that were causing me to feel ill. When I realized what I had done, I let go of feeling sorry for myself and once again came out of a meditation feeling healed.

I was glad Doug had witnessed this. Now as an all grown up, big, strong, handsome, feet-on-the-ground, successful business-man, if he ever sees me slipping back into not feeling well, he tells me to stop and check my chakras.

Six months later, in the spring of 1994, I again caught myself unconsciously bringing on illness. It happened at a weekend study group in New York. Forty people had gathered for morn-ing and evening meetings at a couple's home outside New York City. I was a newcomer to the group and I noticed a big black man come in whom everyone was happy to see. When we spoke, Sampie, originally from South Africa, alluded to the fact that he was a "big, top corporate executive from New York City" (my interpretation). "Big deal," I thought, and couldn't understand why everyone else liked him so much.

During a morning session, he shared a dream he'd had about a lake in South Africa with South African animals around it. Our teacher's interpretation of the dream was that he needed to make a pilgrimage back to South Africa to help his people fight against apartheid. "No," he replied, "I can't leave my job, what I am doing is too important. I'm not needed in South Africa."

One year later at the same conference, I again noticed Sampie. He seemed different. Not physically. He was still a big black man, he was still friendly, but something had changed. There was now a quiet resolve about him.

This time he shared the fact that he didn't know where he was going to live or what he was going to do, but he had resigned his job and was going back to South Africa to help his people. He was at peace. Everyone was jubilant for him. I even shed a tear.

And then I started falling asleep.

I felt like I was drugged.

I was flopping from the sofa to the floor to a cushion.

I couldn't stay awake.

We didn't have an afternoon session, so I asked someone to take me to the hotel so I could nap. I couldn't even think of meditating, I was way past that stage. All I wanted to do was drop on the bed and pass out. As I was falling off to sleep, I heard my little inner voice (that I was now used to) say, *Greedy, envious, jealous, and angry.*

That woke me up with a start.

Oh, my gosh, I thought. I wasn't happy for Sampie. I was greedy, envious, jealous, and angry toward him. I had always been. When I'd seen him at the first conference, coming in bigger than life, jubilant and happy, I'd been jealous. So, the tear I'd shed in the session wasn't in happiness for him, it was in sadness for me. I wanted to be a big, black, affable man from South Africa with apartheid to fight. It wasn't fair that in one year's time he'd found his life's path when, I'd been consciously looking for mine for so many years.

I so burned to find my passion and purpose that I was terribly envious of him. He hadn't even been looking and he found his. I wanted his inner peace. And I so wanted to instantly be an accepted part of the group; I was envious when it seemed so easy for someone else.

No wonder I wanted to hide feelings like this from myself. Who at 44 wants to admit she is behaving like a greedy, spoiled, jealous child? I was envious of someone else's direction in life. I was jealous of his belonging and his breakthrough.

After all this information became apparent to me, I got up from my bed, went to the hotel pool, swam laps, and was awake and alert the rest of the conference. When I shared my discovery with everyone at the conference, Sampie, with a laugh and gracious as ever said, "Patricia, you are welcome to accompany me to South Africa."

Now, instead of comparing myself to others, I honor their process as another example of our collective human spirit, and *I don't have to get sick.* When we vibrate the higher energy of joy, instead of low energy of jealousy, fear, or anger, there is room for all of us to shine our light.

Sampie is now a high public official who continues to help his people. I am bursting with pride for him.

After successfully catching myself slipping into illness when I'd deny or repress emotions, I decided it was now time to look over my past to see if there was an incident where illness might have served me. To quote Vernon Howard, "At first, your new insight will seem like a dim light in a dark tunnel. As you proceed, you'll begin to have more courage. The more you're able to walk forward, the less the old fears will have control over you." I soon learned that being brutally honest about myself and motives didn't hurt. It helped.

I stripped off my rose-colored glasses and reviewed my past. Using all the tools I'd gathered—meditation, divination tools like tarot and runes, even skilled practitioners to guide me in "child within" and other therapies like Hal and Sidra Stone's voice dialogue, where you speak with different aspects of yourself—I found example after example of how I used illness all my life as a survival tool.

It started when I literally was the "child within."

This may seem far-fetched to some, but there are people who believe we, as spirit becoming human embryos, understand what is happening while we are in our mother's womb. Accept that for a moment. Now picture me, my light body conscious even though I was but a speck floating around in all that uterine fluid in my mommy's body. I knew I was the second daughter in a family that wanted boys. I also knew this was not good. Mommy was not going to be happy when the long-awaited beloved *son* didn't pop out to bind her and Dad's relationship.

My older sister was called "George" the whole time she was in the womb. At least I was spared that. Nonetheless, here I was, preparing my physical body for birth while my "light body" was worried about the fact I wasn't a "him." I announced my discontent at this intolerable situation by not breathing when I was born. I'm sure the doctor did what he did after my birth to get back at me for scaring him. After much feverish activity during which time he got me to take my first breath, he told my mother to "make her cry and scream for everything to strengthen her lungs."

Before I get all teary-eyed about my poor little baby plight, sad as it was, I have to say that while my crying and screaming for food and love over the next few years might not have helped my emotional stability, it certainly helped my singing voice.

At birth I had thrush in my mouth. Louise L. Hay, a metaphysical lecturer, teacher, and author, wrote a book on the probable emotional attachment to illnesses, called *Heal Your Body*. In it she says thrush is a result of anger over making the *wrong* decision. Well, that was right on. How about my decision to be another girl in a family that wanted boys? *Wrong* . . .

When I was born, it wasn't "the thing" to nurse your newborn, and Mom made the decision not to. I, clever little baby, reacted by being allergic to everything but mother's milk. I was named Patty because as I'd nurse, I'd pat my little hand on my mother's breast as if to say, "There, there, Mommy, it's okay I'm not a boy. You'll see, I'll make you love me." Later, when the nurses tried me on soymilk and found I could tolerate it, I was deemed "cured" and allergy-free.

But I wasn't. I'd been allergic to coming into the world. You don't cure that with soy milk. People didn't realize back then that sleep could be an allergic reaction. Mom complained that when I was a toddler, she had to carry me everywhere because I'd pass out on her when we'd go out. That was probably why I was deemed "the child who requires more sleep," or perhaps, clever child, I'd just discovered another way to be cuddled in mother's arms.

I learned at an early age I could get the adoration I so desired by being adorable, special, and entertaining. Showing anger, hurt, disappointment, and fear was not behavior that got me kudos, so I repressed them. On the rare occasion I didn't, Dad or

Mom would instantly reprimand me to get me back to the "pretty, perfect, little Patty" they knew and loved.

I started singing at two and began my professional career at age six in Kodiak singing and dancing to "Ta Ra Ra Boom Te A" for the USO. Looking back, I realize being "on" or good all the time was exhausting, but I so loved seeing how proud my parents were that, as they say in the theater, "the show must go on." Joy and lightness shone.

When I got exhausted from being perfectly adorable all the time, I'd catch a cold or flu. That's when I discovered how one was treated when one got sick in the Kimbell family. We were rewarded! Mom nestled me on the sofa in the living room with lots of comfy blankets and toys, made my favorite foods, and gave me her undivided attention. Dad would come home from work, call me Princess, and let me stay on "his" sofa. *Ta Ra Ra Boom Te A!*

Illness indeed served me. Since I didn't know how to turn "off" the energy I used to impress everyone and still get attention, I used illness to rest and recharge and start up all over again. What a cycle to start at such an early age.

I hit the big time in the illness department at ten with a positive tuberculin test. At that time my sister was hitting the other side of puberty. At 14, she had everything: budding breasts, attention of boys, and everyone in the family sewing 30,000 sequins on her cute flag-waver's costume.

I was a 10-year-old with nothing out of the ordinary happening. I remember thinking my brother has a radio, my sister has a radio, I don't have a radio. My brother has a dog, my sister has a cat, I don't have a pet. After moving from Alaska, I was feeling very left out in our new home in Chula Vista near San Diego. In Alaska, I had been a star, singing and dancing and performing for the USO. Here? I wasn't anything special. I wasn't getting the attention I so desperately craved. TB sure won out in the attention-getting contest. Mom and Dad had to coax me into taking my "horse" pills, telling me time and again how good they were for me. I felt good already. I loved the attention.

If anyone had been even a little bit conscious about what was really going on with me, TB would have been the perfect illness to point it out. I was suffocating myself with so much envy over all the attention my sister was getting, I could hardly breathe. TB was a big arrow pointing right at my lungs.

During my school years, my using illness was helped along by the fact I didn't like school. I never admitted to anyone how much I dreaded it. Knowing what I know now after helping my son with learning disabilities, I realize I had a form of them. It wasn't evident, because I'd become really good at covering up weakness. And my strengths were pretty astounding. I didn't have to take the Evelyn Woods speed-reading class in high school because I was already reading faster than the course could teach me. I could ace English without effort and was good at math. I got A's until I hit high school and was given homework and had to start memorizing things. My grades plummeted. My learning disability was not knowing what to study or how to memorize something in which I had no interest. I had no trouble memorizing songs, singing was something I loved to do. Memorizing multiplication tables and algebraic equations, remembering names, dates, and poems was grueling because there was no up side or reward for me. I needed someone to show me how and what to study and to teach me how to memorize something in which I had no interest. Faced with working alone, I couldn't do it, and it made my life miserable. I'd go into my room, shut the door, and do anything but homework so my parents wouldn't think there was a problem.

I saw my chart in the guidance counselor's office while I was in high school. I was a natural when it came to testing, so my test scores on aptitude tests and SATs were much higher than average. Actually they were so good, they got me into college. The comment I read in my folder that stuck with me? "Not performing up to her abilities." I felt terrible. Now, using my new tool of discovering "how everything that happens serves us" to go back and find out why I was not "living up to my potential" or how a learning disability could possibly help me, I discovered another pattern emerging.

I'd seen the reward one got for being intelligent and clever in my family. Four years before, when my sister had started high school, her superior brain began to show. She maintained a high average, and she and Daddy got along terribly. He constantly taunted her at the dinner table about being a "Miss La Te Dah" know-it-all. The message became clear: a girl shouldn't excel over men—it makes them feel inferior and crazy. Dad continually chipped away at my sister's burgeoning intellectual brain and confidence, fearful his own was being diminished. That wasn't what I wanted. I wanted people to like me and be kind to me. I wanted to get away from my feelings of not being good enough, not have someone chip away at my ego. If being all I could be meant I'd have to lose love and attention, then forget it. My greatest fear from birth was that I'd have to go it alone because I wasn't wanted. None of this, at the time, was conscious, of course.

When I finally found the wherewithal to go inside for information, I learned there is a cycle of emotions and illness that works within us. Many teachers, from Brugh Joy to Louise Hay to Christiane Northrup, have dedicated their lives to helping people become more aware of this body, mind, soul connection.

It's a circle.

I'd repress feelings, which would stress my immune system.

My stressed immune system would signal the body to become ill.

The illness it chose was my messenger pointing right to the exact emotions I had repressed.

Round and round we go.

6

IT'S TOOL TIME: Guidelines to Self-Discovery

On my pilgrimage to health and higher consciousness, I collected six basic foundational tools, four insights, and a technique called heart-centering that have changed my life. I know I've said there is no right or wrong way to make a transformational journey, and now here I am, giving you the "right" tools to build a foundation. However, these tools are universal. They have been and can be used anytime or anywhere. Most metaphysical and conventional religious teachers teach them one way or another. Each, though simple in theory, has the ability to provide powerful shifts in the perception of everyday life for whatever direction you take. They build a foundation from which to spring.

I also suggest cleaning your own emotional house. Anyone who accepts the charge for doing his or her own inner work before accessing higher awareness can be gifted. Prepare. Look into the past to see what emotions might be lurking behind a pattern that doesn't serve you. Use professional help by finding someone trustworthy to guide you in the psychological field, talk to your minister or rabbi or friend. Read books on the subject and meditate. Become an observer of your own life and be open to what materializes. Let go of hurts, resentments, and ego-based attachments.

Once the veil is lifted, there's no turning back.

For me, this process has become so fascinating, I don't want to turn back.

It hasn't been without challenges, though. I discovered the ability to heal with my hands long before I was ready. There was no instruction book called *The ABC's of Healing Hands* to which I could refer. I was so overwhelmed by my new talent, instead of hanging out a shingle as a healer, I treated it like a party trick. At social events, I'd heal someone's headache here, bring relief to a knee injury there. It took me years to become comfortable with how to use this new ability. Eventually, using the following injunctions and tools, I found an aspect of myself that was ready to accept and use my new talents with the reverence they deserve.

I just said, "Once the veil is lifted, there is no turning back." Of course, there is. We have choice. We have free will. It's just hard once you start becoming conscious to slip back into unconsciousness.

The following six tools help prepare a solid base to unfold in whatever direction you wish to take.

1. Beginner's Mind

I liken beginner's mind to live theater. A show is rehearsed for weeks. Every night it's the same show, same costumes, same actors, same words, same movements, and same songs. Yet, even if it's been done 30 times before, it is never approached as something to be tired of or skeptical about. Each night it starts anew. The curtain opens, the lights come up, the collective heartbeat of the audience eager for entertainment starts pulsing with the actors' hearts—all become one. All are fresh, alert, open, and energized by the possibilities of a brand-new evening.

A beginner's mind enables us to see old things in startlingly new and exciting ways. A way to practice a beginner's mind is to start viewing things seen all the time with the same awe and joy felt the first time the heart warmed at its sight. A daffodil, a husband, a wife, a sunset, a child, a home. It's contagious. Play a favorite piece of music, any piece that triggers the same incredible feeling it did the first astounding time you heard it. That's beginner's mind.

From beginner's mind, you are able to see things not seen before. Try looking at a forest differently. With unfocused eyes look just over the tops of the trees and "see" the white glow or aura emanating up into the sky. It's something new, "seeing" energy! On one beautiful bright day, I was out riding a pontoon bike on the Gulf of Mexico off Pensacola Beach, Florida. I'd peddled way out from shore, and when I turned to go back in, I could see the entire length of the barrier island. I noticed both ends were glowing. As I got closer, the ends of Pensacola Beach kept radiating light up into the bright blue sky. Since I'd had enough sun for the day, I climbed into my rental car and took off for either end. Both ends of this sandy barrier island were filled with trees. The light I'd seen was the energy radiating from the trees.

Coming from a *beginner's mind* frees us to accept what is. A beginner's mind is letting go of everything we have learned or experienced before. We know nothing, so we're open to everything. We are newborn babies, all fresh and willing to learn. No past or prejudices cloud an experience, because nothing has ever happened before. Now everything that happens is viewed with childlike wonderment.

Many new things open when we let go of our own imposed limitations and go into a place of the *non*knowing of a beginner. Look at a flower like you've never seen a flower before—or your husband or wife as if he or she were a stranger. Recapture the awe.

2. Make No Comparisons

One morning when I rode my bike to breakfast at Downey Flake in Nantucket I found the entertainment section of a newspaper left on the only available table. There was the perfect story to emphasize "make no comparisons." Linda Ronstadt and

Emmylou Harris were being interviewed about their upcoming concerts together. The interviewer asked Harris about the first time she saw Ronstadt sing. She said it so intimidated her, she stopped singing and concentrated on writing songs for a while. When Ronstadt was asked the same question about Harris, she replied that hearing her the first time was a crisis for her. She felt Harris was doing country rock so much better than she. Ronstadt told the interviewer that this was the time when she had to say to herself, "I can either let this make me feel really terrible, and I won't get to enjoy Harris' concert, or I could accept it as really great music and enjoy it. And that's the choice I made. It was a great lesson, because music isn't a horse race, and you can't have it be a competition. There's room for us all, and we all have our own stories."

So many times, we determine our self-worth by comparing ourselves to others. Who's got the smallest waistline, the biggest bank account, the highest education, the smartest kids, the best address, the brightest ideas. Instead of comparison, we need to accept whatever and whoever we are and do the same for others.

We've all been in the presence of a person in a heightened state and felt our own state heighten. Hearing a great singer, visiting a holy man, meeting a famous artist. Just being in their presence makes us realize that the potential of the human race is unlimited, and it changes the way we feel about ourselves. We revel in each other's accomplishments as fellow human beings on life's journey, instead of feeling we've been eclipsed.

In this process of transformation, feeling inferior or comparing yourselves to others on their paths can make you want to stop.

Now, when I feel I am not measuring up in life, I ask what it would take to make me feel good, and I do it. I take responsibility for my own emotional and spiritual work and allow others to do the same whatever way they choose.

I saw a great license tag. It's a good thing I was behind the car a long time, because I'm terrible at deciphering initials. It read: UBUNIBME. For those of you like me, it's: You be you and I'll be me. Next time you feel a comparison bubbling up, remember this and let it go.

3. Make No Judgments

It's been easy for me to slip into criticizing, since I grew up with a father who would say, "That's good, but try it this way." He called his almost constant disapproval of anything we did "constructive criticism" for our own good.

When I first learned this injunction, "Make no judgments," I had trouble deciding whether I was judging or intuitively reading a situation or person. I now know. If I am judging something, there's an emotional charge to it. When I'm intuitively reading a situation, I'm calm and dispassionate.

Not long ago, a friend wanted me to accompany her to an intensive workshop given by a woman who was one of the first hands-on healers of the New Age movement. Almost instantly, I disliked this teacher. It started with her appearance. Too much makeup, too much hair, too much weight adorned with tight and unattractive clothes. It only got worse when she spent the first four sessions talking incessantly about herself and her life with seemingly no point in mind. To top it off, she judged everything and everyone, making people feel small if they questioned her knowledge or held a different opinion.

It took me a while to realize I was doing the same thing with her. I was sitting in judgment because she was a disowned self of my inner psyche, or simply put, someone who, in the deep recesses of my mind, I was afraid I might become—an overweight, oversensitive, psychic know-it-all. She was my shadow side. No matter what I'd do, I couldn't stop how I felt, everything she did bugged me. Things finally turned around when I saw her doing a healing demonstration. This was where her intention lay, at heart level, awakening others into energy work so they, too, might become healers. When she went into healer mode, all the superficiality about her fell aside and I was able to really see her, with compassion.

The King James version of the Bible, Matthew 7, cautions, "Judge not, that ye be not judged." An important injunction, but not easily followed. Judgment is a behavior acquired through conscious or unconscious conditioning from parents, teachers, or peers. When we find ourselves sitting in judgment of another, we are most likely expressing an opinion that was acquired from the belief system of someone we loved or admired. I have to work hard at being nonjudgmental.

When I find myself mentally pointing a finger at someone in judgment, I now realize that three fingers are pointing right back at me and my own "stuff." Many times, when we judge someone, it is because we are afraid of becoming the very thing we are judging. We can acknowledge it and try to find where the person's heart lies and meet them there, or walk away until we are able to view the situation from a different perspective.

Try this exercise the next time you criticize someone. First, pretend you are pointing a finger at them and see the three pointing back at you. Then think about what you were saying about this person. Consider the possibility that these may also be deep-seated things you don't like about yourself.

4. Delete Your Need to Understand

At many of the conferences I've attended, I have spent the majority of my time in a state of total confusion. My *need* to understand wasn't kept secret. Unlike most people who'd sit quietly in the back, waiting for things to work out, I'd hop right in and question, "Wha-a-a-t?" While one aspect of me "understood" and accepted all that was happening without question, another needed answers to concrete, everyday questions, "What does this mean? Is this for real?" and, "This is all bull! What am I doing here?"

Over the years, I've finally arrived at a place where I can let go of *needing* to know. As a result, answers come through, and miracles flourish.

When my mind is going a thousand miles a minute, sometimes I'll go outside and lie on the ground. Breathing in the fresh air as I lie on my back, I'll gaze at the sky and feel the enormity of the universe. I connect to the Earth and recognize that spirit is everywhere, every tree, bush, blade of grass, cloud, piece of dirt, rabbit, bee—everything. I let go mentally, physically, and emotionally, and feel unconditional love pouring in from this communal spirit. I release my *need* to understand why I can connect in this way, and just let myself fill up.

There is nothing wrong with understanding, but a *need* to understand gets in the way of awareness. With the mind clear of *"needing to,"* it can simply receive direct knowledge. The need to understand freezes the mind on a single thought, so brain receptors are less open to receive unforeseen information. Needing to know is trying to control what simply *is*.

5. No Expectations

I'm always getting hung up on expectations, especially surrounding what I expect of other people. Men in particular. You poor guys. As I grow into my own person, a woman capable of taking care of herself, I am slowly, slowly releasing my "Knight-in-Shining-Armor-Coming-to-Save-the-Damsel-in-Distress" image of every man I meet. It makes it much easier on them and lets them be who they are and not someone I've conjured up in my mind to relieve me from self-reliance.

I set intentions, not goals. Goals indicate an *expectation* of what is to happen. I now know if a "goal" gets me to a place, almost nine times out of ten it's not why the universe has guided me there. Semantics, I know, but it's helped me. My cave dive in the first chapter with my expectation of nothing less than Hollywood enlightenment is a good example. Once I let go of my expected goal, I received the name of my book. I'd not considered it paramount to my "transformation," yet it changed everything.

Now I'm open to whatever comes. I set an intention and keep it flexible. Whenever I feel myself anticipating what I expect to happen, I let it go. I can then experience and enjoy what happens and relish life as it really is.

Having no expectations about others and ourselves frees us to be who we are. We can enjoy things in the present because we're not expending valuable energy toward making a result happen. Although you can still set your intention, you have no expectations about the outcome.

The next time you have an expectation of how an event, party, or date should go, stop the chatter in your mind, take a deep breath, and let every expectation go. Now enjoy yourself and others with no anxiety, no fuss, no muss. Apply the same technique to your spiritual development and watch your spirit unfold.

6. No Attachment to the Outcome

The Golden Rule was probably the hardest belief for me to unlearn from my childhood. I thought that "Do unto others as you would have them do unto you" was an ironclad guarantee that if you were nice to people, they'd be nice back to you. What it really meant was to treat others as you'd like to be treated. All my life, I've given the best, biggest, most expensive, and most extravagant presents. For this, I hoped to receive the equal or better in return. After all, wasn't that the Golden Rule? Most times, I'd sit with a forced smile on my face as people gave back to me what they wanted to give me, not a full measure of what I felt I'd given.

I began to recognize what I was doing when I met my match in the giving department. Alfred, my late husband, was the most extraordinary giver I have ever encountered. Alfred was wealthy in money as well as in the love he'd give. But there were strings. He unconsciously wanted people to give back in the same portions. I'd see his constant disappointment when he'd measure what he'd so generously given against the return. I also realized that most people couldn't respond in kind. They didn't have the means or the need. Feeling how it hurt him when friends always let him pick up the check broke my heart, but it also began my awakening. Retraining myself to give unconditionally without attachment to the outcome is still one of my most difficult lessons.

Movies are like waking dreams, the ones we like and the ones we don't can tell us a lot about ourselves. In the thirties, there was a movie with Irene Dunne and Robert Taylor called *Magnificent Obsession*. I saw it once or twice and found it remarkable. It was remade in the fifties with Rock Hudson and Jane Wyman. It's a perfect example of having no attachment to outcome. Rock Hudson played an impolite, spoiled, rich playboy, Bob Merrick, who foolishly wrecks his speedboat. The rescue team resuscitates Merrick with new equipment that then is unavailable to use when its inventor, the town's local hero, Dr. Wayne Phillips, collapses with a heart attack and dies.

Merrick ends up falling for Phillip's wife (Jane Wyman), who, of course, under the circumstances wants nothing to do with him. When he learns about Phillips's unspoken rule of conduct, to give selflessly and in secret, he tries it in a ham-handed way and causes even more suffering to Phillips's wife. He learns the hard way that anything given with the requirement that it be selfless and without remuneration can't be done as a means to an end. This kind of giving had to be with no repayment of any kind expected or accepted, though the good deed could be passed on to someone else. Hudson's character ends up going back to medical school and eventually becomes a selfless, giving person. At the end of the movie he winds up saving the life of Mrs. Phillips, and wins her heart. While it might seem a bit soap opera-ish to some, this movie speaks to me every time I see it.

Having an emotional attachment to a result can negate the desired outcome. Holding on tight to a desired ending doesn't allow the universe room to work its magic. And, it gets in the way of enjoying the present.

Look for ways to give anonymously, *selflessly and in secret*. A computer to a local school, a bouquet of flowers left on the porch for an elderly neighbor, or cash in a church box for an example. Forget about a tax write-off and give *unconditionally* from your heart without the recipient knowing you're the giver. If you can find ways to be anonymous, you will learn that the best outcome is one you never could have imagined.

Insights

1. The Observer, or Witness

Alfred would have died four months earlier than he did, had I not been able to go to the detached state of the witness. Arriving at the Palm Beach Airport, he walked into a men's room and collapsed from a fatal cardiac arrest. The only reason I heard him was I'd forgotten to give him the roses I'd bought him when he got off the plane, so instead of sitting across a wide hall to wait for him, I was standing next to the bathroom exit so I could surprise him. I heard him fall. I stood for a second calling in, "Alfred, Alfred!" and then rushed in to find him on his back, not breathing. I ran to a counter attendant and told her to call an ambulance and tell the EMTs my husband had had a heart attack in the men's room.

Racing back, I fell to my knees and immediately began CPR I'd learned at a course I'd taken three years earlier. While my hands were shaking, my mind was clearer than it had ever been. Even though my husband was lying dead on the floor in front of me, my brain remained in the detached state of the observer or witness as I performed CPR for seven minutes until help arrived. Moving from his side to his chest, back and forth, back and forth, I'd close his nose and cover his mouth with mine and breathe for him. Then I'd get up, adjust my long full skirt, and straddle him so I could use the weight of my body to force his heart to beat. Alfred was a big man.

I was beyond fear, beyond feeling. Totally focused on giving Alfred back his life, in the place of witness, I observed my petty annoyances, like how hard the tile was on my knees, and stayed in the place of healer. While I had some mental chatter, physically I did only what had to be done.

After a sheriff arrived, I still continued to do the rescue breathing while he began the chest compressions and his helper was trying to set up a hand pump breathing apparatus. When the paramedics came and were setting up, I was still on my knees breathing for Alfred. Looking up between breaths, I saw the woman paramedic having trouble getting an IV into a vein in Al's hand. I became angry and thought, *I don't believe this, I, who don't know what I'm doing, have kept him alive all this time and this "professional" is going to blow it?*

Calmly, looking up at her between breaths, I asked, "Do you want me to do that?"

She asked, "Are you a nurse?"

I said, "No, but I can do intravenous and shots."

I swear that if she'd said, "Okay, you try it," I would have.

Instead she immediately succeeded in getting the life-giving IV into his vein.

Even when things were getting under control, I didn't stop. I told the paramedic not to cut Alfred's favorite leather jacket if they could avoid it; he'd be upset. I took off his watch and put it into my purse. When the airport manager came, I reached into Al's pocket, took out his tickets, pulled off the luggage tags, and handed them to him, asking if he minded having Al's bags taken to my girlfriend waiting in the maroon convertible out front. "Oh, please tell her what happened." When we were leaving, I told the paramedics I would catch up with them at the ambulance and hurried to call Alfred's heart surgeon, Francis Robicsek, in North Carolina. Francis called ahead to Palm Beach emergency room to alert the doctors to Alfred's history and what to expect.

I went to the calm, detached place of observer and was able to surrender all fears, emotions, and annoyances.

Eighteen years earlier, I hadn't reacted as quickly. I was a new mom holding my infant son, when he stopped breathing. He didn't move or cry. He just started turning purple. Before I could respond, my mother grabbed him from my arms, turned him upside down, and patted his back. It worked. He started screaming in protest. My mother went into "witness" mode before I could even think. We all have a witness mode available inside us that can react without panicking.

While no one wants to get stuck in the dispassionate place of witness or observer, it needs to be available to us, and is extremely helpful in higher-consciousness work to "get out of yourself."

The Spirit meditation in the appendix can connect you to this place.

2. Don't Take Yourself Too Seriously and Remember Your Sense of Humor

"Be yourself," my mom used to say when I was growing up. Pretty confusing to me, since I didn't know who or what that was. I'd always "acted" sweet and loving, but was that "me"? Or was there some other self, a true self I hadn't yet met? While spending a lifetime finding the answer, along the way I discovered humor makes the journey a lot more enjoyable.

In this kind of enlightened work, looking holy or acting sacred doesn't get you there. I soon learned not to worry whether there was a certain way to look and act. So I was myself, questioning, irreverent at times, humorous, and even obnoxious about wanting concrete steps to enlightenment when my "inner teacher" wouldn't come forth with answers. I was and am, though, always respectful in situations that evoke respect.

Often at conferences, people thank me for my humor. I found that while this can be a reverent process at times, it doesn't always have to be a serious one. I've had fun, a lot of fun. I'm still having fun.

Different lectures I've given, *Stripping to Your Higher Spirit*, *Even the Big Guys Have a Sense of Humor*, and *May I Introduce You to Your Archetypes*, furnish me a venue to combine humor and spiritual work. Opening to higher consciousness and good health can be amusing if you're not always caught up in the grandeur of it all.

Lighten up and enjoy the process—the journey is about joy.

3. Pause, Center, Shift

I use this tool all the time, not just on a road to higher consciousness. Before I walk into a room of strangers, or give a talk or concert, if I'm playing really bad tennis, I momentarily pause, center, and shift to the more heart-centered aspect of joy. From there I can switch to the poised guest, knowledgeable lecturer, talented entertainer, or the "Chrissie Evert" tennis player aspect of my personality and go on with what I'm doing with confidence.

When you find yourself in a head place you don't want to be in, take two seconds to Pause . . . Center . . . and Shift . . . to a better aspect of your personality or to evoke one or more of the tools here. Take that second of *nothingness* and *stillness* when you pause to center yourself. I do this by envisioning a line going straight down my body from my head to my feet. I "*see*" each side shifting to a balance with the other and both centering in the middle. Then I shift to another more settled aspect and continue on a better course.

4. The Law of Attraction

A friend told me about a book called *Excuse Me, Your Life Is Waiting* by Lynn Grabhorn. In it, the author tells about getting a little buzz or high by focusing on joy and emanating that energy out to others. I decided to try it one night before I left to attend a party. On the ride over, I focused on being joyful. I did this by smiling a secret smile, connecting to my heart, and thinking of something that brings me joy, like my son, or the view from my house. I instantly raised my vibration to a higher level. The evening went beautifully. Everyone was happy to see me, and there was not one time that night that I felt alone, or not good enough.

The author also suggested a 30-day practice. Each day focus on something you like about yourself, so the moment you start thinking about something negative, you can quickly switch gears by saying your affirmation. I had no idea how much I'd slipped into negativity. That first day, I couldn't think of anything nice about myself, I wasn't happy with my weight, I usually like my hair, but I'd recently colored it myself as I usually do and noticed I'd missed a big spot in the back that looked like the black hole of Calcutta. I finally settled on, "I play a good game of tennis," for what I liked about myself the first day. Do you know how many times that day I had to say, "I play a good game of tennis," to counteract slipping into negative thinking? I couldn't believe how morose I'd gotten. A funny thing happened the next day, I was out running errands and had decided my hair was okay, so my positive statement was, "I have beautiful hair." That day I had four compliments about my hair.

Not only is it the Law of Attraction, it's also instant gratification.

You get what you give. If you vibrate a very low negative energy, that's when things like illness, muggings, car accidents, and worse happen to you. If you are vibrating high energy, like joy and love, that's when you can conjure up anything you want from the universe.

Everything is energy—you, me, a rock, a tree, a dog, a cat, money. All are energy. Energy vibrates. Energies vibrating the same frequencies attract and hook up. That's why I love walking into empty churches. Many times I find their designated sacred space vibrates a high, loving, peaceful energy.

Think about it. Whenever you have had something bad happen to you, illness or accident, weren't you down on yourself or fearful about something? Be honest. And just the opposite, if you've ever had some kind of a "spiritual" breakthrough, or felt very close to your universal source, haven't you been vibrating love, joy, energy, or been willing to surrender?

Try this. Whenever you feel negative, if you're going around grumbling and mumbling, stop. Breathe in joy and say an affirmation. Think of something you like about yourself, something beautiful, as a way to jerk you out of negativity.

If you've been negative for a while, don't be surprised if you notice some resistance in your body. The second night of my 30-day joy exercise, my foot cramped up more than it ever had. Apparently my body was reacting to letting go of negativity.

Heart-Center

I saw a miraculous change in a man I became close to at a Dark Side Conference I attended in Paulden, Arizona. Unbeknownst to me, Harvey came to the conference with an old pattern of looking at every situation with pent-up anger. His anger served him well because he never had to be disappointed when a situation didn't measure up. Of course, the flip side was he never was satisfied with anything or anyone. While he'd learned to heart-center at a conference several months before and had given up excessive drinking, heart-centering really hadn't clicked. He was still using anger as a motivator.

At the closing ceremony of our conference, he said he was amazed to have discovered that a dark side didn't have to be about something *dark*. He realized his dark side was passion and pleasure—things he resisted feeling before. When Harvey heart-centered, he stopped comparing and judging everything from a place of anger and made an instant and total transformation to coming from a state of unconditional love and joy.

Anger, like love, can quicken the heart and get adrenalin pumping. Sounds almost helpful, doesn't it? In the long run, anger destroys. Bodies, minds, and emotions fueled by anger will eventually suffer from illness, heart attacks, depression, abuse. Anger stresses. Certainly people around us suffer when we come from anger. If they are balanced enough themselves, it hurts them to see us hurting ourselves. If they are teetering, they think the anger is their problem.

Heart-centering is the one recurring theme that seems to thread through all the popular books and teachings. I see it in all of them. HeartMath is a corporation that teaches Fortune 500 companies how to use heart-centering in business. What a concept: people coming from their hearts in a down and dirty business deal. It doesn't state it that way, it's businesslike and offers to "enhance business performance through science-based solutions." Heart-centering is spelled out in *Joy's Way* and, at his conferences, Brugh Joy teaches it by doing it. The underlying message in all these teachings is that heightened states and universal guidance are best received when coming from a place of heart, joy, and unconditional love.

Heart-centering is simple and is experienced exactly as it sounds: centering on the heart. Coming from the heart with joy and love is the single most important device in my transformational journey. It creates a foundation of balance, protection, and stabilization. I can now heart-center in the lowering of an eyelid. I simply breathe in and think of the word "joy." I feel it filling and expanding my heart. It's a high that costs nothing.

I heart-center all the time, while meditating and before giving a healing session. I guide everyone in the audience into heart-center before I give a lecture. I connect to my heart before writing and before brushing my teeth. Well, maybe not before brushing my teeth, but as much as possible, I switch back to joy and live heart-centered. When you become heart-centered, anger slips away. Envy, jealousy, hurt, resentment, all things that keep us from being that which we truly are, evaporate. I consider heart-centering the cornerstone for this work.

The heart-center meditation in the appendix can be done whenever one feels so moved. If you are already into a certain meditative practice, heart-centering will augment it and take it deeper. You might try it now.

Once you find your center, your heart-center, everything can be tested against it for authenticity. From center there is an innate knowingness.

By using these tools to build a foundation, I gained the wherewithal to go back into my family history and begin a dispassionate search for patterns that had influenced and were still influencing my life.

7

MEN, DADDIES, AND GODS:
Looking for God in All the Wrong Places

Who Am I?

Certainly not Dad.

I look like him
Talk like him
Think like him

Oh, please, don't let it be.

I am myself.

What's so hard to see?

All those years
searching through
Men, Daddies, and Gods

Only to find me.

From the moment I came singing and tap-dancing into the world, I thought my daddy was God. He was a tall, handsome, distant man who acted as though he knew everything. Sounds like some people's description of God.

In my childhood estimation, the Sun rose and set because of him. As far as I was concerned, Daddy could do no wrong. Dad was also the first man who failed to live up to my expectations of a man making me feel safe and secure. While I was growing up, I had no knowledge of things hidden. I didn't remotely know or understand what motivated my father until after his death in 1997.

At 78, after Dad suffered a series of mini-strokes, he became incapacitated and was moved from his home in Dallas to a full-care private room at the Presbyterian nursing home. My sister, brother, and I had been agonizing over this day for years, thinking that when the time came, Dad would have nowhere to go because he hadn't done what we asked and gotten on a waiting list at a graduated-care retirement home. As it turned out, we'd worried for no reason. All was taken care of by his doctor without a hitch. When we got there, he was in the best nursing home in the area. We hoped Dad would do the physical therapy and emotional counseling recommended for his recovery and come out the man we all thought he would be when he got old—a loving, emotionally appropriate, proud, aging father and doting grandfather.

Just a dream, just a dream.

Instead, after Mom's death two years before, Dad had been chasing after (with his walker) sweet young things anywhere from age 19 to 21. He explained to me in a whisper not to worry, "I'm not doing anything with them cause I'm impotent." This was one time in my life I said exactly what I wanted to say. My reply? "You don't have to screw them, Dad, they're screwing you." The girls charged huge bills on his credit cards, got him to sign on three car loans, and took everything of value out of the house. One girl, Vanessa, a banker at his bank, tried to clean out $3,000 from his checking account before my sister and I put an end to it. Before Dad went into the nursing home, there was nothing we could do—he wasn't incompetent. He was just living out his dark side and loving it. He tried to explain his behavior away to me one time by saying Mom had given him permission to do anything he wanted when she died. I don't think so.

Whatever was happening to him, whether the little mini-strokes he continued to have caused his irrational behavior or if he just didn't care, Dad was in for a rude awakening in the nursing home. He soon discovered the only way to stay in this nice place, where everyone waited on him hand and foot, was to follow the rules, act appropriately by not making passes at the women doctors and nurses, and do the very painful exercises to get back muscle mass. He refused to exercise but did lighten up on the women staff. He still told them how pretty they were, he just didn't overdo it. He completely laid off flattering his woman psychologist, who from the way my sister described her, sounded like Nurse Ratched in *One Flew Over the Cuckoo's Nest*.

He was content to lie in bed in his private room for the next two years, watching television and resting on his somewhat tarnished laurels. His only desire was to live until he was 80. For some reason, this was an important milestone for him. On his 80th birthday, I think he intended to blow out the candles, eat his last bite of carrot cake, clutch his heart, and ceremoniously die.

When his birthday came and went, he was disappointed he hadn't died on cue. He decided to change his plan, exercise, get his strength back, and move out. He'd waited too long. Nine months later, frail, the beard he was so proud of shaved because it was too much trouble for the nurses to keep clean, with bedsores here and there, he passed away alone in his sleep without fanfare.

While I feel that if people need us to be there when they die, they will make it happen, of all the people who have died in my life and in spite of all that happened, I wish I could have been there with my dad.

At Dad's funeral, as at my mother's three years before, I found myself standing on the dais of the little stone chapel nestled on the grounds of the Restland Memorial Cemetery in Dallas. Once again, I was singing "The Way We Were," the family standard I sang at all my parents' anniversary parties.

My mind wandered as the familiar words came out my mouth:

"Memories—light the corners of my mind. Misty watercolor memories—of the way we were."

I had choked back sobs at my mother's funeral when I sang those words. I truly missed the way we were when she was alive. My little mom. Five-foot-two, maybe a 105 pounds soaking wet, forever perfectly coiffed and dressed. She always greeted our surprise trips to Texas with open arms, big smiles, and delighted laughter. Since we knew how much she loved our visits, whenever we could, my sister, brother, and I would make big detours in our plans so we could pop in and surprise them. Here, at Dad's funeral, I realized tiny Mom had always kept us from really knowing our real six-foot-two dad. I could see them dancing at their 50th wedding anniversary, Dad's chin resting on the top of Mom's head. So connected to each other.

"Scattered pictures of the smiles we left behind, smiles we gave to one another for the way we were."

Smiles? Singing for Dad, I was trying to control an almost irresistible urge, no, not to smile, but not to burst into hysterical laughter.

"Can it be that it was all so simple then? . . ."

Oh, sure. "Simple" could really describe my family. My older sister, Kat, wasn't at the funeral. Kat has a fragile beauty and a brain that makes her an incredible executive in the computer field. I think of her as a short-haired blonde, a medium-length redhead, and long-haired brunette because she's been all and more. Kat inherited mother's size, though taller at five-foot-six, and Dad's skin, which is not particularly good in the sun. Eight months before, she had flown to Dallas to celebrate Dad's 80th birthday. I think she had enough of him on that visit. Whatever her reasoning, I didn't care. In my book of rules, everyone came to their father's funeral. Besides, I wanted her there. I wanted family.

". . . or has time rewritten every line? If we had the chance. . ."

I wanted one more time to pretend we were a loving, caring unit. I wanted my big sister to take care of me. I wanted, I wanted, I wanted.

My younger brother went to the other extreme and brought his entire family—wife and four daughters—from Pittsburgh. At five-foot-ten, I'm a tall woman. Jack at five-foot-ten is considered a medium-height man. He is nice-looking with a shocking small white forelock in his full head of brown hair. Always being in great shape might have something to do with his being an executive for a chain of country clubs. His four daughters all look like their mother, brunette, petite, pretty, and so musically talented, it's almost unnerving.

Jack requested an open casket so his daughters could see their grandfather dead. *Why*, I asked myself, *do the men in my family always insist on an open casket?* This time Jack. Last time, Dad had to have Mom's casket open after she'd been brain-dead for two years with Alzheimer's. Maybe an open casket was some kind of machismo "everyone needs to experience death" thing with the men in my family.

". . . to do it all again, tell me would we, could we?"

My son Doug hated seeing his grandmother as a skeleton dressed in her favorite beige St. John knit suit. He was 18 then and a big, strong, six-foot blond Arnold Schwarzenegger look-alike. Doug was angry with Dad for having Mom's casket open. He wanted to remember her as the vibrant woman who took him to all his swimming and tennis lessons and to the penny arcade for video games during the summers he spent with them in Texas. For that matter, so did I. Doug didn't fly down for Dad's funeral, either. He was busy starting a career. No, that wasn't it. He had burned out, too.

"Memories, may be beautiful and yet . . ."

I didn't care what anybody's reasons were. My daddy-god had just died, and nobody seemed to care. I wanted to see life through my rose-colored glasses one more time.

". . . what's too painful to remember . . . we simply choose to forget . . ."

This funeral certainly wouldn't be one I'd forget. I came early to the chapel to rehearse, looked in the coffin, and gasped. "You've got the wrong body. That's not my father!"

Everyone panicked for a moment until I realized the man in

my father's coffin who looked like a slick Italian count was, in fact, Dad.

"... so it's the laughter, we will remember ..."

It was funny in a macabre sort of way. The mortician had slicked back Dad's hair, waxed his mustache, and given him a face-lift by pulling the skin taut around his eyes, mouth, and chin. With the weight Dad had lost lying in bed for two years, he looked more like Count Ernesto from Sicily than "General Bull Moose," my big Texan father.

"... whenever we remember ..."

We hadn't remembered to give the funeral home a picture of Dad to go by.

"... the way we were ..."

Of course, if we'd had a closed casket, it would have been a nonissue.

"The—Way—We—Were ..."

Things would never again be the way we used to pretend they were.

Dad dead wasn't who I wanted him to be. My sister, who wasn't at the funeral, wasn't who I wanted her to be. My brother, in attendance, wasn't who I wanted him to be; and my prodigal son, who hadn't shown, wasn't who I wanted him to be. Nobody was living up to my expectations, my hopes, my dreams.

As we say in the higher-consciousness transformation game, when you point a finger, three are pointing back at you.

What really was going on?

Simple.

I wasn't who I wanted to be.

Dad's funeral was another big opportunity for me to wake up.

On my father's birthday, December 7, 1997, three months after his death, I was back in Dallas attending a weekend conference with a motivational "guru." My friend Jody liked this teacher and had suggested I come. She would be there working as an aide and her husband, Bill, would also be attending. I decided to go.

Since I felt it would probably be the last time I'd be in Dallas for a while, I went to Dad's hometown to see if I could find information surrounding his father's mysterious death. All we were told growing up about our grandfather, Jack, was that his death had something to do with a debt of some kind.

Through relatives at Dad's funeral, I had found out my grandfather died on October 6, 1927, and that he'd been a national baseball star and a local hero. Like my father, he was purported to be a tall, good-looking man who could charm you at 50 paces. He retired from baseball due to a hernia, and then struggled to make a living any way he could. I went to the Mesquite, Texas, library and looked up the October 7, 1927, newspaper. There was nothing. I assumed it was no big deal and was about to leave when I thought maybe I should look up the next weekly paper.

When I saw the big, bold, one-inch headline, my heart stopped:

JACK KIMBELL IS DEAD, JOHN S. LAWRENCE OUT ON $15,000 BOND.

The story went on for the entire front page and was written in a shell-shocked, hysterical tone because the journalist, like dozens of others, had witnessed the murder in broad daylight in the town square.

He reported that a scuffle had broken out between John Lawrence, who was the mayor as well as the president of the bank, and granddad's brothers, Oscar and Charlie. It started when Lawrence asked them about a $55 loan their father owed the bank. Charlie is quoted as saying, "Just sit steady in the saddle; we're going to pay you every cent we owe you." Some pushing ensued and when Lawrence said, "Don't crowd me, men," my grandfather walked up and replied, "You've been crowding me for three years."

What lay beneath my granddad's remark and all the hard feelings was my grandmother. This was the woman beloved by everyone in my family; the woman I'd always been told I take after. In later newspaper stories, it came out that Grandma had been involved in an affair with the mayor. At the time of the murder, she was separated from my grandfather, and Granddad was suing the mayor for $50,000 for "alienation of affection."

When my grandfather jumped into the fray with Charlie and

the mayor, he allegedly hit Lawrence with a pair of "brass knucks." Lawrence pulled back and ran through Herndon's store, demanding that Scott, the store owner, give him back the gun he'd dropped. Scott refused, telling him to go back to the bank and cool off. Lawrence went back, picked up his .33 Winchester rifle, and ran around the front way.

Before dozens of witnesses in and around the town square, Lawrence stood at the corner about 90 or 100 feet from where Oscar and my grandfather, Jack, had walked. First leveling the rifle on Oscar as he ran off to the left, it was said, Lawrence very deliberately turned it to my grandfather and fired twice in rapid succession. The first bullet went wild, but the second one struck Granddad on the right side and went through his kidneys. Grandfather took a step and faltered, another step, and then throwing out his hands, he fell, first on his hands and knees; then he keeled completely over into the entrance of the Herndon store. He yelled out, "First he wrecks my family and then he tries to kill me?" He was rushed to the St. Paul Sanitarium and was fully conscious during most of the night. He died shortly before seven o'clock Friday morning.

I stayed in the library all day, checking and cross-checking articles in different papers. I read, reread, and made copies of everything. There were stories in the Dallas papers as well as the local paper with events of the trial reported daily. I tried to take it all in and relate it to its time, 1927.

Kevin Rayburn wrote about the twenties that it was "the first truly modern decade and, for better or worse, created the model for society that all the world follows today, and, though it was an era of towering intellect in the arts and sciences—perhaps like none before or since—it was also an era of pettiness, ignorance, and poverty."

That was the part that caused my grandfather's death: pettiness, ignorance, and poverty.

I talked to my elderly great-aunt, my grandmother's sister, who was very sympathetic to my grandmother's side of the story. She said my grandmother had gotten fed up with my grandfather's inability or lack of desire to feed and shelter his family when he quit baseball because of the hernia. Grandma was stuck with three babies on a small dirt farm outside of town with only oatmeal to feed them many days. That was when Grandma accepted the attentions of John Lawrence, a dashing, rich married man with a reputation for womanizing.

From what I learned, my own father was at his father's side as he lay dying. He heard his father say to his uncle, "Take care of my baby for me," nodding toward his ten-year-old son.

His uncle gave him no help because my dad stayed with his mother. Everyone on his father's side of the family must have blamed her for the death. I'm sure with emotions running so high, no one took my father aside to say, "Little Jack, this had nothing to do with you. You couldn't have saved your pa's life or your ma's reputation." He probably harbored thoughts that if he'd been a better little boy, none of this would have ever happened.

Lawrence was sentenced to jail for 50 years, served two as a trusty, was paroled, and then was pardoned a year later by Governor "Ma" Ferguson. Rumors of bribery circulated, and the number of pardons the "pardoning governor" gave during her term became the subject of political jokes in Texas.

Nothing was ever done to assuage a young boy's need for justice regarding the cold-blooded public execution of his father and hero.

Twenty-two years later, in 1949, Lawrence again ran for mayor of Mesquite. He said he would only run unopposed on the Freedom ticket. When he was installed in 1950, Dad moved all of us from Pensacola, Florida, to Kodiak, Alaska. Seven years later, he wanted to take us to Jakarta, Indonesia. Mom put her foot down and insisted we come back to the States. Dad couldn't seem to get far enough away.

I realize now that it wouldn't have mattered how far Dad traveled; the man who had murdered his father ruled Dad's life his entire life. Dad didn't return to live in Texas until the mayor died around 1975.

It was always at Mom's insistence that we even visited Texas twice. We had cousins, first, second, and third; uncles; aunts;

great-aunts; and great-uncles I never got to know. Of course, I never met any relatives from the Kimbell side of the family. Dad grew up with his mom, whom the Kimbells blamed for their son's murder. As a result of all this my sister, brother, and I grew up with no sense of family. Even the five of us living together in Alaska for seven years did nothing to unite our little clan. Since my parents have died, my siblings and I know nothing about one another's daily lives, nor do we seem to care.

I uncovered a lot more than my family's scandal during the Saturday I spent in the Mesquite library. I discovered how much my own life had been clouded by an unknown past.

"The sins of the parents will be visited upon the children even unto the third and fourth generations" (Exodus 34:7).

What a prophecy. Dad's feelings of inadequacy, due to his inability to save his family when he was 10, were passed down to everyone who came in contact with him. With my sister, brother, and I, nothing we ever did was good enough. While my father called it "constructive criticism" and said it was for our own good, he was really just coming up with ways to feel better about himself and stay in control.

When a neighbor started a weekend project to build a new backyard planter, Dad took over the job, implying it wasn't being done right. I'm sure he did this with business associates, too. Many let him do his thing and bowed out. Why not? Dad did their work for them. Instead of encouraging us to do our school projects, he did them for us. One time he built me a beautiful scale model of the United Nations. I was mortified when I had to lie to the teacher and say I had done it myself. No matter how well we did, Dad could even come up with a better way for us to get an A.

Dad also helped us stand out from the crowd. He had an ability to do anything to which he set his mind. He even helped Mom make my costumes for my song and dance recitals. I'd have the best ears on my bunny costume and the most ruffles on my cancan skirts. I was proud to have the best costume. I liked feeling special.

Eventually though, at age 20, when I left my family, Dad's constant corrections and criticisms became my own inner critic.

As far as I was concerned, nothing I did was ever enough. There was always more to accomplish or better ways to have achieved it. I'd go out for a 20-minute walk when I had CFS, which was a feat in itself, and come back berating myself for not doing 30 minutes. Like Dad, I had to prove to myself over and over that I was as good as or better than everyone else. We were going for *perfect* in the Kimbell family.

Because of all this, a superior/inferior tug of war began inside me. Wanting to be noticed because of being the second daughter in a family that wanted boys, I created a side of myself that seemed totally self-assured. This side I presented to the world when I'd sing and dance on the stage.

The other side of me had been conditioned by my father's criticism. I was so attuned to "being open" to pleasing my parents, I became a "sensitive" who could pick up everyone's thoughts and emotions and take them all to heart. I was extremely thin-skinned and easily hurt over the smallest sign of dissatisfaction from anyone. Since I liked feeling special, my life became a struggle to always feel special about everything I did. Not a good combination—an outgoing, "look at me, aren't I great" sensitive.

Men

I guess it wouldn't be a stretch to say Dad is probably the reason I always go for exciting, dynamic, rather difficult men.

Before we were married, Bruce, my first husband, and I would drive down to spend a few days at his parents' weekend farm in the Blue Ridge Mountains of Virginia. We were young. I was 20, he 23. We'd arrive on a beautiful sunny day to fields of jonquils and daffodils greeting us from the 400 acres of rolling hills, creeks, and pond. We'd be looking forward to a fun weekend of hiking, skeet shooting, tractor rides, and visiting with his family and friends. Instead, I'd end up asleep on the sofa in the kitchen most of the weekend with my head filled up, tired and unable to participate in the family gatherings. After 20 years of no allergies, all of a sudden I was allergic again. Now it all makes sense.

Right before I met Bruce, I was in denial about everything. I didn't want to go back to college after my year off, nor did I want to continue working and living at home. So when I went with a former high school boyfriend to a party at three bachelors' apartment, I "accidentally" forgot my guitar. Unconsciously I decided that, when I went to retrieve it, whoever answered the door would be the man I'd marry. Bruce answered. Great! He was good-looking, a former captain of our rival high school's football team, and from a nice family that was wealthier than mine. To me, he seemed full of potential to be the man of my dreams.

He asked me to marry him on May 9, 1967, we got a ring on July 4, and were married September 2 with all my expectations fully in place. As far as I was concerned, he would give me the same safe and secure lifestyle that his father, the acting director of America's supersonic transport, seemed to have given him. This included, in my mind, a successful career, a big house in Alexandria, Virginia, and a 400-acre farm in the Blue Ridge Mountains of Virginia, just like his parents.

Unfortunately, for all my grand schemes, out of a whole family of magna cum laude graduates from Stanford, Bruce was dyslexic and couldn't conquer it. Back then, dyslexia carried the stigma of "the child's not trying" or, worse still, "he's dumb" instead of "he simply learns differently, let's find out how." Forty years ago, no one really knew how to help a child who had trouble learning. Bruce had wonderful, loving parents. However, when Bruce got a car stuck on a rock at the farm, I remember his father treating him like he was a continual screw-up. His mother always made excuses for him. Not a great combination to help him with his particular problem.

My father had drummed into my head that all of his own problems related to his lack of a college education. He thought the same would happen to Bruce. Now I realize Dad's problems had nothing to do with college. Dad and his friend Hank Ketchum, both wonderful young artists, drew the "We Want You" posters for the Navy's Uncle Sam campaign when they were 20. Dad stayed in the government, to have security, and Hank went on to create "Dennis the Menace." Dad's problem wasn't college.

It was not feeling good enough about himself no matter what he could do or accomplish.

I didn't realize any of this at the time I was married to Bruce, so I felt Bruce's dyslexia and his inability to finish college were getting in the way of my dreams. I had had visions of me putting him through college and law school, just as my sister had done with her husband.

Now, add to all this my real expectations for marriage. I thought marriage would be a haven where I would always feel safe and secure. I believed my husband would forever "have my back." He would be a provider—not just financially, but mentally, emotionally, spiritually, and physically.

What impossible tasks I set up for Bruce with all he and I brought to the table.

It's a shame I never saw Bruce as he really was, because in truth, he is a handsome, charismatic, wonderful guy. When I found out early in our marriage he wasn't going to be able to go back and finish college as he said he would, I was despondent, though I didn't voice my thoughts.

Six months after we were married, I was lying on the sofa crying. I think I realized I'd made a mistake and that he couldn't be the person I'd envisioned. When I wouldn't or couldn't explain why I was so unhappy, Bruce said maybe I should go back home to my parents. The possibility of admitting I'd made a mistake to people who told me I was making a mistake kept me from crying for the next seven years. I polished up my rose-colored glasses and "made happy." I tried living my mother's example of being "the little woman behind the man." It wasn't all that hard, we did have wonderful friends and fun, fun times together. However, after he'd had 11 different jobs in seven years, I couldn't close my eyes anymore. This was not what I'd signed up for.

It wasn't until years later, when I had to fight to find the proper schools to support our son Doug's severe dyslexia, that I realized what Bruce had gone through. After seeing what Doug has accomplished in his life, finding and then pursuing his passion with abandon, I realized what having people around who believe in you can do.

After I left my marriage to Bruce, "Safe" and "Secure" became capitalized words in my vocabulary. Finding safety and security became linked to the things I thought he lacked. My next "Savior" would have an education, job security, and money.

On July 4, 1975, I left Salisbury, Maryland, with half the furniture, $5,000, and our handsome, tow-headed, 18-month-old son, Doug. Though I didn't voice it except to myself, I was going back to Washington, D.C., to find someone better to take care of us. Because of the years I'd spent in banking in my first marriage, I quickly found employment as the assistant marketing director of a small bank in D.C. I decided this would do until I could find a well-paying singing job (an oxymoron if I've ever heard one). I moved back to the same apartment complex in Alexandria, Virginia, where Bruce and I had lived seven years before, and hired a great babysitter.

All these, in my mind, were just temporary measures to give Captain Marvel time to find us. To my way of thinking, here was a beautiful, tall, blond young lady with the asset of a beautiful, bouncing, blond baby boy. I saw Captain Marvel not in a super-hero's tights and cape but as a knight resplendent in shining armor around the corner reining in his impatient white charger. Seeing Dougie and me, he'd swoop us up off to his castle (or an equivalent four-story Victorian town house in Dupont Circle), where we would live happily ever after.

Never did I anticipate being a single working mommy for five years.

During those five years, my business confidence grew until I made my way into mortgage banking. In one month on straight commission as a mortgage banker I made half my former yearly salary as a banker. I was achieving more than most men.

People marveled at what a success I was at motherhood, a career, and dating. Me? I was thankful I no longer had a nine-to-five job, so I could still excel and fudge my hours. Unconsciously I'd begun wrestling with how doing better financially than most men was going to serve me in finding a man to take care of me and my son. It became hard for me to get up in the mornings. I was exhausted. The only thing I seemed to learn by earning a man's wage in a man's job was that I still wanted a man to do it. Unconscious to me, I had been deeply programmed growing up not to exceed my father's accomplishments.

I had another big surprise during the years I was a single, working mom. Never, in a million years, would I have guessed I'd date older men. As I look back now, I realize the older men I met had several things in common: they were financially secure, educated or intelligent, and had clout in their various fields. They met the safety and security standard I'd set of education, job security, and money. On their side, they were probably so happy to have a younger woman around to make them feel young—they didn't mind me bringing a child into the picture, as did some of the men my age.

I met my second husband, Michael, on a blind date. He asked me to marry him that night, and I accepted nine days later. We were married two months after that and bought one of the castles I'd dreamed of (*the* four-story Victorian town house in Dupont Circle).

Since incidents like that proved to me that I could have hopes, dreams, and expectations, and they would be met, I suppose I was thinking when I'd marry so quickly, *Why wait to get to know a person before marrying? If he isn't exactly what I want, I'll turn him into the person I envisioned.*

Right. That philosophy had worked so well in my first marriage.

Michael already was heady stuff. A lobbyist, he was known as the guru in the health field on Capitol Hill and was credited with single-handedly turning around the treatment of the mentally ill in the United States back about the time I was born. This all began through his exposé writings as a young journalist and then a best-selling book called *Every Other Bed*. The title referred to the fact that a mentally ill patient was in every other bed in a hospital. It was *Reader's Digest* condensed, became a Book-of-the-Month selection, and Michael was named Jaycee of the Year. He was the first journalist to be awarded the prestigious Albert D. Lasker Foundation medical award for journalism. President Harry Truman asked him to come east to serve as his aide in the health field. After being in Truman's inner circle, Michael stayed in Washington and lobbied in the health field for the next 40 years.

His friends were famous people. Congressmen and senators called for his advice. The world-renowned heart surgeon Michael DeBakey was his best friend and best man at our wedding. Mary Lasker, credited with being the last of America's grande dames, gave us our wedding reception at her huge U.N. Plaza apartment in New York City. Among all the artwork of Chagall, Monet, Matisse, Picasso, and Renoir, we drank magnums of Dom Perignon and gorged ourselves on Beluga caviar and Norwegian smoked salmon with capers. Her dearest friend, Abigail Van Buren (Dear Abby), attended. Yep, heady stuff.

Now, while all these extraordinary happenings were going on, there were also signs the size of billboards shouting at me, telling me what I was really doing. I was so in my own little dream world and bedazzled by the glitz, glamour, and celebrities, I couldn't read the signs even when they *did* come in threes.

One: My husband was older than my father.

Two: He had my father's birthday, December the seventh.

Three: He had a daughter named Patricia.

Pretty black-and-white even with my rose-colored glasses.

Not black-and-white enough for me to get the message in 1979, however. Even though Michael, at 65, was 33 years older than I at age 32, I refused to see that I might be marrying a father figure. When some people made snippy comments about me looking for a daddy to take care of me, I told them I had a perfectly good father of my own.

The truth? This was the best offer I'd had in five years to stop growing into my own power, to stop the struggle to succeed and not to succeed on my own. I wanted a break from the fear I had and the "looping" I was doing. Succeed/not succeed/succeed/not succeed. I wanted the safety and security I felt I'd only find through a man. And to give the naysayers their due, here was a ready-made situation for me to make a relationship with a father figure into one that made me feel safe.

However, wouldn't you think having two men in my family with December seventh, the date of the bombing of Pearl Harbor, as their birthday, I might have gotten a clue as to what was going on? Nope. Never did see a connection between one of the most dramatic events in modern U.S. history, the huge denial of our entire country concerning a possible Japanese invasion, and the chance there might be some explosive denial going on in my life. Instead of hearing all the messages that might lead me inside for the real reasons I was marrying Michael, I stuffed them.

Very shortly after the marriage, the mornings I couldn't get up when I was a single mommy/mortgage banker turned into Chronic Fatigue Syndrome. I'm sure the physical aspect of me being inundated with brick and plaster dust while renovating and living in our Dupont Circle house didn't help matters much. During construction I'd go over to a neighbor's house and nap when I couldn't function. In Louise Hay's little blue book, the probable CFS emotional attachment is "fear of not being good enough." Was it fear of not being good enough to be my own person or of not being good enough to be in the illustrious company I was keeping? Take your choice. Fear had me vibrating at a very low energy.

When I married Michael, I had envisioned myself sitting at his knee, lapping up knowledge. Unfortunately, for all Michael's prestige and awards, he had terrible insecurities about himself and about not feeling good enough. He was a caustic Irish Catholic who got his entertainment out of attacking the egos of others. Boy, I'd really done it this time. I'd married a richer, more educated version of my father—a cynical man who was a mirror to my own and my family's past insecurities.

Michael's greeting on a morning when I wasn't feeling well was, "So, what's your disease of the day today?" The man could go out and save the masses, but couldn't deal one-on-one to save his life. He once said to me after a fight, "If you think it's hard for you to live with me, you should be in here," pointing to himself.

You have to grant him witty. Oh, what a wit master he was. After five years, we had an amicable divorce and ended our eclectic partnership. Getting a divorce from me is like sending a kid to camp. I found Michael an apartment, rented him furniture, hung art on his walls, and cooked his first meal.

You might think I would have begun to realize that if all the men I attracted had repressed feelings about not being good enough, maybe it was a sign for me to look at this in myself? What we resist persists? Not yet. I wasn't that awake yet.

Alfred, my third husband, was the love of my life. He was the only man who lived up to my expectations. It's embarrassing to admit what made me so happy. He gave me everything I wanted. Everything—houses, cars, clothes, jewelry, purses, shoes, antiques, art, fine Oriental rugs, vacations to exotic places. He had me hire the top music men in New York to help put together my one-woman cabaret show. He sent me anywhere I wanted to go to look for a cure to my health problems. He was generous, loving, and kind, and always, always happy to see me. I'd sit on a curved stone bench out front of our house and wait for him to come home just to see his face light up like a Roman candle when he saw me. He was everything I'd ever dreamed of. Alfred came the closest to making me feel safe and secure through the abundance and unconditional love he continually bestowed upon me.

But then, Alfred died.

Once again, thinking I'd finally attained lasting safety and security through another person was an illusion.

When I had allergies right after Bruce and I became engaged, it wasn't because I was allergic to the man I was marrying.

When I became sick with CFS after marrying Michael, it wasn't that I was sick about the man I was marrying.

When I didn't get well during the time I was married to Alfred, it wasn't because I didn't love the man to whom I was married.

What was making me allergic and sick and not able to get well were the *reasons* I was marrying the men I married.

I wasn't marrying men. I was marrying situations.

Situations I hoped would make me feel safe and secure,

The same safety and security I wanted but didn't receive from Dad.

From the time I was a little baby I thought my Daddy was God.

And there it was.

I was looking for God in all the wrong places.

We look back through our history to find the patterns we live out and repeat in our lives. Not to obliterate them, but to recognize and honor them. All my life I was Sleeping Beauty waiting for the handsome prince to awaken me to my own radiance with a kiss.

Finally, long after my handsome princes were gone, I awakened.

**The essence of feeling safe and secure
comes not from connecting with another person,
but from connecting to our own higher self.
Security only comes from within.**

8

WOMEN, MOMMIES, AND GODDESSES:
Sacred Space and Archetypes

Women need sacred space.

I never knew that until I moved to New Mexico. I kept finding myself creating sacred places, both outside on my land and
inside in my home. It's said the veil between is thinner there. I
have to agree.

It's commonplace in New Mexico to honor one's connection
to the universe. Without any self-consciousness, niches are built
into the walls of homes to hold religious objects that honor
deities and bring in sacred energy. This part of the country is so
steeped in blessedness, no one thought it odd that a woman
from the Northeast would create a large, sacred garden constructed as a replica of an old stone chapel ruin.

When I bought my property, I realized the rock wall the previous owner had built around the garden was poorly constructed. I decided not to be judgmental and to regard this flaw
as part of the charm of the place. Almost the first night after I
moved in, the wind gusted to nearly 75 miles per hour. Back on

my former little island of Nantucket, the natives call blustery weather of that velocity hurricane force "Nor'easters." At 7,000 feet in New Mexico? They're gusts. Welcome to the Wild, Wild West. Things were whipping that night. The long, big wind chimes had to be taken down so the clanging wouldn't drive my houseguest and me nuts.

The next morning was beautiful, and I started my "first light" ritual that day. Watching the day awaken from the converted sun porch off my bedroom, I repeated a Sun Meditation I had copied from the *Book of Runes* by Ralph H. Blum.

> *You, who are the source of all power,*
> *Whose rays illuminate the whole world—*
> *Illuminate also my heart*
> *So that it, too, can do your work.*

Then I went outside for a walk. With decaf in my favorite American flag mug, I wandered around my eight acres in my nightgown, coat, and beloved "Ugg" boots on this early December morning.

My property is situated on a bluff with uninterrupted views of open land for miles in all directions. As I strolled toward the garden taking in all around me in the dim light, I had a vague sensation something was different. Too enchanted by the distant morning light playing on the far prairies to let it enter my consciousness, I let the feeling go. I turned to view the glow of the Sun's first rays on the top of the Ortiz Mountains miles away, and said out loud, "I am the luckiest girl in the world." Turning back, I soon reached the middle of the garden. As I scrutinized the situation in the dawn's early light, I realized that, *yep*, my instincts had been right, something was very different. My funky stone wall was gone. Three sides had blown over during the night. I was standing in the middle of a garden of rubble.

My first thought, bringing out my best I'll-turn-lemons-into-lemonade was, *Oh, goody, a real physical exercise project outside on the land. I won't have to do "fake" exercise in a gym. I'll rebuild the wall myself.*

I set down my cup and decided to put the first few stones back in place that moment. As I bent over, I noticed the cement was so dry and crumbly, it simply fell off. I surmised that was good, it wouldn't have to be tediously chipped off to reuse the rocks. I envisioned the whole project complete in a couple of weeks.

The rock wouldn't budge.

"Bend your knees, Patricia. Don't use your back," I said to myself, and tried again.

It was anchored to China.

It seemed my large rocks were heavier than a gym's eight-pound weights.

I put out the word I needed a stonemason, and the synchronicity began.

My new neighbor, Wendy, brought up her handyman extraordinaire, Angel, who could not only handle the stonework, but was also a carpenter, a painter, a contractor, and a sweet young guy who spoke only Spanish. With my two years of high school Spanish, both of which I had to repeat in summer school, we somehow managed to communicate.

My "simple little project" required at least 10 times more rock than I anticipated to complete the "chapel ruin" plan that unfolded in my mind as the work progressed. Rocks are expensive. I use to think of rocks as hard dirt. Dirt's everywhere. And with that clever deduction, I figured I shouldn't have to pay much more than the cost of transporting them to my property. Not so. The rocks we were matching were *quality old* rocks. Apparently, rocks with good lineage such as mine are right up there with fine art and antiques.

We (as in the *royal* we) decided to make the walls look like ruins by building up the corners higher than the sides. I'd noticed on actual ruins the corner joints are stronger and disintegrate last on old adobe buildings, so the walls slope down from the corners into the middle.

Instead of putting one of the original garden gates back up, I searched for double arched doors and found them at a local place called Jackalope. New from India, they're made to look like old

Mexican doors painted a faded-looking light blue. What the heck, I was going for the *illusion* of chapel doors, not authenticity.

Inside the garden, Angel created a flagstone walk in the shape of a Celtic cross. Where the arms of the cross came together, I had him fashion a round circle of rose-colored stone bricks with a morning star pointing north, south, east, and west. At the end of the east arm of the cross, he made a small stone altar where I placed a two-foot bust of Buddha to honor Eastern practices. To the west we built an altar for a two-foot marble cross with carved flowers entwined honoring Western religions.

When Angel finished the stonework many months later (not the two weeks I'd first anticipated), he constructed a raw wood arbor with straight benches for the middle of the garden, curved benches to go around the circle in the cross, and two large chairs with high backs for the two inside front corners. Finally it was time to create the garden itself. Our local gardener helped me find plants that would thrive on my blustery, sunny bluff.

One morning, as my gardener, Linda, showed her workers what to set out on another part of the property, I carried her 18-month-old baby girl into the sacred garden and sat in the arbor. This darling little girl put her head on my shoulder and became so still and peaceful, I thought she was asleep. I sat there for a quarter of an hour thinking how connected we were at that moment. A feeling like this had also washed over me the first time I'd seen her, when she had been sick and I'd given her healing. At that time, I thought it was healing energies going back and forth. Yet here was the peaceful feeling again. This time, however, it seemed different and deeper than healing energies, though still vaguely familiar. As I sat there with incredible unconditional love pouring in and out of me from this completely trusting little baby girl, I began to realize what was happening.

Sitting in the garden, we'd tapped into a connection of something ancient. This child had taken us into a peace that originated before time. And then it dawned on me, she'd linked us to a state of grace. Her mother, always amazed at her daughter's serene behavior around me, came over and told me she was not asleep, just totally content.

The baby's name?

Grace.

I want to reiterate the powerful metaphors in this story. I think it all quite remarkable.

First the wind blew over the old stone wall. Next a *Wendy* brought me a handyman named, perfectly enough, *Angel* to build a chapel ruin for me. Sitting in this newly constructed space holding the daughter of my gardener, *Linda* ("beautiful vista"), I once again experienced an awareness of peace beyond experience and a connection to all that is—or to a state of grace. *Grace* and I initiated this site into sacred space.

Friends now come to visit and leave icons honoring their religions. There's an elephant deity, Ganesh, from Hinduism; Quan Yen from Taoism; Saint Francis of Assisi, patron saint of animals; a Native American Morning Star; a Jewish Mezuzah; and a statue of Our Lady of Guadalupe. All religions are honored in my sacred garden.

Now all who enter experience grace.

Women need to be thought of as sacred space.

I knew that in the core of my existence and now recognize it in every fiber of my being. It's not a religious thing. It's true of every woman no matter her looks or sexual persuasion. Women who attain this way of living, being honored for the light within them, can range from feminists to Playboy bunnies. A good buzz phrase sweeping the country calls this light "goddess energy."

Inside my house, like outside in the garden, a wonderful tiny sacred space unfolded to honor this energy.

I'd resolved when I moved here to set up my first official home altar. Of course, like always, I wanted to find a book called *All the Steps to Creating the Proper Home Altar.* When no book was forthcoming, I decided home altar rules must be about creating a quiet, out-of-the-way place where one might sit and meditate and feel the energy the sacred objects brought into the room. Until I could decide where this space was to be, I got into the habit of placing objects that to me represented sacred energy on top of a built-in chest in a small alcove in the hall leading to the bedrooms. When settling in over the first few weeks, as I'd walk back and forth from the bedrooms to other areas of the house, I began to realize how much I enjoyed seeing my sacred objects several times a day.

I started making a little ritual. Every time I'd walk past, I'd do my "heart-centering in the lowering of an eyelid" and instantly drop into a more centered place of compassion, innate harmony, healing presence, and unconditional love. Soon the alcove became an uplifting reminder to connect to my higher self or source every time I passed.

I finally surrendered to my need to have "rules for sacred space," and asked a neighbor who is an artist/sculptor to give the little alcove a tiny old New Mexican chapel-like atmosphere.

Munson created a colorful masterpiece devoted to "goddess energy." This small space, no bigger than four feet by three feet by eight feet, has a built-in dresser and a window. Now the ceiling is painted with faux arches and a Michelangelo-like scene of hands depicting the moment of Creation. The back wall has rolling green hills and bright blue sky and columns that look like they're holding up the beam above the window, over which hangs a framed piece of leaded, beveled glass. The sidewalls look like ancient cracked adobe with four painted images of stained glass windows that contain full-length likenesses of three of my women friends who I feel best live their goddess energy. I am in the fourth window looking as I envision my higher self—slim, ethereal, and eternally youthful (once again going for illusion, not authenticity). Each is holding her hands in a different heart-centered, receiving, giving, or honoring position. Every time I walk past, I see my three goddess friends, Laura, Valery, and Jody, gazing down upon me, encouraging me to let my light shine.

I have a ritual I do when I turn on the light in this little space in the morning. Looking at the goddess who has her hand over her heart, I place my hands over my heart and say, "I heart-center with compassion, innate harmony, healing presence, and unconditional love." My eyes move to the goddess beside her, whose arms are at her sides with her hands facing out in an open position. I place my hands in the same position and say, "I receive." Looking across at the wall where the next goddess lives, I copy her hands by placing my right hand on my heart and my left up, open, facing out, and say, "I give." Going to the last goddess, whose hands are in a Namaste position, I copy her by holding my hands in a prayer position at my heart and say, "I honor."

Then I go about my day joyfully treating myself as sacred space.

Women

The women I picked to hold a place of honor on my indoor chapel walls and in my heart are all testaments to the fact that one doesn't have to lead the protected life of a Stepford wife to stay in goddess energy.

One of my goddesses chooses to live in the wild kinetic energy of Southern California. She, her husband, and two wonder dogs have lived through their house burning to the ground in the Malibu fires, floods when the rains came in the spring, earthquakes, and rats eating holes in screens and invading the house they rented until they could rebuild. Throughout all this, she also continued her work as a corporate "healer" (going into Fortune 500 companies advising them what to do to become even more successful), plus studying for a Ph.D. in mythology at Pacifica.

Another goddess, who has a loving husband of 30-some years and two beautiful children, fights against her family's love and support. Until recently, she never really took to heart the honors and accolades bestowed upon her, as she found herself on the way up the corporate ladder from account representative to president of the corporation. She keeps saying she wants the traditional life she expected, where the man makes the living, not her. If she wasn't Latin, I'd think she was following the Egyptian tradition of the evil eye, fearful that if something looks too good on the outside, ruin will come to what's inside. She might be afraid that if she admits she has it all, someone will either take it away or expect even more of her.

My last goddess is in her mid-thirties, has a new, handsome, virile, and intelligent husband, and two mystical cats that mimic their masters' moods. Everything in her life is on a time schedule: exercise, marriage, babies, desired income, and amount of security she needs before certain events (like getting pregnant) will be allowed to unfold. She has been an editor/ghost writer for several famous people and has finally accepted the truth that she is an incredible writer herself. Her new son has taught her all about schedules, or the lack thereof.

My thorny, nongoddess-like side?

Not hard to guess. It was my proven ability to unconsciously withdraw into illness the moment I get scared or hurt thinking that someone might not like me for whatever it was I was doing.

My goddesses have also had their health problems. Between them, there was a hysterectomy, a miscarriage, and an operation to have fibroid tumors removed.

Yet, despite all of them not having totally rosy lives, they all live their goddess energy. They are unafraid to be feminine and to let their own light shine. All are incredible examples to me.

Every woman's individual goddess energy began the moment our spirits sparked the decision we made to be female instead of male. At the same instant in which we chose to be rich, wet, full, soft, and curvy, our goddess energy flashed on. It's always there. It's circumstance that sometimes pushes it to the background.

I met a woman at a conference in Hawaii who owns and runs a large personnel agency. At the airport, she looked tired and afraid, hair pulled back, shoulders slumped, clothes baggy to hide that she had gained extra weight. This successful executive looked mousy and helpless. She remembered me from another conference when I'd complimented her on her hair, and now she wanted to connect with someone she "knew." The next day when I saw her at the pool, I asked her to join me. She was wearing a royal blue one-piece bathing suit. After she sat down, she got back up and walked across to a cabana to buy some tan lotion.

When she returned, I went with my intuition and said, "You should walk in clothes like you do in a bathing suit." That startled her. She asked for more. I explained that it seemed in a bathing suit, exposed for the world to see, she touched back into her goddess energy. Shoulders back, stomach in, breasts out, almost on tippy-toes she was so light in step, she floated, not her former way of almost skulking around.

That comment started us on a two-hour healing session.

As she talked, she realized she felt that not only had a man "done her wrong," but she had also allowed him to suffocate her goddess energy. As a result, she had become confused as to just how much of a woman/goddess she could appropriately be at home and work.

Now, if you use the Law of Attraction theory here, at the time this man "done her wrong" she must have been very insecure about how to handle her position as an executive woman.

We talked about goddess energy and how it isn't about low-cut blouses, short tight skirts, or laces and bows. It is about how goddesslike you feel in your body. Like she seemed to be in her body in a bathing suit. Even in the typical unisex business suit, identical twins could look totally different if one was in goddess energy and the other in beaten or fearful energy. Age, weight, height, and education have nothing to do with it.

After our poolside session, Carol was a changed woman. The next evening, I left the conference session early to get a table in the hotel restaurant. I was waiting for the hostess and saw Carol having dinner out on the porch. The change in her was remarkable. Her lovely blond hair was down and soft, her face enthusiastic, and she was wearing a new dress—light blue, when her colors before had been beige and brown. Bodice cut, the dress accentuated her ample bosom in an attractive way. The skirt was ankle length and flowing. Her image was finished off with a fresh pedicure and new sandals. She was glowing. I started over to say hello and see if I might join her for dinner when I noticed behind the column a handsome, animated man sitting with her. I smiled, did an about-face, and sat at another table where some other participants joined me.

Carol called me after she'd been back in California for a while. Her wardrobe had altered along with her attitude, from frumpy clothes with elastic waistbands to appropriately fitted clothes. She was now shining her inner spirit for all to see. She would flip a collar up on a dress, add scarves and feminine soft blouses to suits, pin an overflowing handkerchief out of a pocket, and wear silk and sexy underwear. Away from work, her clothes were gauzy and flowing. Everything she wore honored her lush femininity. I use the word "femininity" on purpose. I want to reclaim it as a word to describe a full, sensual, lush, wet, warm, practical, intelligent woman. Feeling feminine takes nothing away from my friend being head of the company. In fact, she says living her goddess energy seems to give permission to other women to do the same. The men? It brings out a gentlemanly admiration. She is honoring the light within her, her goddess energy, and treating herself as sacred space. Being around people who let their own light shine is a fast way to become inducted into our own light.

Nelson Mandela used the following words of Marianne Williamson in his inauguration speech: "As we let our own light shine, we unconsciously give other people permission to do the same. As we are liberated from our own fear, our presence automatically liberates others. When we live life honestly, as our true selves, everyone is drawn to our light."

At the same conference in Hawaii, I mentioned to a very heavyset and extremely lovely lady that she was certainly in her goddess energy that day. The comment made her ecstatic. She asked me how I knew, what I did, and told me she wanted to attend any conferences I might give on that subject. Four or five other women standing around who had overheard our conversation expressed their interest. This encounter made me realize women want their goddess energy back. It was so apparent when an off-the-cuff comment of mine about noticing goddess energy brought such elation and interest. Apparently, my tiny acknowledgement opened a door a crack. There inside was the glimmer of a lost memory of feminine essence they wanted to retrieve.

How does this energy get misplaced?

When we build up a shield to past hurts, the shield may keep out future barbs, but it also blocks our light from reaching out into the world.

Mommies

My mother was a tiny five-foot-two-inch bundle of energy who lost her goddess light at the end of her life. She had always taken her job as the little woman behind the man very seriously and thrived living her femininity. People used to say she looked like she stepped out of a bandbox. If that meant her makeup was perfect, hair coiffed, clothes hemmed the proper length, shoes and matching bags cleaned and polished then, yes, she stepped out of a bandbox. She glowed. After 20 years as a homemaker and mother, she went back to work as an executive secretary for the government to help Dad with upcoming college expenses for my sister, my brother, and me. While she might have felt some guilt about not being there when my 11-year-old brother and I, 16, came home from school, she wasn't unhappy working. She was a super executive secretary. It gave her an outlet to nurture more people and shine her light.

If Mom knew about Dad's family's scandalous past, she seemed to be able to live with his denial during their first 30 years together. When Dad was crushed that he didn't receive the promotion he wanted at age 50, he retired early, had her retire early, and moved them back down to Texas.

In Texas, Mom had to come face-to-face with living Dad's lie. In 1997, when I was researching Dad's history in Mesquite, I talked to the librarian, who said she remembered a visit my mother made to the library twenty years before. It hit me that Mom had seen all the information I'd found on the scandal and murder. Mom told the librarian she and Dad would come back to attend some of the Mesquite town functions. They never did.

Mom was not ready to retire from life or join Dad in his ever-growing depression. In Texas they came smack up against the lie Dad had been living, that everything was fine and he knew best. Everyone in Texas knew about Dad's family's past, yet Dad was still acting like it hadn't happened and that it didn't affect him. When Mom lost the connection to their formerly precariously balanced truth of "everything is beautiful," she lost herself. She began wondering who she was, who she could be.

Instead of delving into his pain, Dad blamed "women's lib"

for Mom's behavior and spent more and more time in his recliner in front of the television. He was relieved when it was discovered he had adult-onset diabetes because he had something else to blame for "retiring" from life. When Mom found they couldn't have the life in Texas she expected—friends, card games, trips, and fun—she became angry that Dad had taken from her, her life, friends, and family in Washington, D.C. Dad, in turn, became angry with Mom for being angry, and of course, neither knew why they were angry or what it was they were angry about.

When Mom couldn't take the duality of "everything's okay" when it wasn't, she shut off her mind and ever so slowly began slipping into Alzheimer's.

That was in 1984. Back then, we had no knowledge about Alzheimer's disease, nor any idea about what was happening to Mom. During this hideous disease's onset, Mom would look at me and plead, "Patti, help me."

I didn't know then the protective, pretty little world she'd set up had been shattered and that the only way she could cope was to close everything out of her head. Not being allowed to live life as it was, she could no longer pretend that Dad's denial about his family's past didn't affect them. Her Alzheimer's lasted eight years.

I couldn't visit Mom the last year. Though she was brain-dead, Dad kept her body alive with antibiotics and intravenous feedings. His actions were not open for discussion. One didn't question Dad on anything, much less something of this magnitude. I think I was fearful that if I visited Mom as the living dead, I might have the ability to take a pillow and, *Patti, help me. . . .* If I'd ever had a conversation with Mom before she became ill in which she told me she wanted to die with dignity, I just might have taken matters into my own hands. I'm not sure I want to know.

Statistics show my propensity to contract Alzheimer's is incredibly high with my mother and grandmother dying from it. I think we have a choice. I don't believe we are bound to our genetic illnesses once we discover and release what is really being passed down from generation to generation. Since I have brought to light our core family problem—denial of reality and continual repressing instead of releasing feelings, Alzheimer's doesn't have the same breeding ground. With the knowledge I now have about living a conscious life, I feel I have a choice not to contract our family's illnesses.

Check with me in 20 years or so.

At some point in my babyhood, I disconnected from my body. I used to tell friends a good caricature of me would be me walking around with a balloon. My body would be just that, a physical body. The balloon, my spirit. My balloon spirit would be looking down in wonder, saying, "That's an odd creature. Why doesn't it know basic things about itself, like when it is hungry, tired, angry, hurt?"

One night in Nantucket, I went to sleep petitioning for information about my health and ever-fluctuating weight. When I awakened during the night, I sat up in bed and decided to pull a tarot card from the Voyager deck to help me retrieve information. The sleepy meditative state I was in was perfect for divination work. The first card had, among other images, a picture of a very pregnant woman. I thought of my mother, who by then had been deceased for several years. When I received all the information I could from that card, I asked for more information and pulled another card, my mind being guided from card to card. In a very short time, I'd pulled six cards. I had been guided into seeing my mother (my sister and I would have paid good money for our problems to have all related to our father) violently cleaning and reaming out my tiny baby orifices after I'd mussed a pretty little outfit through my diaper.

I've seen pictures of myself when I was a baby and toddler in Pensacola, Florida, and how beautifully Mom dressed us. We were always in immaculately washed and ironed little white ruffled dresses. I have childhood memories of everyone marveling at how good Mom was at training our pets. She kept a spotless house—no room for accidental messes.

If Mother did do what I saw in the meditation, it would

explain when I lost contact with my body and why I had 45 years of constipation. I would never again make a mess and make Mommy angry with me.

As much as I didn't want to believe this vision, it could also explain why I wasn't an intact virgin even though I waited to have sex until I was married. Perhaps, my "Father Knows Best" Mommy took my virginity in a cleaning frenzy. Whether I had conjured this vision up to come up with a neat little package to explain away unanswered questions doesn't really matter. It helped me move on.

I realized, in this event I saw, Mom wasn't angry at me over a dirty diaper, but was venting her frustrations about me not being the boy she felt she needed to make her feel "safe and secure." In Mom's family, her father had walked out when she was two, leaving her mother with three little baby girls to raise alone. When I looked at that situation from Mom's point of view, in her mind, if she or one of her sisters had been the long-awaited son, her father might have stayed.

I did lose touch with my body at an early age. I've never had knowledge of it. My periods, like clockwork every 28 days, were a constant surprise to me. I've never known when I was hungry or when I was full. I never even knew I was thirsty. Plus I didn't know when to go to the bathroom; I never recognized signs like pressure or fullness. Every bodily function worked from the emotional standpoint of "protect Patti from remembering, protect Patti from feeling."

Fortunately, about two years before my menses stopped, I became conscious about being female with all its richness. I actually started honoring my periods for those two years. I enjoyed feeling the pressure, the bloating, the rich, earthy redness. I think I got in touch with something quite primal. I found myself proudly announcing, "I am having my period" (actually to only a close few—not over a PA system). I suppose that was the beginning of my return to my body.

In my mind, I devised rituals I adapted from American Indian women's traditions. They were "banished" to a menses tent by the men because the braves knew how powerful a woman is during her moon. They believed at that time she could steal a man's power. In a menses tent, the women were honored and served by women not on their cycle. They spent the first part of their stay reviewing the month past and the second part planning the month to come.

I started doing that. During my moon, in my mind, I'd go to my menses tent and honor myself as a powerful woman. I'd review the previous month and plan the month coming. I wish I'd known to honor my cycles all along, but I was glad to get those two years. They were a blessing. I found when menopause started, I missed my bleeding. My periods were never terribly bad like some women's, with mass bleeding, clots, or horrible cramps. I had some long periods, but that was about it. I found when my periods stopped, I missed how it punctuated my wonderful femininity. Looking back, I realize how comforting it was. It was like a touchstone to my female self. I was so fortunate to have honored it for two years.

I know of a woman who rubbed the blood from her period over her in the shower in a ritual to honor her process; another went outside, squatted, and bled into the ground reconnecting to the Earth. Wish I'd known.

All this new discovery of my body and its systems was why I didn't want to take hormone supplements during menopause. I'd just gotten into honoring my regular body cycles, and I didn't want to miss honoring my cycle into elder-hood. I wanted to fully experience its richness. Yet I was so tired and weak, and my brain was fogged. Doctors told me it was menopause. I explained I hadn't had a period in two years and had had no major problems; why now? They had no answers, but they had solutions. I tried hormones concocted just for me that are rubbed on the skin—didn't work. I tried troches, more hormones that dissolve in your mouth—no change. I tried being treated for borderline low thyroid, and it almost flipped me out. At night I felt like my skin was crawling and my brain was becoming unhinged.

Finally I lay on the sofa and incubated. Eventually I got to the point where I thought to look inside myself for answers. I noticed my health problems were corresponding with a bigger change in my life: finishing this book. What was really happening was that I wasn't ready for the uncertainty of what was next in either situation. When I finally let go of any expectations and attachments in either sphere, everything started to balance.

Me as a mother? We could have killed the fatted calf, because first try I got the prodigal son. If I'd known about dyslexia and the continual struggle Doug would go through to feel good enough about himself (sound familiar?), I wonder if I'd have been kinder about some of his acting up and demanding his own way. I now know these are traits of learning-disabled children. Of course, they are also traits of spoiled, longed-for beloved sons, so it might have been a toss-up. Being so independent and demanding, I suppose he could have been called a "difficult" child, but since he was the only child I ever had, he seemed perfect to me. He was and is handsome, daring, personable, bright, clever, witty, brave, and loving, and has amazing manipulative powers.

Dyslexia served Doug in one obvious way. The entire time he was growing up, I worked to find ways to make him feel good about himself since he felt so bad about his inability to read. He learned there was no shame in not being the same as everyone else. He learned if he failed at something to try again and, with what he'd learned about failing, he'd most likely succeed the second time. So, through no consciousness on my own, the "sins of the father" being passed down—in the form of my father thinking nothing he or we (his children) did was good enough—ended with Doug.

Doug's natural father, Bruce, was a German-descendant Protestant who loved and respected both his parents. Doug's second daddy, Irish Catholic Michael, didn't like women much, revered his hard-drinking, abusive-to-women father, and despised his long-suffering mother. But third dad Alfred, raised Orthodox Jewish, revered his mother and womanhood.

I think things balanced out. Doug loves women and thinks they are essential parts of his life. When he was 13, on his first

111

day of boarding school in Connecticut, I called to see how he was settling in. The young man who answered told me Doug was out with his girlfriend. Knowing Doug knew no one at the school, I asked him about "the girlfriend" when we talked later. In his wonderful adolescent wisdom, he said, "Mom, there's four guys to every girl here. You've got to get one fast. You know, girls enhance your life." Something worked. My son recognizes the goddess in women.

Goddesses

Looking back on my own school years, it is amazing to me that I managed to slip through and graduate as well as I did, with almost no ability to remember names, dates, or places and with nary a clue how to study. Good thing I test well. When we had a few days of mythology in high school, having to memorize names of gods and goddesses in that period of time left me with absolutely no interest in anything mythological. It seemed to me a total waste of time.

Years later, in my studies of healing, higher consciousness, and self-discovery, mythology and goddesses as archetypes (the original model on which something is patterned) began coming up again and again. I still didn't get it. Why should I care what ancient goddesses did or didn't do?

Then I learned that Joseph Campbell, a mythologist and scholar, referred to a connection between these ancient stories and the emotional concerns of modern life. "Aha." A light began to dawn. Campbell's travels took him to Paris and Munich, where he discovered the ideas of Sigmund Freud and Carl Jung, James Joyce, Thomas Mann, and modern art. He saw parallels between mythic themes in literature and psychological lessons such as those revealed in dreams. More grist for the mill.

Gods and goddesses of ancient Greece, Rome, and Egypt being revered in modern times finally began to make sense to me. They tell our stories and they awaken our dreams. If we identify what aspects of goddesses we are playing out in our lives, we are given keys to why we act out in certain ways; and as always, with more information comes more choice. These ancient tales used to explain natural order as well as *disorder* have more to them than we realize.

I can now intuitively pick which god or goddess someone is acting out. The one I have most acted out in my life? After reading the preceding chapter on men, daddies, and gods, you have to ask? It's Aphrodite, of course, the Greek Goddess of Love and Beauty. Most people identify her and Venus, her Roman counterpart, with the themes of love and desire. Some of the most compelling myths, however, deal with the consequences she suffers as a result of being the victim of love. When Aphrodite falls madly in love with Adonis, she tells him, "Beware how you expose yourself to danger and put my happiness at risk. Attack not the beasts that Nature has armed with weapons. I do not value your glory so high as to consent to purchase it by such exposure."

My Aphrodite-like self would get blindsided by my efforts to live my life as the Goddess of Love and Beauty. Feeling I'd achieved this "love and beauty" when I married and turned my happiness over to each of the men in my life, I'd wonder why I felt at risk. Each husband had problems of his own that would take him into "the dangerous grip of his own beasts of insecurity." Not being the gods I expected them to be, they couldn't take on the responsibility for my happiness. And I? I'd leave the marriages before I would have to consent to pay the price to help them with their problems. Had I known more about mythology, I might have become conscious of the pattern Aphrodite energy was playing in my life again and again. When Adonis was killed not heeding Aphrodite's warning, she cautioned the Fates that her grief would endure. This paralleled my husband Alfred's heart problems, my warnings to him to take better care before his death, and my everlasting sorrow.

Now, I don't go around living my life guided by fables and myths, but they certainly opened my eyes to the patterning others and I live. My real-life "goddess" friends on my "chapel" walls can easily be identified with their archetypes.

Laura would be Persephone. One day this Greek Goddess of

the Underworld was out picking flowers when Hades grabbed her. Though Persephone cried out to her father, Zeus, king of the gods, and mother, Demeter, Goddess of Agriculture and Fertility, Hades took her away to his underground world. There she was tricked into living half of the year in the dark underworld and the other in the light with her family.

My friend Laura is the head of a large corporation with a supportive husband and two beautiful children. She is a born ruler and leader like Zeus, father of Persephone, solidly grounded, Laura regains her strength from the fertile Earth like Demeter, Persephone's mother. Like Persephone, half of her life is in the darkness of thinking she wants something she doesn't have (staying home and being a wife and mother), and the other half in the limelight at peace with abilities and position.

Jody is Artemis, Goddess of the Hunt and Protector of Children. Aloof and free-spirited, Artemis is not constrained by husband or hearth, remaining eternally a virgin. As the daughter of Zeus, she enjoyed the status and privilege of an Olympian and was free to pursue her interests and was often found frolicking in the forests.

Jody has a husband and beautiful home that complement her, not contain her. She will eternally be the virgin with no children of her own to prove otherwise.

Valery is living her Isis energy. Isis, the greatest Egyptian goddess, was a vital link between the gods and mankind. Able to foresee traumatic events, she was also a great magician. She was considered a beneficial goddess and mother whose love encompassed every living creature. Isis was thought to be the purest example of the loving wife and mother, and it was in this capacity the Egyptian people loved her the most.

Valery is truly a muse. A direct link to the gods. When she is around in a capacity as editor, writers have incredible dreams and breakthroughs. She is a nurturer to all, humans and animals. Her cats mirror her moods. She rescues little spiders in her home. Happily married with a beautiful son, she uses her studies in psychology to better her relationships.

When we recognize our archetypal patterning, we become

aware of symbolic messages in our ordinary lives. With more information comes more awareness; with more awareness comes more choice on how to live our lives—honestly, as our true authentic selves.

PART II
healer

9

PAST LIVES AND PARTY TRICKS:
Past-Life Regression and Healing Hands

*Here died my mother. Herein was I born. But it is mere
idleness to say that I had not lived before—that the soul has
no previous existence. You deny it?—let us not argue the matter. Convinced myself, I seek not to convince. There is however, a remembrance of aerial forms—of spiritual and
meaning eyes—of . . .*

—Edgar Allen Poe

In 1996 when my favorite teacher, Brugh Joy, announced he
might be retiring, I decided to take the conferences I'd put off
attending during the previous three years. In two months I took
four back-to-back conferences. The first was the Dark Side. This
one I'd been scared to take because of my fear of what I might
still have hidden from myself and the world. The information
sent to me on this conference didn't allay my fears. "Only those
who are serious about inner development and are prepared, as
best one can be, to explore disowned and difficult material
should consider this conference."

We were also told to bring a costume that best represented our hidden dark side. My thought was, if it was hidden, how was I supposed to know? I wondered if I was the only person who was better at hiding things from myself than from others. I settled on dressing as a happy, innocent, naive little girl. I wore black Mary Jane shoes and white ruffled socks, a black pinafore dress with a full short skirt of black fluffy tulle, and a white blouse with a big pink bow. My hair was in two ponytails with pink ribbons, and I toted a blond doll around by one arm who was dressed exactly like me. The teacher got a good laugh about how "hidden" that persona was. To me, until that point, the fact I had a scared, naive, trusting, little child inside me was hidden. Now when she is ruling my life, I mentally tell her to go play with her toys, I'll handle it.

We were shown movies to trigger deep feelings. During a movie called *The Straw Man* in which a police captain was lured to an island so the townspeople could sacrifice him for the crops, I found I felt no emotion whatsoever as the effigy of the straw man in which he was placed burned. Yet in a movie called *The Devils* with Oliver Reed and Vanessa Redgrave, when the townspeople turned on Reed, who was their beloved priest, and burned him at the stake, I felt like a truck had hit me. I lay on the floor curled in the fetal position after everyone left, wondering why I couldn't move. What was the difference?

The second movie touched my fears of not being able to count on people in my life who had professed love and honor. At that point in my life, I didn't trust myself to take care of me and had found out I couldn't trust others to do it for me. *The Devils* personified all my troubles at the time. I was beginning to see a void that I didn't know how to fill.

The next conference, The Call of the Ancestor, was one in which I wasn't especially interested. With my ancestral history of denial, it's no wonder. It, however, turned out to be my favorite conference. We explored the "One Human Being" and the latent potential of human consciousness, plus our own lineage and ethnicity. Finishing this conference, I started to feel I belonged to a family—the human race. I left with a new concept of how we truly are all one.

The third was called Drinking From the Well, which was intended to nourish our souls. After my discoveries in the first two conferences, I drank deeply from the well.

Then off I went to Kauai, Hawaii, to a Sacred Space conference. We did intensive dream work and deepened our abilities to tap into our own dream interpreter. It was at this conference that I had my enlightening experience with the cave dive I described earlier.

I had so few brain cells firing after two months of such intensive work, the only thing I was totally clear about was that I couldn't immediately go home to Nantucket and pick up life where I had left off. I needed to go to my proverbial cabin in the woods to process all the incredible new information I'd garnered.

My sister and I had helped Dad go into a nursing home a few months before, so the closest, quickest, and least expensive "cabin in the woods" where I could be blessedly alone was Dad's suburban house in Dallas. My whole life was in question. Everything I'd believed in and everything I repressed was out in the open, upside down and inside out. I felt like I knew nothing and knew everything. I was just beginning to learn the possibility of what was available to us as far as help from the universe. The glimpse of its unlimited potential was overwhelming. The veil to the other side had been lifted—the side where living with a more aware consciousness, universal guidance, and unconditional love was the only way to go. Daunting.

There was no turning back. I'd hit bottom and needed to build up again, but this time from a strong foundation with no feelings of whether I was worthy enough to get up in the morning. This period I was going through is what some people call "spiritual madness." A period where the balance between old and new consciousnesses collide. This is a time that handling what seems like such blinding awareness and a nonstop input of information from the universal is overwhelming.

In Hawaii, my teacher suggested I find a Jungian psychologist "to guide me into my descent mystery." Whatever that meant. I decided I'd try. I went to a meeting of the Jungian Institute in

Dallas and asked for a recommendation. They mentioned a man's name and pointed to some books he had written. I leafed through the books, thinking they seemed lofty, hard to read and understand, but since he was my only choice, I decided not to be choosy.

I expected this man to be my savior and have all the answers to my unformed questions. Oh no, the "e" word again—expectation. I was looking for him to fill the void I felt at the pit of my stomach, which I had yet to find out couldn't be filled by anyone else. At my first appointment with him, I was given a sign. He looked like a young version of my father and acted like he knew everything, though he didn't understand what I meant by wanting him to "guide me into my descent mystery." I certainly couldn't tell him.

I so wanted to feel better, I stuck it out for a few sessions. I told him about my husband dying, the huge estate battle and lawyers wanting more money than it looked like I was going to receive. I told him about my being ill, healing, discovering I had healing abilities, and about my whole world turning upside down with my new ways of looking at life.

His reply was that it would take him a long time to help me.

He also had no idea what I meant by my wanting to live as my highest self or about heart-centering with compassion, innate harmony, healing presence, and unconditional love. You'd think I would have walked by now.

It finally happened after a particular session in which his therapy was to not lend me a pen with which to write him a check. I had gotten out my checkbook to pay him and couldn't find a pen. Asking if I might borrow one, his reply was, "No." I thought it odd he didn't have a pen in his office, but let it go and said, "Okay I've got one in the car, I'll go down, get it, write you a check, come back upstairs and slip it under the door so I won't disturb your next session."

As I was leaving, I asked about our session times for the next week. We walked over to look at the calendar on his desk, and there was a pen. I picked it up and said, "Oh here's one, I'll write your check now." He took it out of my hand and said, "No, I told you I wouldn't lend you one. You should be responsible enough to bring your own."

If this was done to teach me independence, it hit the mark. I left his office in tears, went home, and typed him a long letter about Rome burning while he was fiddling away missing the big picture. I called, read it to him, stopped seeing him, and didn't pay for that last session saying, "Sorry, can't find a pen."

While I had been seeing this Jungian psychologist, I was also trying another therapy recommended by a person in Arizona who channels a higher evolved being. This therapist told me to take several 20-minute baths with two cups of salt and two cups of soda to cleanse my outer energy field and equalize it with my inner energy field. I was also instructed to combine the baths with a special breathing exercise called "dolphin breathing."

Dolphin breathing is taking a deep, deep breath into the gut area and then blowing it out as hard and fast as possible, making a dolphin "pah" sound and imagining the breath is hitting the wall in front of the tub. This is done to help release issues from the past that might be holding us back.

When I first did this, I'd choke and gag. Something didn't want to release. I persevered and went through this routine daily. When I eventually got to where the choking and coughing dissipated, thoughts and feelings started passing through my mind, one after another. Soon I became aware that something else was happening. It unfolded as though I was watching a movie. I saw in the long-ago past a young girl going through her day.

I was instantly aware I was witnessing myself in a past life.

Now, I wasn't a total novice about past lives when this popped up. Back in New York, I had gone to a well-thought-of woman who used her Ph.D. in psychology to guide clients into past lives. Also, after Alfred and my mother passed away, I'd read two books that had turned me around about death, Betty J. Eadie's *Embraced by the Light* and a book by the former Yale professor, Brian L. Weiss, M.D., *Many Lives, Many Masters.* Both books dealt with life after death and past lives.

In the past life that came forward with dolphin breathing, I was an innocent 14-year-old girl with long, wavy chestnut hair during the time of the Salem witch trials in Massachusetts. I was dressed in burlap clothes of the period, barefoot with a burlap scarf around my shoulders. It was a little town, clean, in spite of thatched huts with dirt floors and dirt roads.

I was at a neighbor's, holding her dying baby while she ran to get the priest. When she left, I continued to sit and hold the baby close. I felt such unconditional loving love and compassion for it. With no effort on my part, I let these qualities pour through me from the universe into the stricken little body. Without thought, I moved my right hand over the child's heart, letting a golden flow of light and love enter. The child responded immediately. When the mother came in with the priest and the townspeople and saw the now healed, happy gurgling baby in my arms, she screamed, "Witch."

In the next scene, I was running barefoot as fast as I could across a green field toward the woods with men, boys, horses, and dogs chasing me. They caught up with me on the side of the field in a ravine with trees. I was bitten, beaten, and stoned to death.

Back in Nantucket sometime later, another past life came forth. I was supporting a friend who wanted to start group past-life regressions. During the first session, I was briefly taken to another past life. All I saw were Pilgrim-like buckled shoes on cobblestones and knew I was a man in England.

For days afterward, I felt that something more about this past life wanted to come through. I called my girlfriend, Sheri Perelman, to lead me back. Sheri is a healer, a light worker, and Nantucket's best sacred space holder. While her specialty is Jin Shin Jyutsu, she had also studied with Brian Weiss, so I knew she could assist me.

This "new" past life of mine unfolded as soon as she guided me in a meditation through a tunnel out into the light. She told me to observe what I was wearing. Once again I saw my black shoes with brass buckles and the cobblestone streets. I looked up and saw typical English town houses. In the next scene, I realized who I was. I was a well-respected seventeenth-century male English medical doctor. I not only had impeccable educational credentials, but also had healing hand energies that I used to help diagnose and heal my townspeople and their animals.

Everyone loved me and thought me more than kind and generous. It didn't matter to me. I was despondent over how little anything meant. There was so much hatred, killing, and war in the world. I felt so inadequate to the task. I ended up killing myself because I felt the part I could play was insignificant in the grand picture.

As Edgar Allen Poe said, "I seek not to convince you." Whether these past lives are real or not isn't significant. If they are products of a vivid imagination, it matters not. What matters is the guidance they brought me. I now knew why I was reticent to accept myself as a healer in this lifetime. I was fearful of outside and inside persecution. What people might think about me and what my inner critic might do to me. Experiencing these past lives made me aware of influences that could be stumbling blocks to finding and accepting my purpose in this lifetime. They showed me trouble spots I needed to work on.

With these two past lives, I no longer had to go outside "to be guided into my descent mysteries."

My inner teacher was doing it for me.

My first experience with healing others happened at my initial two-week heart-centered transformation conference in July 1993.

It was a lazy, sunny day in the deserts of Arizona. The only sound was water flowing down the rock waterfall into the lodge swimming pool. Tanning and dozing, I was awakened by a splash and looked up to see that my friend Bill had dived into the water to cool off and swim laps.

Even though we'd been told we could nap in a session or even miss one and still "get it," I nevertheless felt guilty when I reluctantly skipped that afternoon's class on energy exchange. I'd reached overwhelm. I felt I couldn't possibly take in any more information until I spent time resting, processing, assimilating, and finding compartments in my brain for all the new life tools we'd been given.

As I opened and closed my sleepy eyes and watched my friend's tall, fit body glide back and forth through the pool, my mind wandered over yesterday's session when we were experimenting with body energies. We were working in twos, and Bill and I were partners. As instructed, he took the first turn lying on the massage table to be the receiver. I stood next to the table and with my hands was to be the giver of energy. We were told not to communicate by talking, but to read signals from the partner on the table. One finger meant too little energy, two meant just right, three meant too much.

After mentally visualizing connecting to a higher source (I envision connecting to a higher source in the universe, but it could be a childhood image, or a religious belief), I was told to pass my right hand about three inches over Bill's body and note any sensations or temperature changes. Then I was to practice being guided by intuition as to how much and where energy was needed. Bill seemed quite content and almost euphoric with the energy I was sending him.

Enmeshed in these thoughts, I was startled back to the present at the pool when I heard a loud, "Ouch!" as Bill let out a painful yell. After several laps, he'd swum to the stairs and raised his hand to grab the handrail, and a wasp sitting on the water ferociously stung him between his thumb and forefinger. Bill quickly came around and sat next to me, holding his rapidly swelling, inflamed hand. I hopped up, doing a kind of a "jumping up and down, turning three circles, waving my hands to give myself time to think dance," saying, "I had a son, but he never had anything wrong with him. What do we do? Ammonia? Mud?"

Bill looked at me calmly, held out his hand, and said, "Heal it, Patricia."

Oh, I thought, *Okay, they all must have learned how to heal at the session I missed this afternoon.*

I suppose my naiveté helped at that moment. It never dawned on me I couldn't do what he asked. There was no code of belief or dogma in my background that told me only "special" priests could hold healing masses, or only "gifted" sainted people became healers. I just assumed everyone had learned to heal with his or her hands at the session I missed. Our teacher said we would "get it" whether we were in the session or not. So it only seemed logical to me I had the ability to do what was asked of me.

I put my right hand over the now hugely swollen fiery red sting. The chatter started in my brain. *Am I doing this right? Am I doing this wrong? Am I giving too much energy? Too little? Is it too long, too short?* Suddenly the chatter quieted. A peacefulness settled over me, and I knew it was time to stop. I took my hand away and all evidence of the wasp sting was gone. Completely No swelling, no redness.

And that's how I became a healer—because I didn't know I couldn't.

At that moment, though, I was totally unwilling to appreciate the magnitude of this extraordinary gift even for a second. My first thought after healing the wasp sting was, *This'll make a great party trick.*

As much as I'd always wanted to be special all my life, no way was I ready for this one. I immediately negated the magnitude of what had happened.

True to my word, I started "playing" with this new "trick" whenever the opportunity arose. At the end of the conference, my sister came to pick me up. When she drove up to the lodge she complained of a bad headache. I said, "No problem. I can fix that." And, whomp! Right hand on her forehead, left at the back of her head and her headache disappeared.

This was going to be fun!

She and I went off to Hawaii, and during a group tennis lesson, a fellow student backed up against the fence and was stung by two wasps. Somehow he relayed that he could go into an anaphylactic shock, and he, along with the ten other participants, began to panic. For some reason, I calmly walked over to him, put my right hand on the sting on his neck and my left hand on the sting on his left hand as he quietly stood there. Soon he said, "The sting is going away," and then he said, "It's okay now." I took my hands away, and the stings had disappeared. He and his wife invited us over for drinks that night and regaled the other guests with what I'd done. I said, "It's nothing, anyone can do it."

I continued to make light of my new talent and went blithely around treating it as a kind of party trick. My not being ready to accept this gift didn't seem to bother other people. Ready or not, clients began to find me.

My first client appeared when I went home from Hawaii to my condo in Rehoboth Beach, Delaware. Friends of mine there knew I'd cured myself of multiple allergies and asked me to work with their 28-year-old daughter. Melissa suffered terribly with allergies. She also wanted to learn about meditation. I decided to use Barbara Biziou's meditation tape. I'd listened to that morning as an introduction for her.

Melissa was a slim, young woman with pretty chiseled features and jet-black hair pulled back into a tight bun at her neck. When she arrived, she told me it was her birthday. She was in anguish over becoming 28 because of her expectations of being married and having children by then. I explained perhaps she was exactly where she should be and might it be possible she was still single because she needed to learn the lesson of no expectations? We talked about setting intentions, not goals, which would leave room for the universe to work its magic.

I prepared her for guided meditation, explaining there was no right or wrong experience and to have no expectations about it. Putting the tape in the recorder, I pushed the play button. Nothing happened. Not wanting to break the energy by messing with the plug or the electric box circuit breakers, or doing what I really wanted to do, violently shake the boom box that had just been working, I calmly said, "I'll guide you in meditation."

Right . . .

This was my first time guiding a meditation. Poor Melissa. She got a smorgasbord of every meditation I'd ever experienced. I must have tapped into some kind of guidance, because she survived. I heart-centered her, introduced her to her child within, her wise woman, her masculine and feminine consciousnesses, and her warrior. I took her down a path to a special safe place, which turned out, for her, to be her grandmother's house. I took her to a library that has no ceiling because the books go on to include 50,000 years of collective consciousness and the answers to any question. I guided her through the purple flame of transformation.

After the meditation, I asked her to tell me anything she wanted to share about her experience. She talked about her ugly little inner child—I took her back into a meditative state to have her hold and nurture the child until she became soft and pretty.

By the time Melissa left, she felt well. No stuffy head or allergies. She had a songlike quality to her voice and practically skipped out of my condo. That night at the dinner party in honor of her birthday, her parents would have genuflected in front of me if I'd let them. Across the table from us was their formerly morose daughter glowing, loving, happy, and having a ball becoming 28.

Now, what I hadn't learned with the healing powers I'd received were boundaries. The next morning my son, then 20, and I decided to spend a play day together. At 10 A.M., after driving race cars at the amusement park, we hit the video arcade at Fun Land.

All of a sudden my head began to fill up and I started talking through my nose. My eyes became puffy and almost swollen shut and my lips swelled up like I had had a collagen injection. I looked like a prizefighter who had lost. Doug was scared. Nothing like this had ever happen before. He looked at me and said with great concern, "Mom, what's up? Are you okay?"

No, I wasn't, thank you very much. Thank goodness I'd seen Ellen Burstyn's movie, *Resurrection*. I remembered that the healer she played sometimes took on other people's illnesses. I knew that was what had happened. I'd taken on Melissa's allergies. Doug and I quickly left the arcade so I could sleep it off. The next day, 18 hours later, I woke up fine.

This was not acceptable. I'd been sick long enough myself without taking on other people's illnesses. What was I doing wrong?

A couple of months later, I didn't even think about taking on illnesses. I was visiting Washington, D.C., when my girlfriend called to say she was really looking forward to our dinner at the Palm restaurant the next night. She said, "I need some stiff drinks." I told her I didn't understand. Dee explained she learned that afternoon that it looked like the breast cancer she had beaten three years before had reappeared as cancer in her ovaries. The doctors wanted to open her up immediately—that Friday.

I said, "Dee, we're not going anywhere, I'm coming over, and we'll do some healing and meditations and at least get you more centered and balanced."

I laid Dee down on the floor and checked the energy in each of her chakras. I held my right hand over each one to see how it felt, feeling compelled to hold my left hand up toward the universe. I now could feel a very definite energy exchange between someone's chakra and my hand—almost like a slight vibration, sometimes like a heat source. Dee's heart chakra was the strongest. Knowing Dee and the width of her open heart, I could have guessed. Keeping my right hand at the heart area, I placed my left hand over the ovaries and uterus area and told her we were using her own energies to send healing to the suspected area. I asked her to visualize an image. She saw chocolate Pac-Men in the form of Reese's Peanut Butter Cups going in to gobble up the cancer.

The doctors told her to be at Sibley Hospital at 8 A.M. and that the procedure would be done at nine. We spent the day talking, meditating, laughing, and centering until 4 P.M., when they finally got around to her. During the day, I spent time balancing her chakras, and if the energy was up in one and down in another, I'd tell Dee to bring it up or down, and then swoosh my hand over her body. They'd stay balanced until a doctor would come in and tell her it'd be another two to three hours. We read her tarot cards, used a pendulum to ask yes or no questions, and were open and positive to the information we'd receive. When her husband came back, I went down and bought a big box of a hundred Reese's Peanut Butter Cups, and we all had a good laugh.

Dee told her doctor that no matter what they found, she wanted a hysterectomy. There was nothing I could say to change her mind. She felt if everything was removed, there'd be no place for cancer to go. When they opened her up, she was cancer free but there was bad scar tissue, so they went ahead with a hysterectomy. When Dee came out of the anesthetic, her children had lined the Reese's Peanut Butter Cups up like little Pac-Men marching all over on top of windowsills, on picture frames, and above the doors all around the room. To this day, Dee credits me with there being no cancer and keeping her sane. There's no way to know. I'm just glad I had the opportunity to be with her.

Later that year I went to Canyon Ranch Spa in the Berkshire Mountains in Lenox, Massachusetts, and met a lovely couple from Montreal. The husband had been troubled by a leg problem and had had a slight limp for several months. Bob and Ruth, his wife, had a very successful clothing business that was now going through growth problems. He wanted to learn about meditation and how to heal his leg. When we both had a free half hour from all our classes, I found an empty exercise room and led him in a guided meditation. At several different points in the meditation, I could feel his energy change. I began to know when I was getting close to the answers to his problem by the way his energy would tighten or relax. I found I was being guided by Bob as to what I needed to say and where the meditation should go. In regard to the business, he was coming from scarcity and fear—it had been successful for 20 years, but now needed to undergo major change. Bob didn't want to "step" forward into the new. We worked on releasing fear and showing him he had the answers, as well as the ability, to make necessary changes. He came out of the meditation jubilant, with no pain in his leg. He went around Canyon Ranch singing my praises.

Bob wanted me to work with his wife whom I'd briefly met, but there was no time before they left. They invited me to stay with them during the Montreal Jazz Festival. He said I'd have time to work with Ruth then. He told me so much about his wife, I felt as though I knew her. A month later I flew up to Montreal from New York. We had a great time at the festival. On every corner in the downtown area there was a great jazz combo. At night we'd go into the clubs to hear the headliners. We saw

Bo Didley's son, who was wonderful. By the last day of my visit, I still hadn't worked with his wife. I hadn't really ever talked to her, just to him about her. I wasn't picking up on what was really happening. She didn't particularly want to do a session. I suggested to her we work during a free hour we had before we were to go to lunch with the girls. I took her through my smorgasbord meditation that now had become something of a specialty.

I could feel during the meditation something was missing. Afterward I asked her how it was. She sat on her sofa and said it was fine. *Fine?* I thought. This was not the rave review I was used to. I asked how she felt. She said her thighs (which had been fine before the meditation) were hurting. Instinctively I went over to her and put my hands over her legs. The energy that went into my hands almost blew my hands away, and her legs stopped hurting immediately. In the car, on the way to the luncheon, she said her neck hurt. I put my hand on the pain in her neck, and it too went away. I couldn't imagine what had happened. When I later consulted with another healer, she said, "You probably took her someplace she didn't want to go, and she was putting on the brakes." That was it, I knew it. She'd only agreed to the session because she was being the perfect hostess. She was happy where she was. She'd been successfully denying any problems in her life and didn't want or need to go there. The pain in her neck? I knew what it was—you figure it out.

What I learned from that session is that a person has to ask for help and want to be helped. Someone else can't do it or want it for him. And, by the way, you're right. I was the pain in her neck.

I learn a lot from my clients. Some who came with the slightest problems ended up being the most bizarre sessions. There was a lot more than illness to reconcile. At a conference I attended a woman, whom I will call Sarah, demonstrated her ability to speak in tongues (the capacity to talk in a foreign or ancient language of which you have no prior knowledge). She was short and slim, with lovely medium-length brunette hair surrounding her sweet face. Throughout the sessions, she was plagued by an irritating cough that would not go away. When our teacher asked her to leave a session because her cough was disruptive, everyone felt sorry for her and offered all kinds of sympathies and remedies. She asked if I would do a healing session with her. I suggested we sit out on a quiet patio, and talked with her about setting the intention for our session and asked if there was anything she needed to tell me. Simply, she wanted to know why she couldn't get rid of her irritable cough. Seemed straightforward enough to me. I, with my "no expectations" injunction fully intact, expected to have her cough free in about two and half seconds.

I led her into a meditation, in which she immediately started speaking in tongues again. This time, though, it sounded different. Much, much different. It was a sound I'd never heard before. I, now totally in healer mode, was, thank goodness, being guided in how to handle her. I asked Sarah who was speaking. In her soft, feminine voice she told me it was an extraterrestrial.

Okay . . .

Healer mode unruffled—but other aspects of me had the hair standing up on the back of my neck while screaming in my head, *Oh my God, I got a nut-case here*, and then, *Oh my God, what if I don't have a nut case here?*

All the while, my outward appearance remained calm.

I told Sarah I wanted to again talk with the ET. This time I flattered the entity by saying, "I know you are so much more further developed than we humans, I'm sure you can talk with me in my language. Would you please do that now so that I might understand you?"

It responded to flattery. In a masculine voice about six octaves lower than Sarah could ever speak, the entity started talking in English. Now, while there was still a part of me that wanted to abandon ship, I didn't. I stayed centered—however, my healer mode was in overdrive.

After the way the ET had been jabbering in its language, it didn't seem like a stretch to assume it had something it wanted to say. It did. It talked about the lady, Sarah, fondly but said in a rather patronizing tone that humans were so limited in their development.

I laugh now when I think, here I was having a conversation with an ET and had the opportunity to ask "Big Bang" questions about the universe and what did I do? I asked if it knew why Sarah had the little irritating cough.

It jumped on the question and told me she was choking on things it wanted to say. I asked to speak to Sarah again. When it consented, I asked Sarah if she needed to keep this alien with her because it made her feel special or if she could allow it to leave. She said it could leave. I went back to talking with the alien and asked if it could tell me what it wanted to say and then leave Sarah. He agreed and started talking.

I am so sorry to have to tell you, I have no recollection of what it said. I can only guess that while it was talking, my mind was completely focused on getting this session over in a satisfactory way. I could just see me going back to our conference teacher and saying, "Oh, by the way, do you remember that pretty brunette with a slightly irritating cough? The good news is her cough is gone. The bad news is she is sitting out on the patio looking like something out of the movie *Alien*. Do you think you might find the time to help me turn her back into something human?"

When the alien entity finished speaking, it left as promised. You could almost see a presence leave. Sarah slightly slumped, and I then guided her back into a nonmeditative state. I told her to come back to Arizona, to the Wildflower Lodge, to her body, and once in her body, to wiggle her fingers and toes and open her eyes. Lo and behold (as my mom would say), her cough was gone.

Later, however, when she noticed that the tea and sympathy that fellow participants had been dispensing stopped, her little cough returned. Interestingly enough, it was totally under control during class sessions.

Another unusual case I had was a lady who had nothing wrong with her, but heard me speak at a noonday talk in Nantucket and wanted to study with me. I thought, "Super, an easy one." One of our conversations touched on dark sides. She said her ex-husband thought her dark side was spiritualism. Then Marion shared that her husband was into Satanism.

Oh goody, I'm thinking. *Here we go again.*

She told me that after they'd separated, she slipped back in the house and found their former bedroom in total disarray. It was a horrifying mess, the bed sheets were tied in tight knots, the pictures upside down, and there was a very sinister air to it. She said that after she entered the room, the door slammed behind her, and when she was allowed to leave she had bruises on many places of her body. I believe it was true for her.

I was beginning to understand why I was getting so many clients with such strange aberrations. I was being shown that we could manifest anything we need to grow, or to stop our growth, into higher consciousness—ETs, illness, and Satanic ex-partners.

The more I thought about this lady's strange situation with her ex-husband's Satanism, the more I realized her dark side might indeed have been her spiritualism. What if she had been wearing spiritualism like a badge? What if her piety and spiritual journey was a flag she waved in her husband's face every minute of every day? What if he went exactly the way she feared most to counteract her? And what would have happened if she had lightened up, so he could, and there could have been more of a balance? Does that mean some couples manifest the opposite to balance each other? Of course it does.

A different client, Sue, was an entertainer who felt tired all the time. She asked me in session if I thought there were people who were witches, and could one have cursed her? It was with this client I considered the possibility I might have a sign on my forehead that read, "Only totally odd, strange clients apply here."

My healer mode told her anything was possible, but from her story, it seemed that a woman, jealous of her and her talents, was trying to scare her into silence. I also brought her around to the possibility that she had an aspect of herself afraid to go on stage and wanted an excuse, any excuse, not to follow her passion and purpose.

I'll give you one more example of the unusual client list I was acquiring. A woman I'll call Marie, after we were well into a telephone session, revealed she had stabbed herself in the heart four times after an initiation into heart-centering at a conference she had attended. I'd heard about her and this incident through the conference grapevine but didn't know her name.

First, I asked if she had a therapist. When she answered in the affirmative, I confirmed how important it was for her to have regular therapy. Then Marie told me her sad story. At a heart-center foundational conference, while being initiated into heart-center during a beautiful ceremony, she heard her girlfriend having an ecstatic and wonderful experience. Marie was upset that she didn't "feel" anything. She went back to her room, and stabbed herself four times in her heart.

I brought her around to telling me how the stabbing served her. It seemed pretty black-and-white. Before Marie went to the conference, she and her husband were separating, and she was losing her children and life as she knew it. After the stabbing, her husband rushed to the hospital, concerned and angry with everyone but her. He took her home, back to her former life and family.

Marie seemed to want to top her stabbing story. She revealed to me she thought she was Satan incarnate. I once again mentioned nearby regular therapy. Then I reminded her she had a choice. Dark or light. The light might seem at the moment the less glamorous and less powerful as far as attention was concerned. The dark could be incredibly seductive, all that good badness to glory in. Light can be more frightening to some than the dark. Madness is available on either path—a blissful "no responsibility" for your actions.

I take the word "suicide" seriously. It only takes one moment of madness to leave this life prematurely. There are those who would argue with me and say I am interfering with a person's path by stopping someone. I say my being in their life is part of that path, and I'm a fixer. If someone has asked me for help, and I find I can "fix" a broken person by helping them with the tools I've picked up along the way "fixin'" myself, then I feel obligated to assist.

The things we can manifest to help or hinder our growth are unlimited. Good or evil, light or dark. They are all available to us. I don't believe evil is out there just lurking around ready to pounce on any unsuspecting person that happens by. We have choice. Yet, if we fear evil? That's what the universe perceives, and since the universe only says yes to us, that's what we'll get. If we don't think about it one way or the other? Then darkness and evil are nonissues in our life. It's not as though we have to keep up a constant vigil against it.

For some people, consciousness can be a terribly frightening path at times. That's why I emphasize to people to deal with their emotional baggage as much as possible before starting this journey. Jungian therapists seem to be the best at assisting when the quest is opening to a higher consciousness. They honor dreams as well as mythical archetypes. Again, though, don't do what I did and just run to the first Jungian therapist you find. Take the time to check them out. Ask around, find a friend you admire who has used counseling and try their person. It would be great to find someone to help who understands the heart-center and its four attributes of compassion, innate harmony, healing presence, and unconditional love. When I think back on my situation with the Jungian therapist who looked like a younger version of my father, I realize, while he was a jerk, he was just the jerk I needed at the time. What if I had gotten a therapist who looked like my father, yet didn't act like my father because he was kind and sympathetic? I'd probably still be in therapy, or would have become his slave.

Look for a reason behind what happens. Most things are meant to be. By the way, I do realize that before the idea became popular that someone could get paid to step into the surrogate role of family and friends, people worked things out between family and friends. Try that too.

All these clients were a big lesson to me on truth in healing. Even though it's not my truth, I have to honor my client's truth whatever happens. Whether I believe something or not makes no difference if it is real to them. I later read that Carl Jung discovered this, and it is taught to Jungian psychologists. It makes sense that Jung got this information from his observations and inner teachers, as do I.

We all have access to the same information.

At one conference I attended, our teacher suggested that a man recovering from cancer work with me. This man had been

doing all the "right" things at the conference to deepen his healing experience. He tried hard to be open in sessions. It was
apparent to everyone that Carl couldn't understand what his
dreams represented. The man couldn't make the connection that
he was using illness to avoid situations in his life, such as having
a sexual relationship. Instead, he said he thought the cancer was
back even though doctors at the Mayo Clinic said they could
find nothing. I found that curious. It seemed logical to me that
if Carl had been getting clues his cancer was back, he'd be on
the next plane back to his doctors. When I asked him about it,
he said he'd make an appointment when he got back.

During our session, I started by having him talk. This was a
man who had been extremely successful in business all his life,
and could figure most things out very quickly. I decided to put
my hands on Carl's shoulders and guide him though a short
meditation visualizing white healing light from the universe
coming into his body. As I sent the healing light to the suspect
area in his prostate, I suggested there would be no cancer for the
doctors to find when he got home. Just as I finished saying this,
I felt an almost unperceivable jerk in his body.

The realization went through my head, *Good grief, Carl wants
to show those doctors they're wrong. He's "dying" to show them he has
cancer.* I quickly brought the meditation to a close and sat down
to talk. When he didn't bring it up, I finally said I'd noticed
something rather odd happen when I suggested the cancer was
gone. Carl said he had been really surprised by it, too. He
couldn't believe he wanted his body to have cancer so he could
show up his doctors. He realized that if he had cancer, nothing
would be expected of him except to focus on dying. Eventually
he got his wish; he died a few years later. This man so didn't
want to deal with underlying problems, he'd rather die.

As well as using my healing abilities with the various and
sundry clients that came my way, the entertainer in me continued to amaze friends at parties with her healing hands.

I'd cure a toothache here, scores of headaches, PMS and
cramps there, and once worked on a friend's lover's bad knee at
her son's engagement party. She was the same woman I'd helped

a couple years before, when she was so frightened about starting her own business, she was suicidal. During the fervor of her bitter business partnership breakup, I had her over for dinner. I didn't think of it as a healing session, but there was a fire in the fireplace, the table was beautifully set with crystal, silver, and china, and wonderful dinner music was playing. This is the way I always set up my home when having guests. After dinner, I read gypsy cards for her. They validated her current situation. We laughed at some of the cards, she cried at others, and she left feeling relieved and renewed.

The next morning I awakened terribly depressed.

My assistant, Vita, understood.

She said, "Ma'am, I think you took on her depression."

I was taking on people's illnesses again.

From then on, for months, taking on the illnesses of others got so bad, I couldn't even go out of the house to the grocery store without coming home with someone else's stuff. I could pass people on the street and pick up their moods, their colds, their aches and pains. I was a walking, healing sponge.

I remembered a thought I'd had as a child. I had a theory that you could give your cold or flu to someone else and get rid of it. Well, here it was in action. I seemed to suck their illness out of them. Vita and I got worried. We'd been through a lot during the seven years she'd worked for me. She had helped me through my illness, Alfred's death, the move to New York City, and the move to Nantucket. Now that I was well, I didn't want to feel bad again, especially with other people's physical and emotional baggage. She, too, didn't want me feeling bad again. Vita was so sweet, in the midst of my taking on everyone else's "stuff," she placed a crystal at each door to the outside of the house to remind me to "block" before I went out into the public. Vita, in spite of all her formal Catholic upbringing and background as a teacher in Catholic schools in the Philippines for 20 years, immediately embraced my new ways of honoring spirit, too.

I was really having trouble understanding what was happening. Why couldn't I experience all my new talents with the same grace and ease as the heroine in Ellen Burstyn's movie

Resurrection? When her character has a near-death experience after a terrible auto accident in which her husband dies, she goes to her father's home to recuperate and finds she has the power to heal her own paralysis. She never has a moment's angst when helping others and knows immediately if someone can be healed or not. There is one quick scene when she takes the grandmother of a patient aside to tell her she can't help her granddaughter. She quietly explains that some people need their illness to receive love and attention or to give love and attention. Boom, done, all figured out.

Why couldn't I have it that way? I wanted my life to imitate art. I wanted to know ahead of time which clients were open to healing and which ones weren't.

There was one part of the movie that bothered me. Ellen's character felt if she healed through love, it didn't matter how she got the powers or to whom she'd credited them. Her seemingly irreverent attitude bothered her boyfriend, gorgeous Sam Shepard. He had begun to feel she was the resurrection of Christ, and in her denying this, she was denying God. When she didn't listen to him, he tried to kill her by shooting her at one of her public healings.

Great, and what message should I have gotten from this, this scene straight out of my own past lives' fear of persecution? Maybe that if you don't know where your powers come from, you can get hurt? I was not only taking on illnesses of people I'd heal, as Ellen's character sometimes did in the movie, but I was also taking on everything from everyone. Something was very wrong here.

What wasn't I getting?

10

The Big Golden Healing Circle: Protecting Yourself

And then, it came to me. My answer as to why I was taking on people's illnesses. During a meditation in which I was guiding Vita to let go of anger toward people who had cheated her parents, my inner teacher gave me a vision.

It was big, beautiful, golden, and round. It came from the universe, through me, and back out to the universe.

A Big Golden Healing Circle.

All I had to do was see it, and the rest of the message became clear.

We are not intended to go it alone. When we connect back to our original self or spirit, we can help others without hurting ourselves.

Anything is possible when we are connected to Source.

There was my answer!

When I took on other people's illnesses, I had been creating a smaller circle. I was giving them my energy and when the circle came back around to me, I was taking on their illnesses. From me, to the person I was healing, and back to me. From allergies to deep, dark depression, I was a magnet. I'd heal my clients by pulling the affliction from their bodies into mine. I had been channeling my own energy into my clients in a smaller circle, and like a mirror, it had been returning to me, leaving me vulnerable to whatever energies they needed to disperse. I'd heart-centered without connecting to Source. Brimming with unconditional love, compassion, innate harmony, and healing presence that had no connection, I was being stripped by anyone I came near.

Once I understood the concept behind the vision, I was protected.

Now before giving someone energy from my hands or starting a healing session, I evoke the Big Golden Healing Circle by saying the following to a client:

I want you to visualize a big golden healing circle
See it coming from the universe or Source
Through me
To you
Taking your pain or illness
Back out to the universe.

Thank your illness or pain for bringing you a message
And let it know that you can now receive its message
Without having to have the pain or illness.

Then I'd give them energy until I "felt" it was enough or until they'd say they had no more pain. I also might be guided to move my hands to different places on their body, sometimes not even close to the painful spot. Usually the message their body is trying to relay comes through to them or me, like the time I was giving energy to a man whose hip was bothering him. As my hand radiated energy, he told me about another time it hurt when he was walking unevenly on the beach. That time coincided with a fight with his wife. This time his wife had died. He got it. His hip would go out of balance when his life did. He let go of his need to balance his life in an old way and the pain left.

142

If a client is ready to let go, the pain can go totally away. If there is some message they aren't ready to hear? The pain might lessen but it stays.

When I begin a session with a visualization of the big golden healing circle, negative energy is recycled through the infinite energy of the universe or Source instead of coming back to me. In this simple way, I am protected, and universal healing passes through me. I'm simply a conduit.

I was learning. Life wasn't only my responsibility, nor was healing. Plus, I was made to realize I'm never alone. The small golden circle I'd been using needed to expand, from Source in the universe through me to the Earth to the client and back out to the universal Source. The power is love, but a much bigger, much more unconditional love than one person can ever give to another.

I understood it, without knowing I did, when I was learning about energy transference at the first conference I attended. I'd instinctively hold up my left hand to the universe in the energy exercises at that conference. With that gesture, I was intuitively invoking universal healing by connecting to Source to bring the healing energy through me. Placing my right hand on the patient and focusing on my heart, I was bringing through universal unconditional healing love from a never-ending source with my left hand. A beautiful golden healing circle grounded in the Earth by our human connection, just as I'd seen in Vita's meditation.

There were more times I'd unconsciously connected to Source. I had with my friend, Dee, who'd been told she had cancer. I'd held my hand up to the universe while checking her chakras before setting up her own healing circle between her heart chakra and the suspected cancerous spot. By doing that I protected myself and set up a powerful healing circle for my friend.

I recently went to assist at the same conference I'd attended seven years before, the Foundational Heart-center Initiation. That was the conference at which I'd learned I had healing hands. It was also the conference in which I had done my retreat into sleep 95 percent of the time. While I learned how to heal subliminally, what I didn't learn or hear was something said many times: "Protect yourself, connect to a higher Source, and cut the energy between you and the person you are working with when you are finished."

Once again, I had to learn a lesson the hard way. We were doing an energy exercise. The receiver would lie on the floor and the giver would send, through their right hand, unconditional love from their heart-center to the receiver's heart-center. I was the receiver. I knew the woman doing the exercise with me. We'd been at many conferences together over the years and always enjoyed each other's company and stories. I didn't bother blocking any of her energy. I figured she knew how to connect to a higher source before giving unconditional love. Who needs to block that?

When Sue started sending energy by placing her right hand lightly over my heart-center, (just a little above and between the breasts), I first felt pain at my heart and then instantly had a taste of cigarettes and alcohol in the back of my throat. "What the heck!?" Then it hit me. Since I hadn't blocked, I was sucking up any toxicity she had. She must not have connected to a Higher Source for the unconditional love she was giving. We were doing the "smaller circle" from her to me that I used to do, and I was getting the toxicity from her being a long-time smoker and former alcoholic. I quickly blocked the toxins by visualizing a colander over my heart-center; good things would be allowed through the holes and toxins would stay out.

I made sure after we finished the exercise, we symbolically cut the energy between us. Holding our arms out in front of us, bent up at the elbows, we then sliced our hands down in front of our bodies in a cutting motion.

This experience made me realize I still needed help setting boundaries.

Several months before, I'd worked with a woman in a phone consultation whose expertise was boundaries. In an exercise, she told me to put the phone on speaker and go sit in the middle of the office room floor. She said to draw an imaginary circle

Important!

around me that would be my boundary. I did and felt p₁ good; I sat up taller and straighter and felt protected. Then s₁ told me to take a pillow off the sofa, put it in front of me, ana pretend it was another person. I did so. I was told to draw a boundary circle around it. I did. She asked me to check my boundary. It was gone! In the presence of another person, I'd dropped my boundaries. When she said to draw it again, I sputtered something, like, "No, I can't, I won't be a child of the universe, open and available to everyone."

Now, I realize that sounds like something left over from the drugged out hippie-dippie times in the sixties, but as I said, I hadn't been into that scene at all. So, where was this coming from? Right back to Freud: "A child who can steal one parent away from another grows up without boundaries." Mom practically handed Dad over to me on a silver platter. I so wanted to find the safety and security of connecting to Source through my father, men, and others that I am always open and available to everyone and their stuff.

Perhaps that's why the universe guided me to live on eight acres in the middle of nowhere in the high desert of New Mexico. It was not only a good place to write a book, it was a great place to avoid taking on people's illnesses and baggage while I was learning to protect myself.

One thing I've learned since living in New Mexico, it's known as the Land of Enchantment for a good reason. Many people believe the Earth is changing its vibrational energy. In New Mexico it's quite apparent. The process is speeding up. The new trend here in healing is to do nothing but be a conduit for universal energy. While you still can use your intuitive senses to guide your hands, it seems simply being an instrument for universal healing to come through is quite enough.

I've finally decided, the more I stay connected to my higher consciousness or godlike self, the less I need to worry about boundaries. Once we get to a point in our lives where grace is present, whatever is coming at us will come in and out with no effect—a continuous, always available Big Golden Circle.

11

MOVE OVER GYPSY WOMAN:
Intuition, Tarot, Runes, and Psychic Phenomena

> *The intuitive mind is a sacred gift, and the rational mind is a faithful servant. We have created a society that honors the servant and has forgotten the gift.*
> —Albert Einstein

It was early August 1957 in Kodiak, Alaska. I, ten years old, was stomping around crunching pine cones and needles under my red rubber boots while following a new path through the woods. It was a little chilly that day; my mother made me wear a long-sleeved plaid flannel shirt over my T-shirt. Both were tucked into the elastic waistband of my jeans. My blond hair was tousled by branches I forgot to duck. When I reached a big decaying log blocking the path, I scampered over it and came to a large clearing. Though the grass was long and green from the moist summer, there were still some late-blooming scarlet sage and deep blue lupines peeking through. After surveying the clearing and the tall pines on the other side, my eyes went from the treetops to the crystal blue sky. There I saw God looking down at me.

Yes, I did say God.

The vision was very clear. His image almost filled a quarter of the sky. I saw His head with His flowing beard and long white hair and a nice, rather approving look on His face as He smiled down at me.

Excited and proud, I ran home as fast as I could to tell Mom and Dad. I burst into the living room, saw them playing cards at the kitchen table and rushed over to tell them my extraordinary story.

If they heard me, they must not have understood.

I'd just seen God and I was shushed and shooed away?

When parents notice their child possesses a special ability in the arts or intellect, it's natural to foster the gift until it develops into a skill. Fortunately, more and more parents are now also fostering their children's natural abilities, whether it be the ability to stay heart-centered, intuit life, or use psychic abilities—all traits that help live the human experience putting spirit first.

At the moment of conception when each of us comes in as spirit, we are heart-centered and intuitive. Many of us spend the rest of our lives trying to find or get back to that original authentic self. Some people trek the world looking for gurus in caves on mountaintops to give them the meaning of life. Others visit psychiatrists searching for something they never lost. It would help if we could just remember:

> **We are spirit having a human experience, not humans having an occasional spiritual experience.**

We *are* spirit. We *are* soul. We can't lose it. I remember reading a book by Thomas Moore in which he said all our problems, personal and social, are due to a loss of soul. I understand what he means, but I think the way he says it is misleading. Twenty years ago when I'd just become ill, in despair I said I felt like I'd lost my soul. I wish there'd been someone around to say, "Patricia, that's impossible. While we might lose our *connection* to soul or spirit, we can't lose our soul or spirit. We *are* soul or spirit, always and forever. It's just these human bodies, memories, worries, the DNA that connects us to 2.5 million years of collective consciousness, all these things distract us from our connection to who we really are first and foremost—we are soul and spirit."

I quickly learned from my seeing-God experience at age ten that psychic visions weren't accepted or discussed in my family. So out of my great need to be accepted, I stopped having visions. Other psychic talents surfaced. My ability to intuit the thoughts of others came forth. Like many children, I'd blurt out some shocking truth about an adult, embarrass everyone, and be reminded my comments were not appropriate.

I also knew where conversations were going long before they'd get there and would become impatient and butt in to bring them to a conclusion. I'm still working on that one.

There were fun things, too. I have an amazing ability to win prizes. When I was ten, my first winning, in my estimation at the time, was the world's most beautiful red clock radio. Over the years I've won everything, from T-shirts to cases of wine and designer outfits, from Beanie Babies to a Mercedes-Benz.

I can also call dice.

Always curious about my abilities, I never understood them until I bumped into the display of Pete A. Sanders Jr.'s book, *You Are Psychic*, at the Coliseum bookstore in New York. Sanders, a tall man with dark hair and glasses, was raised by a mother who understood and fostered innate intuitive abilities. When he was a child, she'd take him with her on visits to psychics. At 18, he went to Massachusetts Institute of Technology to ascertain scientific reasons for things psychic.

His book made so much sense to me that I called to schedule time to study with him. I learned many "facts" about being psychic. According to Pete, there are four psychic senses. We all have them, though generally one or two are more dominant than the others. As you read on, I'm sure you will recognize the ones that are more dominant in you. Remei intuitive or psychic.

Psychic Intuition is located at the to head. Psychic intuition means you know thi son to know. Being intuitively psychic can i bigger picture. It is as if you tap into thous lective consciousness directly. An internal awareness, it's nothing you've studied, seen, or read about. It's a knowing that pops into your head from seemingly nowhere. When I learned that my intuitional "hits" could often be about the future, not the present, I instantly became less frustrated about where I was on my path instead of where I thought I should be.

An example of intuition, or "knowing," happened to me during the week Princess Diana and Mother Teresa died. I was surprised that every TV broadcaster wasn't saying what I knew to be true—the timing of their deaths in the same week was no coincidence. It was a message to the world we could no longer leave the pain and suffering of our fellow man up to two lovely ladies. The safeguarding of humanity and our planet had now been passed on to the savior in each and every one of us.

It seemed clear to me.

Here's an exercise. Try intuiting into something you've lost. Take a couple deep breaths to clear your mind. After quieting yourself, guide your awareness upward to the top of your head and out. Allow impressions to pour into your mind. Be open. You may feel a sensation of heightened attunement—your body may start lightly circling. You will find yourself knowing the answer.

This practice has worked for me time and time again. Even six months after I lost an earring, I did this exercise and "became" the earring. As "the earring," I looked around, what I felt and saw was that I was against the sink cabinet in the master bedroom looking at the thick rug. I went to my bedroom, felt along the wall-to-wall carpeting that butted up to the cabinet, and there it was.

Psychic Hearing is located just above the ears. People receive messages either by having acute hearing or by hearing that pop into their heads. Songs will come to them that messages, meaningful words from overhearing other people's conversations will hold an answer. A random dialogue heard in a crowd might have special meaning. Sounds can trigger insightful events.

My friend Jody and I were visiting Nantucket before I moved there. Jody had always felt a strong connection to the island. The first morning, we found that the shortcut to town from our bed and breakfast was across Nantucket's graveyard. When we climbed over the split-rail fence, Jody decided to see if we could find any of her New England relatives in this cemetery. We started combing the gently slopping terrain dotted with headstones. We split up, and by the time we'd covered half the place, I was getting bored and ready to continue into town.

Out of nowhere, I heard high melodic notes of angelic-like singing. They seemed to float on the air. The sound was so lovely, it unnerved me. Shuddering, I hoped when I turned I'd find Jody right behind me and that her alto voice would be responsible for the unearthly high soprano notes I'd heard. I looked up. No, Jody was way at the other end of the cemetery. Okay, I was freaked. What had I heard? The sound had been so clear. I was in the middle of the cemetery, far away from cars, and there was no breeze. I stood there a moment and looked around me. My eyes stopped at a gravestone. It read "Anna and Jacob Belcher." Jody's seafaring relatives.

When I called to Jody, I saw her at the far end of the cemetery stooping down to pick something up. When she came over, she held up a black feather and said, "I can't believe it, Patricia. At the same moment you called, I heard the snap of a wooden ship's canvas blowing in the wind, felt a blast of cold damp air, and looked up to find this raven feather floating down." (Ravens are spirit guides in American Indian medicine.) Jody now understood the connection she always felt when coming to Nantucket. The message she received from her relatives? They were calling her back to be her authentic self and follow her bliss as they had. Jody gave up the consulting job she had that paid good money but gave her no joy, and began her Ph.D. in mythology.

You can practice psychic hearing by going into a meditative state to ask for information about a question with which you are struggling. Then go about your day as usual, tuning in enough to notice the answer when it appears. There might be a message just for you when you turn on the television or radio. You don't have to concentrate on receiving the message, just open your awareness to recognize it when it comes.

Psychic Vision was my most dominant sense as a child. Usually we have one sense that dominates. In my case it is now intuition, but others click in at times. Psychic vision is located around the middle of your forehead area and occurs when you have visions or see things in your "mind's eye."

I have this sense when it comes to finding good real estate. In 1986, a realtor I was working with drove me past a house for sale in Atlantic Beach, New York. Nothing could be told about the house from the front. It had very few windows and was practically an all-wood facade that was not terribly attractive. I immediately told her to go get the keys, I'd go get my husband. In my mind's eye, I knew exactly what the house looked like inside, and I knew it was the house we'd been looking for during the last two years. When Al and I walked in, it was exactly as I'd envisioned. It was breathtaking, and instead of small windows looking out to the water as the other houses had had, this living room and the rooms above had huge plate glass windows and sliding glass doors, exactly what we wanted. We bought it that day.

Again in Nantucket, I saw the outside of the house and knew no matter what the inside looked like, I was buying that house. It was a mess inside, mildew on the walls and ceiling, trash coming out of the fireplace in the kitchen. The little bit of furniture in it detracted from the beauty of the rooms with their tall mullioned windows and angles. With a small amount of labor, the walls washed instead of painted, it turned out to be beautiful and made me a huge profit when I sold it five years later.

Try using psychic vision when you are going to meet someone you've never seen before or when going to a new place. Pause for a moment beforehand and imagine "seeing" the person or the building. Write down your first impressions and check to see how accurate you were.

Another of my favorite teachers is Carolyn Conger, a California psychologist and the most intuitive intuitive I've met. During a two-week intensive one-on-one study session I did with her, she asked me to describe her surrogate daughter whom I'd never met. I closed my eyes and was confused. I saw a slim girl with short black hair and then a young girl with long blond hair, a little heavier. I was right both times. Her daughter had just cut and colored her hair, and lost weight.

Psychic Feeling is located at the solar plexus area. A lot of you will recognize this one. It's gut reaction. Feelings can range from euphoria and butterflies to a vague discomfort or actual nausea or pain.

Back in 1990, my husband and I were visiting new friends of ours, the Sydneys, in England. They took us to visit their grown children who lived in a wonderful old farmhouse in the Oxfordshire countryside outside of London. We were told the house was so haunted by a spirit that our friend, Meredith Sydney, would never stay overnight. This did not make Alfred particularly happy about our excursion.

As we drove up, we could see the stone farmhouse with its large thatched roof and behind it, an old stone barn that stood three stories high. There were aged stone walls delineating borders that seemed to go on for miles and disappear over hills of bright green grass. Thyme and other herbs were growing between the cobblestone roads and paths that connected all the outbuildings to one another. I had such a feeling of serenity, I couldn't image what the fuss was about.

The Sydney's daughter, Marion, and her husband were delighted to see us and offered us a tour of the house. I could tell my big, strong Alfred was still reticent. He begged off and sat on the patio with our friends while I went off to tour. I was excited and wanted to experience the ghost. I assumed from a previous conversation that the story of the ghost brushing Marion's hair when she was sleeping in the living room meant I would sense the ghost in that room. I went into the living room and was hugely disappointed. I felt nothing. As the tour continued, we came to a lovely room where the silence was filled with sensations of merriment, laughter, and light. I felt such peace and contentment in that room, I didn't want to leave. After our tour, I told Marion. She laughed and said, "Oh, that's the ghost's room. That's where I was sleeping when he brushed my hair. He was showing off for you. He likes pretty women." I had "felt" the ghost with an eye for the girls.

This one you probably don't need to practice. Haven't there been many times when you've walked into a room and "felt" the energy? Either positive and happy "vibes" or negative ones filled with animosity and envy? That's psychic feeling. Next time pause before entering a room and see what you feel.

Emotions can emanate from ghosts and real people who have been in the room even if the room is now empty. Many people burn sage, to "smudge" and clear the energy of a room or house. Denise Linn has written a book I refer to often, called *Sacred Space*, on clearing and enhancing the energy of your home.

Divination

The definition for divination in *Webster's* is:

> 1: the art or practice that seeks to foresee or foretell future events or discover hidden knowledge usually by the interpretation of omens or by the aid of supernatural powers
> 2: unusual insight: intuitive perception

I bring this up because of something that happened one night when I was having dinner with my friend and her husband. Laura is used to me and my new skills so I didn't think anything about taking off my cross necklace to use as a pendulum.

Pendulum

I use a pendulum to connect to a higher consciousness, thereby bypassing any emotional or egotistical attachment to an answer. How it works is simple. A pendulum can be a crystal or stone on a string, or any object that will swing freely. I use the heavy gold cross I bought at the Vatican because I wear it all the time and it's available. I hang the chain across my forefinger and let the cross dangle. To test it, I ask it to show me yes. It begins to circle or sway. For me a "yes" always circles clockwise. To test it further, you can ask an obvious question like, "Am I wearing a black blouse?" to validate yes and no. For some people, instead of going in circles, it will swing back and forward, and side-to-side for yes and no. For me, it circles clockwise for yes and counterclockwise for no. See what happens for you. Just suspend any misgivings you might have and let it happen.

The first question I asked at dinner that night was whether I should have the steak or lobster. It swung yes for steak and no for lobster. Then, kidding around, I asked whether my son and their daughter (who were sweethearts in high school and still friends) would marry.

Laura's husband, who is strict Catholic, said, "Don't do that. It's conjuring." Since I have always taken my spiritual path with joy and no fear, I was surprised at his reaction until I later looked up the definition of conjuring.

Look at *Webster's* definition 2, sub (3)a.

> 1: to charge or entreat earnestly or solemnly
> 2: to summon by or as if by invocation or incantation
>   (1): to affect or effect by or as if by magic
>   (2): imagine, contrive—often used with up
>   (3): to bring to mind intransitive senses
>   a: **to summon a devil or spirit by invocation or incantation**
>   b: to practice magical arts
>   c: to use a conjurer's tricks: juggle

No wonder he was upset. I was using the first definition—"to entreat earnestly"—while he was thinking I was summoning the devil.

When I use a pendulum, I am asking a higher consciousness that isn't emotionally attached to an answer, to give me an opinion. An opinion I don't consider sacrosanct. Even if the pendulum had said yes, our children would get married, I know with life's changes, if I asked at a later date the answer could be no.

I don't take any divination as the be-all and end-all. I use it as advice, not the answer. I know that as conditions change so will the advice, everyone has free will. Divination tells us what, at that moment with conditions as they are, can happen.

When I told my son about this incident with the pendulum he said, "Mom, some people are scared. Remember when I was in school in Connecticut and what happened at the girl's dorm?" The girl's dormitory he was talking about is the oldest building in the state and had documented ghosts. Doug told me the story again, "One night, Mom, the girls living in that dormitory got together to see if they could contact the ghost. Cecelia had a Ouija board she'd brought from home on the last break. They all sat in a circle around the two girls who had their hands on the plastic pointer and asked if anyone was there. As the pointer slid quickly over the board to yes, they felt a presence enter the room. The girls ran out screaming and crying to the dorm counselor. One of the girls was so frightened, she went home and didn't return. The rest all slept together in the same room until Christmas break."

Doug went on to say that a male student and a counselor laughed about the girl's experience and vowed to spend Christmas holiday in that dorm. Doug returned to school to find both guys freaked by their experience and that neither would go near the building.

I believe this. Certainly after my experiences with Alfred, my deceased husband, I can't say there are no ghosts and that we can't (the number-one definition of conjure) "charge or entreat earnestly or solemnly spirits to ourselves." Of course we can. We can also "conjure" up bad things. But we have choice as to what and whom we earnestly entreat or conjure. I don't believe evil spirits are just hanging out waiting to jump on us.

It's the law of attraction. If we expect them, they're what we'll get. If we don't, we won't. That's probably what happened to the young students. They put out to the universe they wanted to connect with a spirit and that they were afraid. The universe said yes, sure, you can have what you want. They connected to a spirit and were scared. The school was right in banning Ouiji boards. No one had a foundation to begin this type of work.

While I've had a good time on my journey, I'll say it again—opening to higher consciousness should not be taken lightly or frivolously.

People have been using divination for thousands of years to help them foretell the future, find practical guidance, and receive spiritual advice. We all have the ability to touch into our inner teacher when we quiet ourselves. Readings are just another way to help us connect. They can bring clarity to everyday issues by triggering our innate awareness.

Now, don't get me wrong, readings can and will reveal the glossed-over version of the truth we try to feed ourselves. So if you are fearful of knowing what you are truly capable of manifesting, don't use divination. If you are blind to ways you're thwarting your own progress to a more aware consciousness, and don't want to know about it, don't use divination tools. Divination tools don't sugar-coat.

There is nothing hocus-pocus about divination. It is our normal intelligence being given added light. A reading is information-gathering and many times confirms what we already know.

I did realize, once I became familiar with divination, that newcomers need preparation. If I do a tarot reading for someone who knows nothing about divination tools, I enlighten them a bit first. I tell them in tarot the "Death" or "Hanged Man" card in a reading is most likely foretelling the possibility of great transformation. I say that they're good cards to get if you need big change in your life. Powerful cards, they foretell of the necessity of old ways dying out so there can be the birth of new.

The "Hanged Man" card is usually showing that we are hung up in a situation and need to isolate and surrender to get things moving again.

I only once pulled the "Death" card when I felt it might actually be announcing real, physical death. My client was, after all, 94 years old and complaining about how she had outlived everyone in her life including all the younger generations. Pulling the card allowed us to talk about her death and realize the card was announcing her *desire* to pass on to join her relatives. It wasn't forecasting her death. She was lonesome. The card was telling us she wished she were dead because of her loneliness for past relationships. Subsequently, she hired a live-in companion and is still alive at 100.

I start a reading by having my client join me in a short heart-centering meditation to set an intention. I say something like, "Coming from our hearts with compassion, innate harmony, healing presence, and unconditional love, we ask that this reading be for our highest and greatest good, and give information about _____," and we go on with an informative session.

The Internet

I consider myself a hip, twenty-first-century intuitive. Almost every morning since I've been writing this book, I turn on my computer, press the web home page button, and up pops a free site: www.facade.com. It's an extensive web site with five tarot decks, runes, I Ching, bibliomancy, and other divination tools from which to choose. My favorite, which I've automatically set to come up, is the William Blake tarot deck by Ed Buryn. The web site describes it this way. "The William Blake tarot explores the mystical vision and artistry of the renowned English painter and poet. Through rich interpretations focused on creative undertakings, it has long been the deck of choice for artists, writers, musicians, and thinkers."

I type in the date and my question, pop the mouse on the type of reading I want, and the cards appear with interpretations. Usually I ask for a day card to contemplate, read the interpretation, and go about my day, keeping what I read in mind. To give you an example of how this works for me, one day when I was working on this book and having a great morning, I pulled the card "8 of Music—Discontent." The Blake quotation was, "Clouded with discontent and brooding in their minds terrible things." The reading was, "Disappointment or dissatisfaction.

Troubled emotions below the surface. Feeling at the mercy of circumstances. Possibility of emotional breakdown. Fears of what
may happen. Apprehensive about the unknown. Paranoia.
Feelings of missing out on something. Former values and friends
no longer interest you. Wanting to escape the situation." Under
an area at the bottom of the reading it said, "In the creative
process: Psychodrama and emotional torments can serve as imag-
inative stimulants. Expressing and documenting what you feel
can be artful as well as healing."

Valery, my editor, was there that day. Still a little nervous
about all this, she said, "See, that's why I don't like to pull cards.
That's a terrible reading. It will influence your mood and change
your whole day."

I replied, "I tell you what, I will use the information in this
card to help me write a chapter." I looked at all the chapter
names we had pasted on the bookcase glass doors, and out came,
"Men, Daddies, and Gods." All my father's fears, discontent, and
wanting to escape from memories of his father's murder came
pouring out.

The readings are ours to use as we see fit, not predictions cast
in stone.

Tarot

In the Voyager tarot by James Wanless, my favorite card,
"Illumination, Ace of Wands," shows an X ray of the energy of our
hand. Beautiful colors radiate from the fingers, red, blue, yellow, and
white connecting to all that is. It reminds me to feel our electric-
ity—to live with intensity knowing we illuminate and enlighten.

Wanless calls this deck a vehicle for a journey into the inner
universe of the self, a symbolic pathway to the full realization of
your abilities. It has 78 beautiful, colorful cards, each with a
montage of pictures of mountains, rivers, stones, flowers,
machines, computers, buildings, people, colors, space, planets,
windows, candles, and many other items, an assemblage of symbols in each card that helps connect us to our inner self. When
pulling a card, study it to see what intuitively comes up from the

card's image. Then if more information is wanted, the description can be read in Wanless's book.

Another tarot deck I like is the Osho deck with its simple, beautiful pictures. I kept pulling the "Lovers" card in readings when I asked about a man I'd just started seeing. I, of course, wanted the card to be forecasting that we'd fall madly in love, even though I knew it wasn't to be. Where it lay in the reading among the other cards told me to get my own act together. Harmonize the two warring fractions of my personality, my masculine and feminine consciousness, and then I'd be ready to love again, this time on a more mature conscious level.

I Ching

Years ago, when I first learned how to do an I Ching reading, it didn't "click" for me, I wasn't ready for the rather esoteric writings. Now I find sessions with the I Ching fascinating and the readings "right on."

After I finished the first draft of this book, I did an I Ching reading. I asked for significant information for me at that time. The future hexagram was Number 24, "Returning." That hexagram represents the quality of likely opportunities and challenges arising from changes that are in process now.

Perfect for my situation.

In the reading I was told, "There is a turning point which recharges you and eventually brings successes. It is the beginning of a turn-around. The time of letting go of the old and making way for the new, a time of new beginnings, and it starts with a rest." I was cautioned, "Don't move too fast. The new momentum is just beginning. The turn-around demands that your energy be recharged by adequate rest, so that your life-force will not be spent prematurely."

I was leaving my solitary life of writing to go out into the world with the promoting and publishing of my book. A time of major adjustment. The reading reminded me to take the time to recharge before "switching hats."

The I Ching is the oldest continually used divination system in the world. It comprises 64 basic symbols called hexagrams.

You get a reading for your question by making a hexagram producing six lines. There are various ways to do this. You can use yarrow sticks, coins, 16 stones or marbles of four colors. Then you read the corresponding symbol in *The I Ching* or *Book of Changes*. I only read part one and part three. There's also a web site I've use for I Ching at www.tarot.com/oracle/.

Runes

During the process of writing this book, I kept drawing the same rune that had in its explanation the Sun Meditation I told you about in "Women, Mommies, and Goddesses." Called "Sowelu," it represents Wholeness, Life Force, and The Sun's Energy. When I moved to my eight acres in the middle of nowhere in New Mexico, it really began to have meaning. The rune cautioned, "You may see fit to withdraw, or even to retreat in the face of a pressing situation. . . . Know that such a retreat is a retreat in strength, a voyage inward for centering, for balance. Timely retreat is among the skills of the Spiritual Warrior."

The word "rune" means "whisper" or "secret." I use *The Book of Runes* by Ralph H. Blum, which includes 25 stones with Norse symbols. Depending upon which spread you decide to use, you can draw up to six stones.

I usually pull three runes to give me an overview of a situation. The instructions are to select them one at a time with an issue clearly in mind, placing them in order of selection, from *right to left*. Reading from the right, the first rune speaks about the "situation as it is"; the second (center) gives the "course of action called for"; and the third rune (on the left) states the "new situation that will evolve." Like the I Ching, you look up the runes' meanings in the book. I like these interpretations. They are easy to understand and translate effortlessly into modern life.

Bibliomancy

About four years after Alfred's death, I was at the Frank Lloyd Wright chapel in Sedona looking out at the expansive views of

the red rock sculptures of teapots and sleeping Snoopy formations. I opened the large Bible placed at the front of the chapel
to a passage. The meaning was clear. Basically it said, "Throw
away your widow's weeds and sing a happy song."

In bibliomancy, one simply concentrates on a question or
topic, and using the Bible or some other book, opens it randomly and places a finger on the page. The passage selected often
proves strangely applicable to the query at hand.

Fortune-Telling Cards

I love my Russian Gypsy Fortune Telling Cards by Svetlana
Alexandrovna Touchkoff. They are a set of 25 beautifully colorful cards. Each card is divided into four parts. Each fourth is a
half of a picture. After you shuffle the cards in the prescribed
way, all cards are dealt face-up on a table. If there is a card next
to one with the other half of a picture, you match them up even
if the card has to be turned. Then you look up the picture in the
book.

Years ago when my friend Jody introduced them to me, I felt
I had completely healed from Chronic Fatigue Syndrome. One of
the matches I drew in these beautiful cards was, "You will always
have a chronic illness." I was so bummed. Months passed, and I
began to realize that what it said was true. If I don't do things
necessary to stay well, normal things like eating organic foods,
getting proper exercise, rest, and most importantly, not repressing emotions that stress the immune system, I will be sick. It's
true of anyone and any illness. An illness just doesn't disappear,
it goes away because we've stopped doing whatever hooked us
into it the first time.

Aura Reading

One night I was playing around checking my friends' auras
while we were having dinner at the Summerhouse restaurant in
Nantucket. I told them they could do it, too. My friend's son, a
22-year-old Ivy League graduate, looked at his mom and said,

aura is green." He said his friend's was blue and mine yellow. He, a left-brain law honor student, instantly picked up seeing auras.

What does this information do for us? When properly interpreted, it can reveal a person's mood, intentions, health, feelings, and motives. There is a chapter on sensing auras in Pete Sanders' book, *You are Psychic!* In it he defines what the colors mean. Personally, I like to ask for my own inner guidance to interpret colors, but it's fun to see what someone else has written and whether it resonates with you. If I see blue, I quietly ask, "What does blue mean?" Sometimes my answer will be, "Throat chakra, the person isn't saying what he needs to say." Other times it can mean the person always speaks what they feel. My aura color readings usually associate with the person's corresponding chakra color. Orange can mean the person is in a creative stage or feeling sexy, depending on the person. Yellow can show the person is protecting himself or is ready to conquer the world. That's why I don't give you a list of what colors mean; for you it could be different. Ask your inner teacher for an interpretation. Like the old singing joke, "How do you get to Carnegie Hall? Practice. Practice. Practice." That's how you learn to see and read auras.

I practice aura watching when I'm at an airport and get bored waiting when my plane is delayed. I usually do my unfocused look at people with their backs to me so someone doesn't think I'm staring. I just look at auras. I don't ask for information on them. Not only would that be an invasion of the person's space and privacy, I might end up knowing something I don't want to know about a person, perhaps even something criminal.

When you first practice, it helps if there is a white background behind a person. Don't stare. Look beyond the person and a little above their head or shoulder. Relax your eyes. Let them go out of focus. Your unfocused eyes will notice a white area about an inch or two wide around the head, almost like a reverse shadow. That's the person's aura.

Once you see it, if you don't see a color or colors, *imagine* a color, and you will see or "imagine" a color emanating from the person. "Imagining" takes viewing from your "outer" eye's responsibility into your "inner" eye and moves your awareness up to the third eye area, where it really can "see" colorful auras. Don't force or overconcentrate.

I've found that a way to see what color a person is emanating is to focus on the person's face for moment, then close my eyes and see what color comes up behind my eyelids. If you do this, make sure you are not just picking up on a complementary color, such as seeing blue in a red sweater. Again, when you close your eyes, if you don't see a color, imagine one to get you out of logic and into intuition.

Another way to see energy radiating from your hands is to darken a room and use a black cloth as a backdrop. Unfocus your eyes and look around your hands. You'll see white or colors radiating out from your fingers. On airplanes it's fun to hold your hand up to the window with the white and blue, cloud and sky background, look past your hand, unfocus your eyes, and see the colors shooting out of your fingers. I wonder what people think of me with my hand raised to the window, as I am looking with awe at two inches of blue light streaming from my fingertips.

Intuitive Readings

Before I see a client for a healing or teaching session, I prepare myself for his or her arrival by meditating to see what wants to come through. Sitting in a relaxed position, saying or thinking the person's name, I ask for information to come through for his or her highest and greatest good to help me in a session.

One of the first times I tried gathering information this way was with a male client who was coming to me with complaints of low energy, fatigue, and achy feelings. Among other possible ailments, the doctors had tested him for Lyme disease, since this was Nantucket, with the world's largest incidence of tick fever. Nothing showed up on any of his tests. About an hour before he was to arrive, I started a reading. I didn't think I was getting anything. I kept thinking, "Nothing's coming through. Gee, my face feels numb. Nothing's coming through. Boy, my heart hurts."

Then I understood, it wasn't *my* face or heart I was feeling, it was *his* face feeling numb and *his* heart hurting. I was getting a reading on him kinesthetically. When I asked for guidance as to what these feelings meant, the information that popped into my head about the numb face was that he didn't want to get his face "slapped" anymore (metaphorically), so it stayed numb to keep from feeling pain. I asked about the pain in the heart, whether it was "physical, spiritual, or emotional?" I heard, "emotional, a love relationship turned bad."

With this same client I pulled up images on www.listening-in.com, a web site that has "do-it-yourself creative divination." You ask a question, choose a layout, and different pictures come up at random. Then you intuit their meaning. I asked for information to help this client. The picture I received was of a bearded man walking toward a tree. The first thing that popped into my head was that my client (who also had a beard) was walking into the tree because he needed to become one with nature. In nature he could connect back to his Source and authentic self.

During this man's healing session, when I had him on the massage table in a meditative state, he popped into a past life, sat up, and started crying. Instinctively, I held him and asked what he saw. He said, "I am walking into a tree, and I'm scared." I was ready to jump up and do a little "Oh wow, I did it, I did it, I really connected into universal guidance" dance. But staying in healer mode, I said, "That must make you feel very connected." He switched from fear to wonderment.

As it turned out, he had a long, unhappy relationship that he was reluctant to end. He wanted to move to Telluride, Colorado, yet hadn't told his alcoholic girlfriend of 16 years that he needed to go alone. He became ill at the same time his girlfriend decided she, though not invited, would go on his two-week trip to Telluride. He couldn't cut the cord to a relationship that was now only familiar and draining, not satisfying and nurturing and it made him sick.

The universe provides us tools to gather all the information and guidance we need if we are just willing to open to it. I question everything, even readings, and answers flourish.

PART III

And Beyond

12

AUTOMATIC WRITING: IT'S GOT TO BE EASIER THAN WRITING MY OWN BOOK: Accessing the Collective Essence of Great Teachers

Simon and Garfunkel's song "Bridge Over Troubled Waters" could have been written about the way I felt in April 1996.

> When you're weary
> feelin' small,
> when tears are in your eyes . . .
> I'll comfort you. . . .

I skipped a few lines here about "*I'll dry them all, I'm on your side, when times get rough,*" to get to the "*I'll comfort you*" line. That was my problem. I wanted an "I'll comfort you" person and didn't know where to find one.

I had just taken the four back-to-back spiritual conferences and left Hawaii to go to Dad's vacant house in Dallas. The only thing I was sure of was that I needed balance before going home to Nantucket to act like myself. Who would understand? That "myself" was gone. I wanted a comforting person to talk with about finding a way to peacefully join my old unconscious but familiar life with my newly emerging awareness of how much more the universe has to offer.

My first two weeks of rest and relaxation alone in Dad's house in Dallas could be likened to me sitting in a corner, sucking my thumb, and twirling my hair with my forefinger. While I didn't actually physically sit in a corner, I was in a corner of my mind. I got better the second two weeks. Those days I spent lying on the sofa with the television watching me, eating everything in sight, and throwing up.

I went to see a food disorder psychologist during my two-month Dallas stay. She recommended a nutritionist as well as her own therapy. I wanted help with my "if you can be a little bit pregnant, then I'm a little bit bulimic" problem, which I'd had for 20 years. I felt since I didn't binge and purge often, or since it never "got out of control," then I was just a little bit bulimic. Neither professional could help me do what I wanted to do. I wanted to get to the *hook*, the emotional hook that was locking me into using food as comfort and control. They didn't have the answers I was seeking. They only suggested yet another diet.

No "I'll comfort you" there.

A friend of my parents, Bob Palmer, brought me a copy of Neale Donald Walsch's book, *Conversations with God*. My first thought as I began reading was, "Why am I reading a book by a guy whose life use to be much more of a mess than mine, who's been married five times?" Once I got into the book, I was jealous. Whatever Walsch was doing, whether he'd tapped into a direct line to God or not, he was receiving some very sage advice from somewhere, and his life and others' lives were becoming better for it. This book spoke to me. Like the two books that had turned me around about death, this book rang some ancient bells. A higher being who was nonjudgmental, compassionate, unconditionally loving, and a constant healing presence? Not only ancient bells, it also fit right in with all I was studying and beginning to know as my truth.

While I was in the midst of reading Walsch's book, Bob and

his wife, Sue, invited me to join them at a lecture given by Ruth Montgomery. He told me Ruth was a woman who channeled spirits by automatic writing and had many books to her credit. Her name sounded familiar to me but not in this genre.

I was not totally unfamiliar with automatic writing and channeling. A friend had given me a book a few years before called *Testimony of Light* authored by Helen Greaves, a nun channeling her deceased nun friend. While it was interesting, it didn't leave much of an impression on me because of my lack of connection to things Catholic.

When Ruth Montgomery was introduced, I remembered why I recognized her name. She had been a White House press journalist for six presidents. From my teenage years in Washington, D.C., I could conjure up a memory of her on television raising her little hand and President Johnson saying, "Yes, Ruth." She was one of the first high-profile women journalists.

Now she was doing automatic writing with spirits from another realm? Oh, come on. However, I found myself liking her and her story. During her newspaper days, her editor sent her to cover a séance, fully expecting her to expose everyone as frauds. Instead, her dead father showed up, and that was the beginning of Ruth's automatic writing 11 books from higher spirits.

The emcee was humorous. He said since Edgar Cayce, the famous psychic who channeled healing information, wasn't a writer by profession, his books left a lot to be desired as far as coherence and style. He pointed out that Ruth had been a prize-winning journalist and her channeled books were completely understandable. Not having read either, I couldn't say.

Ruth, being from Washington, D.C., my hometown, comforted me. I knew nothing about Edgar Cayce, except I'd found a book by him in my mother's nightstand after she died. Automatic writing in *Webster's* is defined as "writing produced without conscious intention as if of telepathic or spiritualistic origin." Okay, whatever that meant. From what Ruth said, one person's hand might actually be guided, and another's experience would be more like being a stenographer and writing down a conversation going on in his or her head.

169

I liked Ruth. She was a small, feisty, pragmatic 86-year-old with a lot of presence. A tiny woman with a lot of heart. Someone, during the question and answer period, expressed concern about whether there was a possibility of connecting with evil spirits during automatic writing. Ruth answered in rapid fire, "Oh, I never worry about that, but if you do, say a little prayer about keeping evilness and evil spirits away."

While this might have been too flippant an answer for some, it was just what I needed to hear. It resonated and helped me turn a corner. If she wasn't afraid . . . after seeing Ruth and reading *Conversations with God*, I, too, now wanted to automatic write.

I have to admit, the thought crossed my mind that recording a conversation as a stenographer had to be a lot easier than writing my own book. Connect to a higher power and record a conversation? What a snap! Okay, so how was I going to go about this? As usual, I wanted a rule book. This time I sought and couldn't find an Amy Vanderbilt–type version of *The Proper Way to Automatic Writing*.

Of course, in the far recesses of my mind, I, too, wanted to automatic write God like Walsch had. You would have been proud of me though, as I managed to go into this experiment with no expectations as to who would show up.

I did know whom I didn't want. I didn't want some unfamiliar entity named Orin or Daben or Seth giving me the facts of life.

So, I began.

Since I couldn't find one particular book that gave me all the instructions I wanted, I once again made my own. I'd bought two or three books that could have really confused the situation. One had 15 steps to automatic writing and how to make a totem bag. Another, under "Preparation," said, "Have completed Attuning with Life-Force Energy and Trance Posture and Position exercises in Chapter 6 before doing this process . . . ?"

I didn't want to spend my whole life getting ready for this. Ruth had made it sound easy. I created my own *rules*. I like rituals, so I set up a little same time, same place, same equipment ritual. I kept it simple with childlike wonderment.

At seven each morning, I would go to my parents' round din-
ing room table on which I'd placed three great blue-green candles on a silver tray. I had a large 50-page 12-by-18-inch art pad in
case my writing was big or my guide wanted to draw pictures,
and had several pens and pencils nearby. The rest of the area was
clean, the room was clean, and I was clean and dressed in white.
All of this was my personal preference. I made up a ritual to suit
me. It could be any time that is quiet and uninterrupted, any
table, any color candles, or none for that matter. I got much
more casual about this ritual later.

The rituals you make up are all about what makes you comfortable. Following some tips I picked up from Ruth's talk and
information from a book I'd found on channeling, I heart-
centered and said, "Keeping evilness and evil spirits away." I
asked that whatever happened be for my highest and greatest
good, and got started by going into a meditative trance. This
wasn't hard for me to do after four back-to-back conferences on
accessing higher consciousness. If anything, it was hard for me to
get out of a trance.

By the way, if anything happens during your ritual that
makes you uncomfortable? Stop. You have control, jerk yourself
out of your trance. I have never had any problems. I don't expect
any, and I've always had great experiences.

Okay, Patricia Heller's *Personal Rules on How to Begin Automatic Writing*:

*First, heart-center. With my hands, right under left over my heart,
I called on my connection to Source and the four attributes of heart-
center. Saying and feeling, "Coming from the universe to me and back
out to the universe I feel compassion, innate harmony, healing presence, and unconditional love." This allows feelings of awe and joy to
pour in my heart and being.*

*Second, I said, "I request that whatever happens be for my high-
est and greatest good and that evilness and evil spirits be kept away."*

Third, I did deep breathing to go into a trance/meditative state—

Breath in for four,
hold for four
out for four,
hold for four,
and let my mind go blank.

Fourth, somewhere I'd picked up that I'd see or imagine light-beings who would take me up through the universe to a door, so I saw or imagined beautiful light-beings (mine were lovely white gauzy flowing beings with no features).

Fifth, they would take me up through the universe to a door.

Sixth, I'd open the door and see my guide.

Seventh, I would ask his or her name and whether he or she was for my highest and greatest good. If the answer was yes, and I felt comfortable, then I would start and record a dialogue.

Pretty straightforward and simple. I like things straightforward and simple. Unfortunately, it must not have been straightforward and simple enough because day after day, I'd get up to the door and the darn thing wouldn't open. For 10 days I'd travel up with the beautiful light-beings, and every time I'd get to the door, it wouldn't budge. I didn't give up. Every morning, up at seven, showered body, clean white clothes, candles lit, paper, pens, and pencils, trance, light-beings, door. Nothing. I kept trying. I wasn't terribly discouraged. It was like rehearsals. Actually I might have been building up my resolve for what was to come.

On the 11th day, May 6, 1996, the door opened.

I went through and saw my guide.

Whoa! I thought, taken aback.

I continued as practiced.

I asked my guide, *What is your name?*

He said, *Jesus.*

Shocked, but as rehearsed, I said, *Are you for my highest and greatest good?*

He replied, *The only one higher, Patricia, is my Father.*

I had to smile. I loved it. Fantastic, even the big guys have a sense of humor.

My reply to His comment was in the same humorous vein. I told Him, *I guess you'll do*, and it was his turn to smile.

Let me take a minute here. I beg your pardon? I was automatic writing whom? My entire life, I'd unintentionally resisted Christian ideology. Jesus? I wanted my journey to be about something entirely new and unique. After 10 long days, I come up with Jesus? Why me, why Him? I wasn't raised religious. Actually I was downright ambivalent about Jesus and the Bible. Yet, for some reason, strange to me, my subconscious seemed to be happy with Jesus. Or, was Jesus really coming through?

I decided I'd be open. No judgments, no comparisons, and delete my need to understand. I realized another person automatic writing might come up with no image at all—kind of like Beethoven channeling sonatas. Someone else might envision a more Mideastern version of a Jesus-type figure or an old, wise Chinese man, an elder in an Indian tribe, or something or someone less physical—a nameless, faceless entity.

I agree with those of you who have trouble with Christian ideology. However, Western ideology is what kept coming through to me. I didn't seem to have a choice. I want to live my life guided, not me guiding my life. What was I supposed to say? "Huh, excuse me, I really wasn't expecting you, Jesus. May I see a different selection?" I decided to go with it. I had wanted a higher consciousness to tap into, and for some reason, oddly enough, my subconscious or some Automatic Writer's Association high in the sky decided I should be happy with Jesus.

I want to make it clear that whatever happens when a person tries connecting to a higher place is right. Nothing is wrong—whatever happens, happens—I don't recommend trying to manipulate it to something else. Again, it's about surrender. Once we surrender, then we can tap into all knowing beyond ego—whatever image appears. Maybe that was why I pulled Jesus. Talk about me having to surrender expectations and ego.

Whatever comes through when you have a sincere heartfelt intent is going to be right. In my case, incredibly enough, it was Jesus with whom I was conversing. I knew what He looked like.

I was use to all the Western, white bread versions of Him—tall, not dark but not light skin, slim yet not thin, blondish-brown long hair and beard, dressed in white robes, with a white scarf wrapped around His head, and sandals. That's what I saw. He kind of radiated light. I didn't really see the light as much as sensed it. I felt totally at ease and comfortable and enveloped with feelings of love.

I'll admit it, I was intrigued and curious.

Okay, so instead of fighting it I decided to accept it.

Once I accepted it, my thoughts instantly turned to the fact I must be doing something wrong. We weren't having a rambling conversation the way Walsch seemed to have had with God in his book, *Conversations with God*.

On the second day I decided to ask. *I'm not doing this right, am I?*

His reply was, *There is no wrong way.*

Okay, that was helpful and nice to know. So, if there was no right or wrong way to do this, then I ended up back at full circle. Why me? Why Jesus?

On the third day I got up enough nerve to ask: *Jesus, why of all guides, are you my guide, when I always, in my mind, questioned the authenticity of the Bible and you?*

His answer kept me automatic writing for two months: *Because, Patricia, the way you are developing into a being of light, you can now understand that I did exist and that everyone can exist as I did.*

My dumbfounded reply was, *Amazing.*

It was amazing.

Even at this point, feeling a complete novice, I totally understood what He meant. *You can now understand that I did exist and that everyone can exist as I did.* I got it instantly. Everyone can heal as He did (example my healing hands and self-healing), everyone can be resurrected as He was (by connecting to our higher self), and everyone can love as He did (unconditionally).

Without any religious training, I knew who Jesus was.

He was a man who lived His godlike self as much as humanly possible.

He was an example of how to live as spirit in a human body.

Whether He was God or the Son of God or just a man didn't matter in the exchange I was having with Him. What mattered was that *"everyone can exist as I did,"* living as our higher or god-like selves as much as humanly possible while enjoying our humanness and lush physicality.

On May 18, we had an interesting conversation:

P. *Jesus, can you help me get rid of my blocks to living a fully integrated life?*

J. *Yes.*

P. *How?*

J. *By believing in yourself as you are coming to believe in me.*

P. *Is this really happening? Am I really automatic writing your words, Jesus?*

J. *How do you feel? Stop for a moment.*

P. *I feel a little skeptical. My shoulders are a little tense, but actually I feel great love and compassion—my breasts feel full and sensual—is that you?*

J. *When I come into your "spirit" everything starts working to its fullest.*

On May 30:

J. *Come sit by me.* (We now have a location I usually meet Him. We sit under an olive tree on a stone retaining wall on a hill overlooking a meadow with sheep, green pastures, and a trickling brook. Very tranquil. Lots of light glowing off Jesus.)

J. *How do you feel today?*

P. *How do I feel? Right now, blessed.*

J. *You are always blessed. I am always with you and you are always with me.*

P. *What does that mean?*

J. *It means you are me—exactly like me. Everyone is me. You don't have to die on the cross to prove it though,* He said smiling.

P. I lay my head on His/my shoulder. *Oh Jesus.* Sigh.

J. He puts his arm around me and says, *You're okay, Patricia. You are coming through this transformation just fine. You're trusting your inner wisdom. I know it is hard to give up all you thought you wanted. But your new life is going to be so rich and full and filled* with abundance. *You will look back and wonder how you ever thought "things" would make you happy.*

P. *Oh, Jesus.*

J. *Oh, Patricia.* He kisses my forehead. *I love you so, Patricia.*

P. *I love you so, Jesus.*

J. *This is your cross.* (I realized He meant believing.)

P. *I know. I love you. Thank you.*

After a couple months I stopped automatic writing. I didn't think I was getting anywhere because I kept asking the same question over and over again in different ways:

Patricia: *What is my passion and what is my purpose?*

And I kept getting the same response.

Jesus: *Helping other people the way you have helped yourself.*

I wasn't ready to hear this, so I got bored and stopped writing for several months. I started up again when I was feeling rather vulnerable and thought touching in might help.

December 11, 1998: (I've been typing my automatic writing for sometime now, I put my fingers on the keyboard, close my eyes, connect, and type.)

P. *Hi, Jesus.*

J. *Hello, Patricia.*

P. *I need a hug.*

J. *Come here, dear.*

P. After receiving a hug, I say, *This is hard work.*

J. *It doesn't have to be.*

P. *Okay, what am I doing wrong?*

J. *Nothing.*

P. *Then why is it so hard?*

J. *You're in your own way.*

P. *How do I get out?*

J. *You just did.*

P. *What does that mean?*

J. *That it will start flowing now because you have come back to Source.*

P. *Meaning you?*

J. *No, meaning you.*

P. *Oh, Jesus, this is so confusing. I feel like singing a chorus of*

"What's It All About, Alfie." (Actually I sang my husband's name Alfred instead of Alfie.)

J. Do.

P. *"What's it all about, Alfie? Is it just for the moment we live? What's it all about when you sort it out, Alfie? Are we meant to take more than we give? As sure as I believe, there's a heaven above, Alfie, I know there's something much more, something even nonbelievers can believe in. I believe in love, Alfie. Without true love we just exist, Alfie. Until you find the love you've missed you're nothing, Alfie."*

I get it—the love we've missed is love of and from Source. Love of and from ourselves because we are Source.

J. *By gosh, she's got it.*

P. *Right, Professor Higgins. So, what's my book about?*

J. *What you just said—loving yourself as Source, unconditional love of self.*

P. *What's Source?*

J. *You don't have to answer that—everyone answers that for him- or herself. What is Source to you, Patricia?*

P. *Source is you, Source is the universe, Source is me, Source is the God in all of us. But is there one God, one Supreme Being? One image I have is of Him lounging up in heaven, a huge personage reclining in white robes, long white beard and hair? Who is that?*

J. *That is your childhood God—who is there if you need Him.*

P. *So how did we all begin if there isn't one God starting the flame?*

J. *That's for me to know and you to find out.*

P. *I need to know—now it is time.*

J. *It's an experiment.*

P. *What is?*

J. *Beings—Earth.*

P. *And?*

J. *It is an experience/experiment—souls trying out existence in physical form in which they might experience love/hate, laughter/sadness, birth/death.*

P. *Light side/dark side in physical form.*

J. *Yes.*

P. *To what end?*

J. *To gather more knowledge.*

P. *For what?*

J. *For the Big Bang.*

P. *What in the world—or excuse me, universe, do you mean by the Big Bang? This is getting too far out.*

J. *It is about your experience in coming to find intuition and opening to more than just ordinary awareness. It is about you allowing Source or "God" to come into your life as a lover, a friend, a confidant, a guide. It's about you feeling unconditional love from Source and about knowing the benevolence and having no fear. It is about life as a human being lived on a multidimensional level. With hope, love, and life, everlasting. It is about opening to the universe and all its glories, Patricia. You've got enough.*

P. *I'm not sure I remember all you said it's about. Can you give it to me in a nutshell?*

J. *It is about love, Patricia. Unconditional staying in love and that state of grace.*

P. *My heart hurts.*

J. *Let it go and feel the love.*

P. *Oh God, it is so beautiful. . . .*

A little later . . .

P. *Okay, I'll go and try to decipher all this.*

J. *It's clear-cut, Patricia. The book is about "All we need is love."*

P. *Isn't that rather sixties?*

J. *Not if you approach it right. It's about how you came to love yourself with all your men, daddies, and gods. Finally coming around to self-love.*

P. *I guess I wrote that all wrong* (my fingers had been on the wrong keys for the last sentence and it came out gibberish) *so I would have to stop to decipher what I'd written and really get the point, huh?*

J. *Yes. I love you, Patricia, soul of my soul, love of my life.*

P. *I get it, "love of MY life"—I am living your life. We are all living your life, especially when we open to our godlike self.*

J. *You've got it.*

I suppose I shouldn't have been so shocked when Jesus had shown up as my automatic writing partner. It had just been a few weeks before when I sat in the cave in Hawaii singing the words, "He's a man. He's just a man." In my exchanges with Him, it didn't matter whether He is the Son of God, God, or "just a man." I have come to accept Him as all three. I have come to accept us all as all three. However He is defined, He was a man who lived His God-like self as much as humanly possible. An example for us all.

I continue to automatic write whenever I feel a calling to do so. As I said, I now simply go to the computer, close my eyes, connect, and type.

When you're weary,
feelin' small,
when tears are in your eyes . . .
I'll comfort you . . .

We all have access to the collective essence of the great teachers, even those of us with limited religious backgrounds and beliefs. We must only be willing to surrender and open to their wisdom and comfort.

13

ARE OUR LIVES GUIDED?
Synchronicity, Intuition, and Coincidences

4:44 read the digital clock next to my bed.

"Okay, now it's getting bizarre," I said to myself. This was at least the sixth or seventh time over the last three months I'd awakened precisely at 4:44 A.M.

The first time was in April 1997, in Nantucket. It continued to appear when I went away for the summer and persisted upon my return. It was happening way too often to be chance and not enough to be habit. Knowing that nothing is "just a coincidence," I tried to figure out what could be behind this phenomenon and/or hear the message being sent my way. Try as I might, I couldn't come up with anything that 444 triggered in my life. It made no sense.

In dream work I sometimes add numbers together to get a core number. I played with that for a while, 4+4+4=12, 1+2=3. Three. Okay, maybe it was validation for my book since the title was about threes? Nice idea, but no click. When something is right in my life, instead of seeing a light bulb over my head, I hear an almost audible click of fingers. There was no click with the number three.

I decided, in view of the fact I couldn't figure it out, I'd forget about it.

Not to happen.

444 wouldn't leave me alone.

In the morning, I'd walk in the kitchen to start my coffee, and the microwave would be flashing 4:44. On other days, I'd happen into the bedroom precisely at 4:44. I decided I had to figure out what 444 was about or it would drive me nuts.

I called Brugh Joy's assistant, Mark, to ask if he knew any good numerologists. I explained about 4:44=3, and said I needed to talk to someone about 3. Mark mentioned I might consider it a 4 (novel idea) and gave me the name of a woman who had given a talk on numbers as archetypes at Joy's annual New Year's Celebration at Asilimar, in Monterey. I called her in California late afternoon Nantucket time, got her machine, and left my name and number. She called back the next day when I was napping. My friend Duane brought me the phone and in my groggy state I simply set a time to talk a few days later. When I hung up the phone, Duane said, "You know, Patricia, she called back at 4:44."

DodododoDodododo (the theme for *Twilight Zone* playing in my head).

The next day I went to work out with my exercise therapist, Sherri. She was also the friend who had guided me in the past-life regression. When I told my 444 stories, she said, "Have you read the book, *The Messengers?*"

I said it sounded familiar, maybe I'd read it years ago.

She replied, "No, it's relatively new. It's all about 4:44."

What she was saying didn't quite register with me. I said I'd look it up on the web to see if there was any information. Any information? *The Messengers* not only had a web site, it had a 444 club for people having 4:44 experiences.

I read the synopsis of the book and groaned to myself, "Oh no, not more religious stuff." As I told you, I'd expected "my" path to newfound higher consciousness would be something totally new and unique. Yet, again and again, I kept bumping into things of a Western religious nature. They kept popping up, making me take notice. Like automatic writing Jesus. Maybe the universe was making it easy for me, giving me images with which I had some comfort level and knowledge.

The Messengers is the story of Nick Bunick, an ordinary man having extraordinary experiences with enlightenment. Bunick was a high-profile businessman, the owner of several corporations and directors of others. He, too, had no formal religious training while growing up. Yet, as an adult, he started experiencing flashbacks to a past life.

Now, this was no ordinary past life.

He was Paul.

As in *Jesus'* Paul.

That Paul, the apostle who walked alongside Him 2,000 years ago.

This extraordinary past life caused Nick some dismay. Anxious to share his experience, but convinced his story would seem unbelievable to most people, he kept his tale to himself. Then it started. At 4:44, he, his family, his friends, and even business associates in Japan started getting messages for him to go public. He realized he had no choice in the matter. His story had to be written.

I read on the web site that half the book was on 444 and the other about his journey as Paul. I sighed and decided, whether it had religious connotations or not, I had to read it. I had a feeling if I didn't get the book, 444 would begin popping up 24 hours a day in my life. I ordered the book and read it, once again dragging my heels, kicking and screaming, forever demonstrating why I call myself the reluctant convert to the transformation game.

Through past-life regressions with a trained therapist, Bunick describes his life as Paul, and Paul's relationship with Jesus. In one part he told what Jesus did to help people heal. My eyes widened as I read on, "Aha, this is why I'm reading this book." What Paul (Nick Bunick) said Jesus did was exactly what I did when I helped people heal. I just used different words. I use "repressed emotions" instead of "sins," (greed, anger, jealousy, or intolerance). I say they must be acknowledged and then "let go." Jesus says, "Forgive."

Jesus divided people into two groups. The ones who recognized that their illnesses were self-inflicted and took responsibility for creating their own sickness, and another group who had been born with illness or had become ill through an accident. The latter group needed more help and time to heal by self-acknowledgement and letting go (my words) or through forgiveness (Jesus').

My telephone appointment with the numerologist was after I'd made the 4:44 connection to the book *The Messengers*. As it turned out, she was not a numerologist, she was a Jungian psychologist (you've got to love synchronicity). After talking with her, we both realized we'd attended the same conference in Hawaii. Since then she'd gone on to finish her Jungian studies in Zurich. She was kind and helpful, the perfect example of the heart-centered Jungian psychologist I had searched for in Texas and couldn't find.

She liked the title of my book, *If You Hear the Message Three Times, Listen,* and asked me if I knew it was biblical. I realized it had some religious connotation, but I didn't know what. She told me Moses, Samuel, and Gideon all had to be summoned by the Lord three times before they understood their call. I said, "Well, this is all very nice, and while one aspect of me believes in all this spiritual stuff and coincidences happening in my life, I have another aspect of me that is a Doubting Thomas."

She said, "Thomas had to touch the wound of Christ."

I groaned and said, "Wait a minute, Doubting Thomas is biblical too? My mom used to say, 'Don't be a Doubting Thomas. . . .'"

She said, "Yes, Thomas was an apostle who had to touch the wound and blood of Christ before he'd believe Jesus died and was resurrected."

Oh boy. What was going on? Moses, Samuel, Giddeon, and Thomas. I was in some heavy-hitting company here. I took a couple of days to digest this information. Then I thought to myself, *Okay, if all this is true then why did I have to have all those 4:44 messages sent to me that led me to find a book and then talk to a*

woman who knew all the connections to the Bible? After all, I auto-
matic write Jesus. Why didn't He just tell me?

I decided to ask. Honoring my love of rituals, I awakened at
four-thirty the next morning, went down to my office, lit three
candles, and began automatic writing at 4:44.

This is an abbreviated version of our conversation that
night:

P. *Jesus, what about the 4:44s?*

J. *You weren't checking in with me.* (Meaning I hadn't been
automatic writing.) Then He said something that made me realize the bigger picture.

Also, I wanted to show you what you and I talk about is the
same message others are getting in different ways.

Once again, I knew exactly what He meant. Different people
are being sent the same message of living life with unconditional love, compassion, innate harmony, and healing presence.
People like Nick Bunick with *The Messengers,* James Redfield writing *The Celestine Prophecy,* Neale Donald Walsch's *Conversations*
with God series, James Twyman, *Emissary of Light,* Brian L. Weiss,
M.D., *Many Lives, Many Masters,* Brugh Joy, *Joy's Way* and
Avalanche, and many others. All experience receiving this message in their own unique way and then feel compelled to write
about it. Their different books attract diverse groups of readers
with the same message, "Life can be much more expansive. We
can live as our higher selves. And, come from the heart."

After all this, I decided I needed to meet Nick Bunick. I
started corresponding with his e-mail people and found he
would be speaking at the Arlington Church in Boston a week
later. My friend Duane made ferry arrangements for us to take
the car off the island the afternoon of the talk, but the day
before we were to go, a three-day blizzard started. I e-mailed to
make sure Bunick would definitely be in Boston if we were going
to risk a sea-sickening ferry ride and harrowing drive through a
raging snowstorm. They e-mailed back in the affirmative and
told me to introduce myself to Nick after the talk.

We stayed at the Ritz Carlton, less than a half block walk to
the church. At the time of the lecture, the church was sparsely

filled, about 60 people, but certainly more than I'd expected to see with the blizzard conditions outside. What Bunick had to say was not new to me. Rather, it went right along with what was becoming my truth. What was fascinating to me was watching the faces of the people in the audience as he spoke. Duane was raised Catholic. I realized from the questions after the talk, many in the audience were, too. I'd observe them listening to Bunick, whose parents had been Orthodox Jews, basically rewriting Catholicism, and felt an almost communal sigh of relief.

Bunick told everyone that in the information he received in his past life as Paul, God is not a punishing God. Hell and the devil were creations of the medieval Church, and Jesus was mainly trying to pass along three simple messages: conduct yourself with universal love, universal compassion, and live in truth. Pretty much the same as my heart-centering messages of compassion, innate harmony, healing presence, and unconditional love.

He said that these messages, unfortunately, had gotten lost over the last 2,000 years; sometimes intentionally, as changes were made by the medieval Roman Church, and other times just because of translations. Translations from an ancient language, to another ancient language to another one to, finally in the seventeenth century, English. Messages of love were changed into messages of fear; messages of compassion into messages of guilt. Nick felt God wished him to go back to those original messages, which have been changed and distorted, as Jesus and Paul spoke them 2,000 years ago.

After his talk, I waited in line to introduce myself to Nick. When I told him who I was, he jumped up, came around the table, grabbed my hand, and said, "You're one of the reasons I'm here. I thought if you could come across land and sea in a blizzard to meet me, then I'd better be here." He graciously accepted some of the stories I'd written about my experiences and told me he'd get back to me. A few days later, he sent me a lovely note giving me the name and address of his publisher, telling me that when my book proposal was ready, to send it on with his recommendation. I did.

The publisher read it and asked that I send the manuscript

to him when it was finished. 444 led me to a publisher for the book before I'd really started it. Great incentive to keep going.

In June of 1998, my editor Valery and I got together for the first time. She'd come to Nantucket, and when I told her about the 444s, she asked who was behind my 444 messages. A little taken aback by the question, I said, "I don't know or care. Some nights I simply ask for validation I'm on the right track with my book or life in general and I'll be awakened at 4:44 with a wonderful feeling of peace."

That same day I talked with Carolyn Conger in Santa Monica, the psychologist who's an incredible intuitive. When I told her about 4:44, she inquired as to whether I asked questions when awakened at 4:44. Again, surprised at someone wanting my 444s explained, I told her no, it wasn't like that. I simply felt connected, validated, and peaceful when awakened at 4:44.

That night without any prior petitioning for validation, I awakened at 4:44. I groaned. I knew I had to ask. I knew whatever the answer was to their questions, it would take my 4:44s to a different level. I said out loud, "Okay, who is behind my 4:44 messages?" and lay my head back on my pillow to go to sleep to see what would come forth.

Immediately inside my head I heard, *Gabriel, come blow your horn. Go look him up in your angel book.*

Instead of being excited, I was tired and confused. The next morning when I did my wake-up knock on Valery's door, I said, "I'll be downstairs. I got a message last night about who is behind the 4:44 messages. I have to look something up." Still in my slippers and robe, I stumbled downstairs and went into the office to get my "Angel" book. I knew exactly what book the voice was talking about. I only had one. It was *The Angel Oracle* by Ambika Waters, a book and angel cards I'd bought at the Buddhist Retreat when I'd dragged Duane off to study Tantra. I'd never read or pulled the Gabriel card. I took the book out to the living room with its warm red walls, started a fire in the fireplace, and sat down on the soft beige duck-cloth-covered love seat. I leafed through the book until I found Gabriel.

Under his picture was this description, "Gabriel is depicted

holding a lily, which stands for purity and truth. He is sometimes seen with an inkwell and quill, symbolizing his function
as the heavenly communicator of the Word of God."

The main reading was, "Traditionally Gabriel is the messenger of the Word of God. His name means 'God is my Strength.'
He announces the mystery of incarnation to all souls before they
are born and instructs us as to what our talents and tasks in this
world will be." It went on to say, "All religions honor Gabriel as
the most powerful messenger of the Source. Gabriel helps us to
find the wisdom in our physical bodies and to know our personal truths. Gabriel can help us succeed in developing our individual gifts and fully expressing ourselves."

The reading finished by telling me that "Gabriel's quintessen-
tial gift to us is to nurture our strength and our conviction that we
are each making a valuable contribution to the spiritual development of humanity simply by being who we are. Gabriel lights the
way to the truth within our hearts, and helps us to see what is the
right path for us to follow for our highest good and greatest joy."

These were all the things I needed to be reminded of again
and again. I sat on the love seat, at six-thirty in the morning, fire
crackling in the fireplace in front of me, the book on my lap
with my face upturned and tears on my cheeks. If I needed validation, here it was in black and white. I was being instructed by
Gabriel as to what my talents and tasks in this world would be.
Once again I was being encouraged to recognize and tell my personal truths, simply and honestly, thereby encouraging others to
do the same.

A different type of message began in September 1998.

After parking the car on the Hyannis/Nantucket ferry, I
climbed up the three flights of metal steps to the deck. It was
just before sunset and the harbor in Hyannis was quiet and
peaceful. There was no wind. All sailboats, sails down and covered, were snuggled next to their wooden docks in front of their
gray-shingled Cape Cod houses.

Making ripples out on the glassy water was one lone white
swan.

Knowing swans mate for life, I surveyed the rest of the area for its graceful mate. No, there was only one solitary swan swimming elegantly out in the middle of the quiet harbor. As I watched him, I grew more and more peaceful.

It struck me if this swan could go it alone, completely against its nature, perhaps it was affirming that I, too, could calmly trust myself and my instincts and take care of my concerns with grace and dignity. I had the peaceful feeling that all was okay, I was to go it alone, making my own decisions, until such time I could welcome a partner in my life as an equal, not as a savior.

A few nights later, having forgotten my encounter with the swan, I fell off to sleep with the television droning on in the background. Suddenly I was abruptly pulled from my sleep in the middle of the night by a loud voice yelling, "SWAN—EE." The "swan" part was very distinct. I recognized the coincidence but was so sleepy I didn't give it another thought and hit the "off" button on the remote, falling back into a restless sleep.

The next day, in one of my noncoping moods from not having enough rest, I was lying on the sofa with a fire in the fireplace and the television playing backdrop for the doubts and fears swirling in my head. Totally unable to focus or function, I lay there wondering what was wrong with me.

One thought I had was that someone could make a fortune making Hallmark "Sorry You're Having a Non-Coping Day" cards.

When I get like this, my mind starts looping, questioning everything I'm doing in my life. Now I was working on all that I was coming to believe true. Was everything I was into crazy? Our lives are guided? That's nuts. My inner critic was going on about, "You coulda done this, you shouldn't have done that. . . ." when once again some part of my mind picked up a secondary sound.

On the television, Robert Redford, in the movie *Jeremiah Johnson*, had just been introduced to his Indian bride whose name in English meant "Swan."

Okay, yes, I know, it was three times.

You would think I'd have jumped up, run into the office, and looked up Swan energy in Sams' and Carson's *Medicine Cards*, thereby retrieving valuable "medicine" on how to "walk in balance on the Earth Mother." Instead I walked in and pulled a Voyager tarot card to see if I could get information on what was happening.

The card I pulled—"Energy." "Sure," I said to myself. "Great card for me today, I can't even stand up without wobbling." Instead of trying to muster any intuitive thoughts regarding this obviously wrong card, I went right to the book's interpretation. "Invigorated with lust for life and abundance of vitality. Relying on your physical strength and endurance. Honoring your natural instincts."

"Well," I thought, "that couldn't have been more wrong."

I straightened up as I continued to read, "Looking to animal or totem forces as allies to help you. Multiple or multilingual modes of expression. Gentle guidance. Having the courage of your convictions."

Finally after three signs from swan, and a tarot card guiding me to "animals as allies to help me," I went to *Medicine Cards* to look up "Swan."

I paraphrase its story.

"Little Swan landed in Dreamtime by accident and saw above Sacred Mountain the biggest swirling black hole she'd every seen. Dragonfly flew by and said, 'If you want to enter there, you would have to ask permission and *earn* the right.' Swan agreed to trust whatever the future held as it is presented without trying to change Great Spirit's plan. Swan promised she wouldn't fight the currents of the black hole. 'I will surrender to the flow of the spiral and trust what I am shown,' said Swan. Swan, as an ugly duckling, was swirled down into the vortex in the lake and returned changed into a beautiful white long-necked Swan that learned to accept the state of grace."

I read on, "The Swan card is telling you to accept your ability to know what lies ahead. If you are resisting your self-transformation, relax, it will be easier if you go with the flow. Pay attention to your hunches and your gut knowledge, and honor your female intuitive side."

Shortly after this, I sold my house in Nantucket for a huge profit and was guided to New Mexico, where I continue to get messages from animals telling me to surrender to my self-transformation.

On November 13, 1998, when I went to Canyon Ranch Spa in the Berkshires of Massachusetts, I decided to check in with Jeff Rossman, the head of behavioral health at the Spa, and a Ph.D. in psychology. We'd met five years before, when I was the first spa attendee to ask him to guide me into a past-life regression. While during that session I didn't get back to a past life, I did go to a place right before this life. I was hanging out as a spirit entity, no body or mind, just energy, hanging in the universe feeling good, a state of total peace and patience. I didn't realize then that what we had done was my first introduction into connecting back to Source. I wanted to share with Jeffrey all that had happened during my five years of studying healing and spiritual enlightenment.

During the first visit, I brought him up to date on all the incredible happenings in my life. The 444s; automatic writing Jesus. I forgot to tell him about the swan incident and its message of accepting a state of grace. When I told him about asking who was behind the 444 messages and hearing, "Gabriel, come blow your horn; look him up in your angel book," his body jolted upright a little as if he were startled.

I wondered what was going on? I knew him to be understanding about the path I was on.

He quickly recovered and said, "You know Gabriel appeared to Mary and said, 'Fear not.'" We even stopped and looked it up in the Bible. I let go of feeling he hadn't told me something and said that, at times, fear could almost paralyze me.

On my third visit to him, since I was at Canyon Ranch to lose weight, I requested he put me into a hypnotic state so I could talk about food. Seated in a comfortable recliner, in a trance, I saw myself active, dressed in pink tights, a gray sweatshirt and headband, working out and loving it. When he asked me what was happening, I said, "I am seeing myself after I'd switched to loving exercise. I've made an association to food being nourishing, not being a lover."

We went on gathering information from a trance state with one thing leading to another when suddenly behind my closed eyes everything stopped. I was in a state where absolutely nothing was on my mind. No chatter, no noise, just colors: reds, oranges, pinks, but nothing else. I attempted to describe what I was feeling and couldn't come up with the right word. I tried "peace," but that wasn't it. I tried "nothing." Again, not it. Then I said, "Grace. This is grace. This is what being in a state of grace is."

In a quiet, meditative voice, I explained that as I'd been taking my walks around the grounds, I'd been repeating over and over with each step, "I live in a state of grace, I live in a state of grace," and this was grace!

I told him I wanted to absorb the feeling more and became silent and stayed in that state for several minutes. When I opened my eyes, Jeffrey looked moved.

He said, "Do you want more signs that you are on the right track?"

I looked at him quizzically, and asked, "What do you mean?"

He said, "You have named my children. I was surprised during our first session when you said my son's name, but didn't say anything, thinking it was 'just a coincidence.' I don't think that any longer. Patricia, my children's names are Gabriel and Grace."

I looked at him and said, "I feel like crying."

He said, "I do too." We hugged with tears running from our eyes.

Coincidence? No. Signs. Everywhere there are signs validating that, indeed, our lives are guided, and indeed, we are all one. All we have to do is open our consciousness to recognize the signs.

A little more than two years after the incident when I asked who was behind my 444s and heard, "Gabriel come blow your horn, look him up in your angel book," I was asked to assist at one of the last conferences Brugh Joy gave before a planned two-year sabbatical. It was nice to go back in the status of teacher at the same Heart-center Foundational Conference I had attended seven years before in July 1993. Now in August 2000 in Paulden, Arizona, it seemed to be a beginning and ending, the completion of a cycle. Plus, I knew the number seven indicates spiritual enlightenment, which made it even more fitting I should be there.

Once again we had three days of silence and fasting, which this time went much smoother for me. I had fewer ups and downs, fewer expectations, certainly fewer questions, and my formerly euphoric fasting level was downright nice and mellow. Inner and outer silence had become quiet for me in the years that had passed since my first conference.

During this three-day period, I received many pleasant signs from the universe that I was on the right track. One silent afternoon, a woman from the attached cabin and I were sitting at opposite ends of the covered porch we shared. I was journaling, and had just written in my journal, "I'd like validation that I am really doing the right work." About then we heard the very loud ringing of a phone. Karen and I were both startled and looked at each other with our eyebrows raised. The only phone in the whole place was way up at the office on the other side of the grounds. That couldn't be what we'd heard. I, kidding around, jumped up and went to the platform of the stairs where I could see the sky and raised up my hands and mouthed the words, "Yes, God?" We both chuckled silently. I stood there a moment watching the bright blue sky with its many fluffy cumulous clouds.

There in the middle of this white puffy sky I saw a tiny little cloud that was completely covered with the colors of a rainbow. One little cloud was a bright, bright rainbow. I motioned for my friend to come and look, and we stood with our arms around each other's waists for a long time just looking on. I slowly tore myself away and went back to journaling. While the phone ringing was interesting and the rainbow cloud was beautiful, it wasn't enough of a sign for me. Anybody could have seen it. So, once again I wrote in my journal that I needed a "real" sign I was on my right path.

Just as I was finishing that sentence, Karen came over to me and shook three little crystals out of a small pouch into my hand as a gift. Three for *If You Hear the Message Three Times.*

No, sorry, this was still not enough proof for me to *know* I was still on the right track. Even though she'd come over exactly at the time I was asking for a sign, she knew the name of my book, so her three crystals were too "pat" for me to accept them as "the" sign for which I was waiting.

That night I went down to the pool complex with my borrowed sleeping bag to sleep under the stars on one of the chaise longues. It was quiet and lovely, and I had the area all to myself. I lay there looking up at a magnificent full Moon that had an incredible bright full rainbow circling it, and felt quite blessed and grateful. I didn't know rays of rainbow light shooting out from the Moon was unusual. I figured this was a regular occurrence in the Wild, Wild West. I lay there marveling at the amazing colors that spread out over a quarter of the sky.

When I'd almost fallen to sleep under the protective Moon rainbow umbrella, another participant came down to spend the night at the pool. Since we were in silence and fasting, I couldn't call out and tell her I was there, so I continued on my path to dreamland. She stopped about midway around the pool and didn't see me down at the end. Almost asleep, I'd open and close my eyes now and then to see what all the rustling was about. First, my pool roommate moved a chaise longue, placing it "just so," and meticulously spread out her sleeping bag on it. Then she took a small table for her personal things and neatly arranged them. Retrieving a small chair, she undressed and placed her shoes and neatly folded clothes on it. After a quick quiet swim, during which she could have splashed me she came so close, she dried off, leaned back with her hands on her hips, and looked up at my incredible rainbow Moon. She then retrieved another small chair upon which to drape her towel. Finally she crawled into bed and blessedly settled down.

No, premature thought on my part. Apparently, all was still not right with her world. She got back up and moved another chaise longue in front of her. Back to bed. All was quiet for a moment and I fell back to sleep, awakening two minutes later when she was up again moving another chaise to block her right side. This up and down continued until she had moved four or five chaises and little tables around her, building what I assumed she hoped was an impenetrable Wall of Jericho. All this when the entire pool complex was already fenced in. Finally, when she got up one more time to move her towel from its drying place on a small chair to a chaise, I snapped. Frustrated, I jumped up, eliciting a startled scream out of her. My thought at the time? "Good, she deserved to break her silence." I threw on my clothes, grabbed my sleeping bag, and marched past her fort to go sleep on my porch.

Once again, I'd felt the sting of a small prick of the black needle to my ego. Special rainbow Moon? I was drifting off to sleep feeling I was the only one in the universe for whom it was shining its protective umbrella of radiant colors. Then along comes a disruptive, unaware, intruding, harried, nervous "pool mate" who, in the middle of all her building, stopped for several minutes to gaze upon "my" rainbow Moon. Certainly this couldn't be the sign I was requesting, either.

The next day, I walked into the library at the lodge to kill time. I immediately walked right to a book named *The Rainbow of Your Hands*. This made three rainbows, the unusual tiny rainbow cloud, the remarkable rainbow around the Moon, and now a book.

You would think I would have been able to stop there and say, "Thank you for all my signs, the three crystals and three rainbows, I've gotten the message." Obviously, I didn't want to accept I was on my right path and would have to continue to be self-reliant.

My editor and teacher, Valery, and I had gone our separate ways right before this conference. I was now on my own as a writer. I think what I was really hoping for was a sign I didn't have to finish writing the book and now had a new path. Something easier. Like what, I wondered?

Maybe a charming

Art and Antiques,
Readings,
Natural Fabric Designer Clothing,
Non Toxic Expensive Home
Decorating,
healings,
"No Pesticides" Plants
and Organic Raw Food
Restaurant and Shoppe

in some quaint little town where I could be the owner/chanteuse. The sign alone would be a major investment.

Or, I could always go back to the uncomplicated, unconscious life of looking to a husband to fulfill me and then give myself time off for good behavior with illness.

This is the problem with becoming conscious, old ways no longer work.

The last night of silence and fasting was difficult. I found myself feeling angry. I liked silence and fasting way too much this time. I liked not having to talk to people. I liked not having to explain who and what I am and who I seem to be becoming. I liked not having to decide what to eat, if it was good or bad for me, or worry about whether I'd gain weight. I liked just "being" with nothing to pull me out of it. I was angry because I wanted to stay in silence and fasting, go home and become a very slim hermit. I did recognize the similarities to my former illnesses that allowed me to sleep through life.

Still trying to find a way out, I decided the universe had one more night to give me an unquestionable sign as to whether I was on the right path. Nothing happening on this last night of silence and fasting, in my mind, would negate my other "sweet" signs.

I have done a lot of dream work with a brilliant dream

therapist, Gabriella Lopez-Waterman. Using her techniques of petitioning for information through dreams, that night I wrote in my journal before falling off to sleep and then read aloud:

Dear Higher Consciousness,

Thank you for all that I have and the signs you have given me. Please, if it is your will, in your infinite wisdom, give me an irrefutable sign tonight that I am supposed to finish writing my book, *If You Hear The Message Three Times, Listen*, confirming this is my path.

Much love,
Patricia Heller

I figured I was home free. No sign would mean I was absolved. I could then be on my merry way, not having to "step up to the spiritual plate."

As usual, for me, I awakened in the middle of the night to go to the bathroom. Groggy as I got out of bed, I realized a song was playing so loud in my head, I wondered if it was going to wake up the other women in the cabin. I even thought of the possibility it might awaken everyone in the duplex next door. Then I realized what song was BLASTING over and over in my head and moaned, "Oooh noooo."

Louder than loud, I heard,

BLOW GABRIEL BLOW.
GO ON AND BLOW GABRIEL BLOW.
I'VE BEEN A SINNER, I'VE BEEN A SCAMP,
BUT NOW I'M WILLIN' TO TRIM MY LAMP,
SO BLOW GABRIEL BLOW!!!

Straight out of Cole Porter's musical *Anything Goes*.
Irrefutable.
My Archangel was blowing his horn so loudly for me to hear. How could I not get it?
Are our lives guided?
I'd say so.

14

TANTRA:

honoring One Another, Self, and Spirit

Sex. Sex. Sex. Sex.

In my mind, that word still conjures up visions of Health Class in eighth grade. Sex, the unspoken reason everyone signed up. That was before we knew we'd have to endure weeks of lectures on personal hygiene. Finally the day came. Though we'd all read the clinical version in our book, we still knew nothing except what a split section of the uterus and fallopian tubes looked like, and who cared about that? Our anticipation and excitement building, we waited for our attractive woman teacher to tell us all.

Instead?

Gasp!

She asked for open discussion.

Squirming became universal. The guys were so embarrassed, their faces turned red and funny boy noises emitted from their side of the room. I scrunched down in my seat, for once in my life trying not to stand out. Of course, there always has to be one in the class. Penny Foot. There is always a Penny Foot in life. You know, the self-assured, self-reliant, confident-in-her-own-body one. Her father's a doctor and her mother drives an MG and "*once had a date with the movie star Peter Lorre.*" Penny made us all look like the babies we were. Sitting up very poised, nonchalant, with no embarrassment, she raised her hand to expound upon what I assumed was dinner conversation at her house. We all hated her at that moment and were too busy fidgeting to hear a word.

I think I can pretty much assume that all of us in that class went on to live lives in which we never had an open discussion (much less open observation) about sexual matters. Except, of course, Penny. She probably left high school and shacked up with some sheik of Araby.

It's really quite amazing how taboo the subject of sex is in our culture when one considers the reason we engage in it is because we have such a powerful biological urge to do so. The urge is nature's way of ensuring we procreate. Yea for nature!

We are the only species in the animal kingdom that wraps up sex with love, romance, fidelity, and monogamy. And, for all my talk, I'm glad we do. I wrap it up too.

I am a serial monogamous heterosexual woman. (Different relationships, but loyal to the guy who brung me.)

My sexual background included keeping my virginity until I decided to marry at age 20. I'm not sure where I got the idea. I have absolutely no recollection of having even a remotely sexual talk with my mother or anyone else while I was growing up. When I did get around to having sex with my husband-to-be shortly before we were married, I, to this day, can't believe what I said. When we finished, I said, "Is that it?"

Really nice.

He married me anyway. What I'd meant was, where were all the birds, bells, orchestra, or at least one soprano hitting high C? A fireworks display would have sufficed. Obviously, I'd read too many books idealizing sex and love and seen way too many movies that pan away from the couple and go to a scene with one or more of the above.

Seven years later, when I left my marriage, even after a son, I still felt like a virgin. (To this day, I feel like a virgin, which is a whole other story about the archetypes of temple virgins and sacred prostitutes.) During our seven years together, I never managed to have an orgasm. When I mentioned it to my doctor, he told me to read Masters and Johnson's book *Human Sexual Inadequacy* and to have a glass of brandy before going to bed. I'm not a big drinker or planner ahead-er, so the idea of drinking every night just in case we decided to have a roll in the hay didn't do it for me. I can't remember if my husband and I spent a lot of time trying to find out how I could or why I wasn't, most couples didn't talk about those things back then. I do remember that when I left my marriage, I was determined to figure it all out.

Since it was the 1970s and "free love" was rampant, it seemed a likely proposition. In my "serial monogamous heterosexual non-promiscuous" way, I experimented. While I had a good time and got to where I quite enjoyed sex, I still didn't have an orgasm until 10 years later, when I was 38.

Based on my sexual background, it was no wonder I was intrigued years later when I received what I now refer to as one of my out-of-the-blue life-changing letters. Out of the blue, I received a letter from a nice-looking couple (their picture was in the upper-right-hand corner of the stationery) with happy-looking faces. Their letter explained why they were smiling. Apparently, from what I read, their lives had been radically changed after studying something called Tantra. Their feelings for each other increased. Their sex life became one of passion, love, and healing, all in a frenzy of ecstasy. Life in general was one fulfilling moment after another. They were manifesting all their desires. And, they weren't selling anything. They were just sharing their happiness. They didn't even say with whom they'd studied.

While I hadn't a clue what Tantra was, this letter sure made me want to find out. I did have one condition. I wasn't going to find out alone. I wanted a man around as "protection" on this journey.

I carried this letter around with me for a year and a half before I met the man named Harvey, the fellow participant in the Dark Side Conference I mentioned before. Harvey also wanted to study Tantra. He had just left his second marriage, his job, and alcohol behind to become a better person. He said he wanted to study Tantra with his next life-partner so the two of them could practice what they learned. I wasn't as persnickety as Harvey about having to have my life's mate as my partner. While I didn't think Harvey and I would commit to a lifetime together, I would have studied Tantra with him in a minute. I wanted someone who felt the same way I did about learning if there was a spiritual aspect that could be harnessed during sex. To me, if we both learned this and then went our separate ways, eventually there would be four people with this knowledge. He and I had an incredible ability to play with sexual energy when we'd make love. We could feel energy flowing from each other's hands on our bodies from two feet away. Oh, what we could have done with Tantra!

While I was waiting for Mr.-Right-to-go-to-Tantra-with-me to come along, I began gathering information about classes and teachers. The Muirs in Hawaii had a big following, and Carolyn Muir had just organized her first Goddess Tantric class in Guadalajara, Mexico. I had no idea how 20 women would learn about Tantric sex, but when I talked with her, I was assured it was all on the up-and-up, so off I went to Guadalajara to learn about sex with a bunch of women for a week.

We set up a large room as Sacred Space that we used for all our sessions. The resort staff was told that no one was allowed in or around the building. We slowly eased into our Goddess sessions. We meditated, danced, chanted, sang, and when it was suggested we might dance naked, I was the first to strip off my clothes, feeling as free as any goddess on Mount Olympus. Everyone quickly followed suit, all very at ease with their bodies. We danced with flowing chiffon scarves we picked up from chairs we'd draped to make our Sacred Space beautiful. We were goddesses all—Salome, dancing her dance of the seven veils.

Toward the end of the week, we learned how to facilitate each other in sexual healing. It was a remarkable experience, though not one I could recommend to many of the people I know. To me, it accentuated the healing abilities of my hands. In groups of threes, we assisted each other in releasing long-held fears, anger, and joy. I'm not going into detail, to do so might betray the honor, trust, and faith we had for one another during this experience and turn it into something else.

Suffice it to say, the week I spent at this Goddess Tantra conference convinced me even more that Tantra was something I wanted to pursue with the next man in my life. That's in spite of the fact I was trying hard to go into my next stage of development, that of "I don't need a man to take care of me." In that juxtaposition, I needed to manifest someone to go with me "to be and not to be" my protector. I didn't realize then that the universe only says yes to whatever we ask. I got exactly what I was asking for.

After I got back to Nantucket, my way of going it on my own was punctuated by my ritualistically taking my passport out of my purse. I always carried it with me in case a man asked me to lunch in Paris. Taking it out meant I'd have to *just say no.*

I also remembered my grandmother saying, "Captain Marvel will not come and ring your doorbell, you have to get out to meet him." So, I figured I'd stay home until I learned how to be self-sufficient emotionally.

One morning while I was exercising to a video, the doorbell rang. Dressed in leotards, I sprang up from the floor thinking Vita, my assistant, had locked herself out.

Instead, there was my tall, handsome, auburn, curly-headed UPS man.

Now, if he'd said, "Hi, would you like to go to lunch in Paris?" I would have been fine and would have replied sweetly, "I'm sorry, I can't, I don't have my passport." But, noooo, he said, "I understand from Vita you just got back from a meditation retreat. Would you be interested in seeing a spiritual Indian burial ground in Nantucket's hidden forest?"

Without batting an eye I said, "I've been dying to connect with something spiritual in Nantucket." Then I had a nanosecond's concern about what my toney friends would think if they saw me out with my UPS man. My next thought, "No one will see us, we're just going to the woods," shows how myths play out in our lives. Anybody thinking "Little Red Riding Hood?"

Duane came to get me a couple days later, looking very, very handsome in designer street clothes, slacks with little pleats at the waist, an open pin-striped dress shirt, and expensive leather shoes with tassels and no socks. I felt sloppy in my jeans and baggy sweater. I really believed we were just going to the woods. It's a wonder I didn't throw on a red cape and grab a basket of goodies.

I haven't told you yet about my ability to place my third eye (forehead) on an antiquity and visualize the history surrounding it. When we got to the site of the Indian village, I knelt down and placed my third eye on a rock that had been used to grind grain. I was in the midst of "seeing" a whole former Indian village, when I realized my rear end in my tight jeans was sticking straight up in the air. Duane, standing directly behind me, asked if I'd like to go for drinks at the Summerhouse (only the nicest restaurant on the island).

I quickly popped up to a standing position and said I wasn't appropriately dressed. He said I looked beautiful. Oooookay . . . off we went, over the meadow and through the woods to Siaconset and the Summerhouse Restaurant.

During cocktails, he told me he'd been a realtor during the last market crash in the 1980s. At that time he was also an elected town councilman and had been the head of the land bank for seven years. During the drinks and our conversation, I was beginning to realize he was a lot more than a handsome UPS man. He told me he was a native of Nantucket and had always wanted to stay on the island. UPS provided a way.

So, what do you think I said when he asked me to go on to dinner at the Wauwinet, the other great restaurant in Nantucket? Wrong, I didn't say, "My, what big eyes you have. . . ." It was more of a, "Duh, okay, sure." I seem to remember we also played darts and went dancing somewhere that night.

He was articulate, bright, big and tall and, as I later found out, virile. We became "a couple" and the talk of the town. While it might seem I was postponing learning how to be alone and not lonely, he did seem to be a solution to my wanting a "big, strong guy" with whom to study Tantra.

Right up front I told him if we stayed in a relationship, I wanted us to study Tantra, and showed him *the* letter. I may be naive, but I'm no dummy. I know at the beginning of a relationship you can get a guy to agree to anything. I even got him to go to ballroom dancing lessons with me. In answer to my request of studying Tantra, he replied, "Of course, no problem. Sounds interesting." I don't think in a million years he expected it to happen.

A couple of months after our discussion, he told me he had to plan his vacation time for the next year around some of the others already scheduled. I reminded him about Tantra, and he said, "I'm sorry, that time in January can't be juggled, unless, of course, ha ha, one of the conferences just happens to land on that week."

Not one, but both Tantric masters had scheduled the first week of their three-part courses that same week. Not in a million, my eye. He was stuck.

I decided upon Margo Anand's Skydancing class because she seemed to incorporate more spirituality into her teachings. Her conference was being held in a Buddhist Retreat (I know—I thought it odd, too) in California during the weeklong sessions in January, June, and October.

What I wanted out of Tantra was a vague feeling I could open to more consciousness. For years I'd been studying the art of living consciously. Why not sexually, too? Use our senses to propel ourselves beyond the restriction of physical reality and unite with the true essence of who we really are.

From what I now understand, I think what was supposed to have happened at the conferences was this. First, we were supposed to read her books, *The Art of Sexual Ecstasy* and *The Art of Sexual Magic*, which we didn't do.

I just now opened *The Art of Sexual Ecstasy* randomly to a page that read, "In launching yourself into this adventure of sexual discovery, your first question is likely to be, 'Where do I begin?' Many of my clients," she writes, ". . . come to me assuming the answer is, 'By finding the right partner.'" She goes on to say, "The magic doesn't come from outside—(*all together now*) it comes from inside—loving yourself first." So much for my thought that I needed a man around to protect me during my studies.

Cycle One of this three-part conference was supposed to be about energy, sexual healing, and learning to honor the masculine, the feminine, and the divine. Then we were to go home for three months, practice the exercises we'd learned, and come back for the next cycle to build upon our practices.

Cycle Two was learning to bring the divine into the sexual experience and to relax in the highest states of arousal to allow peak experiences in sexual pleasure, called High Sex. Then we'd go home, practice, and come back in three months to build on these lessons.

Cycle Three would teach us the art of cosmic orgasm, an ancient, extraordinary, and secret way of Tantric union. Using that magical sexual energy to manifest whatever we wanted was supposed to be a done deal.

Now, what really happened?

Off we went to California with Duane joking about the skid marks he was leaving behind as he was being dragged off to sex camp. I laughed and didn't once consider it to be true. I was in my own little world of *There is something I want to know and nothing else matters*, not recognizing that this big, tall, strong, good-lookin' guy was about ready to throw up, he was so threatened by all this.

This was the first conference of any kind he'd ever attended. What was I thinking? His first experience, and I drag him off to a conference where he would be emotionally, physically, and spiritually exposed? Part of his discomfort was, I am sure, the image he had of himself. He considered himself a tall, big, good-looking guy who knew everything about "pleasin' the little woman." Not a good combination. He was beginning to feel his virility and masculinity might be on the line.

I'm embarrassed to admit they were.

The first night at the conference, we were told to walk

around (fully clothed) and greet everyone, give our name, and tell our intentions for the week. I went up to each of the 38 other participants, shook their hands, and said, "Hi, I'm Patricia, I want to find my passion and my purpose," and added, if I didn't think the person understood, "and I don't mean sexual."

The beginning of our first Skydancing week was spent doing exercises that built up trust in one another and in this process. Fully clothed, we did individual breathing exercises and chakra streaming. This entailed lying on the floor and listening to instructions while breathing at an accelerated rate (called fire breathing) with evocative music playing. We were instructed to visualize breathing into the first chakra (the Kundalini) at the base of the spine, and then draw the energy up one chakra to another, Kundalini to regenerative, to solar plexus, to heart, to throat, to third eye, to and out the crown chakra to bliss. Later in the week, we practiced breathing in unison with our partners in a joint streaming of energy. We learned to talk to each other about our fears and boundaries and to really say what we wanted and needed.

Toward the end of the week, in the same big round room we used for our group work, we separated from the group with our partners and created individual sacred spaces in which to do the next exercise. I was having a rough day. I was very tired, which is always a sign that I am afraid.

Our instructions were explicit. Each of the 20 couples created their sacred space. It was funny to see how people concocted their areas. Some surrounded their space with a multitude of backjacks that made a very short mini-border. Others were content making a pallet with lovely cloths and scarves and honored objects. We did both. Then, all of us, dressed in sarongs, "ambulated" (walked) quietly around our sacred space three times, asking for blessings and quietly stating our intentions for the session.

To begin, all couples knelt facing each other in their sacred areas. Bowing, they greeted each other in a sacred salute of hands together in a prayer position looking deeply into each other's eyes. The women told their partners their boundaries, fears, and intentions. I asked Duane that he never take his eyes off me during the exercise and always sit facing the wall instead of the room, afraid his attention might wander to what the others were doing (as I felt it had in other exercises). I also asked that he never do anything to me without asking okay first. My intention was to learn what was holding me back from being all I knew I could be in sex and life. His turn for sexual healing would be the next day, when we would reverse the ritual.

After a half hour of him giving me a gentle, soothing, non-sexual body massage, as instructed, he asked if he might have permission to enter and massage my yoni (vagina) with his finger. Every aspect of this exercise was to be done with respect, honor, and unconditional love. I gave him my permission to enter. We had been told there might be places inside the yoni that were tender, places that might have no feeling, and places that might be painful. If there were, the man needed to stay with his finger on that place and see what emotions might come up for the woman. We had also been told that the man might feel a bump like a sand pebble in these sensitive spots.

When my partner touched a painful spot, and found a small sand pebblelike bump, it wasn't unbearable physical pain. It was more a feeling of loss. I started to cry. My third eye chakra (middle of my forehead) was really hurting and the thought went through my mind, "I am going to *see* something I don't want to see." My internal observer thought, *Uh-oh, what now?*

Shurabi, one of the people giving the course, came over to assist. I was holding my forehead as I told her, through quiet sobbing, about the pain in my third eye chakra. I didn't tell her about the thought that I was afraid I was going to "see" something I didn't want to see. She told me to focus my attention back on the spot in my vagina that was painful and not to concentrate on the pain in my third eye. As I shifted my attention, immediately the thought of seeing something I didn't want to see left. The continuing massage soothed the pain and released the small bump. While I can't positively say I had an incredible healing that day, or that I didn't need to "see" what I was afraid to see, I do know somewhere along the line I released a lot of fear and blocks. Tantra isn't just about sexual healing, it's about life healing.

Duane and I attended the last two Tantra sessions only because we'd paid in advance. The first one had been too much for him. He wasn't ready for what this was about, which was letting go of control and allowing things to be guided. At one time during a healing session, he kept telling both facilitators he didn't have to ask my opinion about what I wanted, he *knew* what I needed.

An example of how hard it was for him to let go happened during another fully clothed exercise when we were to take turns letting go of control. Duane lay on the floor with four people stationed around him, one at each arm and leg. He was instructed to go totally limp, allowing each person to move his arm or leg at random. His arms and legs were so stiff, if you took your hand away, instead of them flopping to the ground like a rag doll's, his arm or leg stayed straight up, rigid in the air.

So, by the time the second conference rolled around, he was pretty much traumatized. The night before we left was spent in the emergency room in Nantucket, with him on his hands and knees on the floor throwing his guts up in a bowl, and we arrived a day late in California. Poor thing, what was I doing to him?

An exercise during the second session made me realize how easily others can influence your energy. As couples, we were practicing "streaming" by rapid breathing from each chakra to the next. This time, however, our partners were seated behind us, their arms gently around our bodies. They were to help facilitate the energy moving up through each chakra by waving their hands in a soft upward motion. This was called "going up the inner flute." One chakra to another. I'm assuming this exercise was done so each couple could start "feeling" each other's energy. Timing and attention between each partner had to be precise. If the music changed, indicating that it was time to go up to the next chakra, and the person doing the exercise wasn't ready, both partners would stay focused on the chakra that needed more attention.

To emphasize the sexual energy we were moving, the one doing the exercise placed her or his own finger over their clothes on their sexual area.

I had no problem moving energy through the lower chakras. As I began raising the energy, I saw the colors of each chakra behind my closed eyes.

Bright red for the Kundalini, life-force chakra at the base of the spine.

Orange for the regenerative, three inches below the belly button, the creative/sexual chakra.

Yellow at the solar plexus, power center, warrior chakra.

An almost Kelly green at the heart, unconditional love chakra.

Blue at the throat, communication chakra.

Violet at the third eye, center of the forehead, psychic vision chakra.

A wonderfully radiant white at the crown/top of the head, connection to all there is chakra.

I was enjoying it. It was interesting to learn for myself that the universally accepted colors of the chakras were also what I was seeing. I was "seeing" energy rising up my inner flute.

During the exercise when we got to the throat chakra, I realized I needed to spend more time there. The chakra felt tight and the blue wasn't as true as the other colors. My partner had been right with me the whole time, gently waving his hand in an upward motion as we moved from chakra to chakra. I expected that he was focused and knew by my energy that I needed to stay at my throat longer. Just as I was getting a nice rich blue behind my eyes and was ready to send my throat chakra as much energy as it needed to become a brilliant blue, the color behind my eyes suddenly turned to violet. I thought, "What the heck is going on?" I wasn't focusing on my third eye, the next chakra, I was still at my throat.

I opened my eyes a crack, turned my head, and to my dismay saw Duane's eyes wide open wandering around the room. When the music made the shift to go to the next chakra, he hadn't been concentrating and had automatically moved his hand's waving motion up to my third eye. My energy had gone with him in spite of me wanting to linger at the throat.

I was angry and sad. I was there to learn magic. Part of me wanted to jab him with my elbow and say, "Get with me on this." Another part wanted to cry at my choice to study with someone who could not go to the places we seemed to be given the opportunity to go.

Now, to be "conscious" about what was going on here, since I'd manifested this particular man to study with, doesn't the old "point one finger, three are pointing back at me and my stuff," say that I wasn't ready for a sexual revolution either? Is that an "aha" I'm hearing??

When we reversed the chakra streaming work, and I was the one sitting behind circling around him with my legs and arms, I really wasn't into it. I was tired. We'd been at it all day, and what I really wanted was to go for a walk in the fresh air. Why did I have to do this exercise with a guy who clearly couldn't focus? What good could it be? When we began raising the energy from his Kundalini up to his regenerative chakra, I almost gasped at the brilliant orange I saw behind my closed eyes. I thought, "I must be missing an incredible sunset." I figured the room had been lit afire from a bright orange sunset. I opened my eyes a slit to see the beautiful orange glow in the room and was surprised to see that the room hadn't changed at all.

The bright orange I was "seeing" was my partner's sexual chakra energy. Now my attention was completely with him, as we raised the energy. I again could see the colors of each of his chakras. None, however, as astoundingly bright as his regenerative. I remembered thinking, "What an enormous energy wants to flow out of here if only we could unlock it."

The third week's session was over the top for my partner. At this last session, we were being taught the art of cosmic orgasm, "the secret way of Tantric union." In our group of 40, we were spread around the room in pairs, again fully clothed. For this exercise, the man sat either with his legs crossed in the lotus position or on a pillow with his legs straight out. The woman would sit on his lap facing him with her legs around him or outstretched behind him. At home this would be done naked and joined. We then jointly began our streaming breath exercises like the ones we'd been practicing separately in sessions before. The object was to bring, along with the breath, sexual energy up through each chakra to the crown and jointly let it out, becoming one in bliss. Cosmic orgasm—secret Tantra.

Sounded great—that's why we were there.

Just as I sat down on my partner's lap, facing him to start this exercise of becoming one with each other and the divine, he, like the young boys in Health Class, began squirming around, emitting funny boy sounds. He then said to me, "When we get home, we're putting you on a diet."

That did it. While I had many revelations during my Tantric studies, secret Tantra was not one of them.

15

YALE—YES! I AM GOOD ENOUGH:
Dreams have No Deadlines

During the first Tantric week in January 1997, we spent the time learning to honor the feminine, the masculine, and the divine. Before then I had no idea that I didn't honor those aspects of myself. The feminine in particular. When I returned home, I asked myself, "Okay, so what can I do to honor the feminine aspect of myself? What will make me feel good enough at age 50?"

The answer was quick, loud, and simple.

"*College*" was the word ringing in my head.

"College?"

"Oh, college."

Some 30-odd years earlier at the age of 18, I moved into the first coed dormitory in the United States at Old Dominion College in Norfolk, Virginia. I'd chosen ODC because academically it had a beach nearby. On the drive down from Alexandria to Norfolk, Dad kept singing, "Rudy toot toot, rudy toot toot, we are the girls from the institute, we don't smoke and we don't chew and we don't go with the boys who do, Nor-folk, Nor-folk, Nor-folk." I was such an innocent, I had no idea why this little ditty was so funny.

I signed up for five courses a semester, way too many with my inability to study. When I wasn't able to keep my grades up, I was asked to leave for a year. Basically, though it hurts to say it, I suppose I flunked out. My advisor told Dad if I'd dropped French the way I'd wanted to, I could have stayed. One less course and my average would have been fine. Dad was crushed because he was the one who hadn't let me drop French. Not only did I feel awful, Dad did, too. There was no "rudy toot tooting" on the way home.

I went to work as a clerk-stenographer for the Defense Supply Agency near my parents' home in Alexandria, Virginia. In a year, instead of going back to school, I met and married Bruce on September 2, 1967. Not going back to college left me feeling not good enough to finish a degree and haunted me for the next 30 years.

In Nantucket, the morning after I'd heard the word "college" in my meditation, I got up early, went for a bike ride, and came back in time for a massage with my friend Laura. She set up her table upstairs in my big bedroom, where we could have a crackling fire in the fireplace and meditative music softly playing. She started the massage on my back, and when I was so content I was about to fall asleep, I mumbled, "I'm thinking about going back to college."

Laura, humming away with her fingers dancing deeply on my spine, said in a cheery voice, "I've got applications to Mount Holyoke and Smith I'm not going to use. You want them?"

Oh, how I love this stuff.

Both schools had programs for older women returning to school. I looked over the applications and found I was too late for Smith. I carefully filled in the application for Mount Holyoke in South Hadley, Massachusetts, and had fun replying to the requested essay, "Why do you want to attend Mount Holyoke?"

I wrote in my essay that I'd spent the past four years studying psychic healing, energy healing, and spiritual healing. I told them that at the first conference I had attended, I learned how to get well from an "incurable" illness from which I'd been suffering for 12 years. I wrote about my new abilities to see auras, feel energy, and balance chakras, and told them through guided meditation and/or using my hands, I'd learned I could facilitate healing in others. I let them know I could now read the tarot and I Ching, and do soul readings. I also threw in that I sometimes know what people are thinking and can see into the future.

I went on to say I knew these gifts were not unique to me. I had not been "chosen" to learn these things. I'd just been open. I informed them I believed everyone has these abilities, and I thought I was supposed to help people recognize this by writing a book.

I said I wanted more learned skills from attending college. I wanted a vocabulary that wouldn't quit. I wanted to be able to write succinctly and fast. I wanted to know what I know, and learn what I needed that I didn't know. I wanted to be more adept at the computer and at public speaking.

They liked what I had to say. After my interview, Mount Holyoke accepted me immediately. I wasn't ready to commit. South Hadley was a sweet little town, but it was way up in midwestern Massachusetts in the middle of nowhere. I sat in on some classes and found the professors at Mount Holyoke young and stimulating. However, through my life's experiences, I realized I wanted to contradict them on several points. I'm happy to say I didn't.

While the University of Massachusetts doesn't have the prestige of Mount Holyoke, I looked into it because they gave credit for life experience. I've never been wild about our American education system that forces students to study subjects in which they have absolutely no interest or talent—all in the name of having a "well-rounded" education. UMASS seemed a way around that. I figured with all my life experience I could get out of UMASS in about two years and then go to a "prestigious" school for a master's degree and a doctorate. UMASS (nose in the air) turned me down, saying I needed to prove myself to them first by going to some small community college near me. I was living on an island 33 miles out in the middle of the Atlantic Ocean. Near me?

When I mentioned all this during a phone call to my girl-friend Jody, she casually said, "Patricia, Yale has a great summer creative writing program. Why don't you go there?"

"Sure, Jody," I said, amazed at her casual suggestion. Like I'd be welcomed with open arms. . . . YALE! The gods must be crazy. Me, go to the epitome of higher education? My educational Mecca! YALE? I'd had a girlfriend whose two sons went to Yale, and she'd acted rather blasé about it. I would have given my right arm if Doug had been able to go there. "Oh, my son, Doug? He's at YALE." I'd always thought it would have been nice to marry someone who went there, so I could glow from his accom-plishment.

Then it hit me. This was my dream. It had always been "my" dream. It had been a boy's school when I graduated high school, which eliminated it from consideration. Besides, while my test scores were good, they wouldn't have been enough to get me in with my average grades. But now? How about being able to say, "I went to *Yale* for a summer to the creative writing school, got 4.0s (A's), and was accepted into their full-time program in the fall." Yes, yes, yes!

Over the years, I'd picked up different bits of information about the type of people Yale liked as students. One man I'd met said he felt his daughter was accepted because of the summer she spent as a trapeze artist in a circus. Apparently, Ivy Leaguers like the unusual, well-rounded, different type of students.

Well, could I do different! I laughed when I thought just how different some of the things I'd done were. I could write my essay on studying sex (Tantra) or on having healing hands. I had a plethora of odd things I could write about. Maybe not on auto-matic writing Jesus, that might be a little too strange even for them. So, I thought, why not try and see if I can write my way into Yale? I had nothing to lose. I was already accepted at Mount Holyoke.

I applied to their creative writing school. I told them about healing myself, discovering I have healing abilities, and that I was writing a book about it. I sent my essay off to them along with 12 pages of my book, and I was accepted!

Tah dah!

Dance, dance, dance.

Glee, glee, glee.

Okay, I'm in, I thought, how do I stay in? After my happy dance, I called the admissions office and asked, "What do I need to do if I want to continue towards a degree in the fall?"

"You'll have to take an academic course to prove you can do the work," was the reply. Poring over the catalog, the only class I could find I was remotely interested in was American literature. I didn't think about the fact I'd be in two writing classes.

Instead of living on campus with the young kids or finding a room off campus, I stayed at the Colony Hotel on Chapel Street. They gave me a great rate for the summer and I didn't have to be distracted with the daily ordinariness of life, since they provided room and maid service. Plus, everyone at the hotel was rooting for me.

Most days, while walking to classes, I'd go through the Rose Alumni Walk and pause at Maya Lin's "Women's Table" sculpture. It is an austere, large, black round fountain with water gently flowing over the important dates for women at Yale. Each time I passed, I stopped for a moment to honor Lin and the controversy she endured as a 21-year-old Yale student when she created the stark walls of the Vietnam Veterans' Memorial in Washington, D.C. Having just found my own self-assurance at age 50, I could admire what she went through at 21.

In the stately old buildings, I'd walk down the wide halls that had wainscoting caked with layers of paint that exuded a wonderful smell of mustiness. I imagined ghostly spirits dancing around me and could almost hear lively, stimulating conversations about this theory or that philosopher. The names Plato, Aristotle, Nietzsche reverberated off the walls. My God! I was attending YALE! My spirit was now a part of all this.

I'd pass by Harkness Tower on my way to attend the Wednesday evening readings, where we'd get extra credit if we read our work to students from other classes. I'd learned on my tour the first day that Harkness Tower had a decorative theme in 1921 that was twofold: to be beautiful and to teach. Leaning back, I could see four levels of sculptures. First were the "Worthies": Elihu Yale, Jonathan Edwards, Nathan Hale, Noah Webster, James Fenimore Cooper, John C. Calhoun, Samuel F. B. Morse, and Eli Whitney. On the balcony and niches of the tower buttresses above the Worthies stood heroic statues representing the careers to which Yale graduates are typically called: Medicine, Business, Law, and the Church. Then the fates or destinies governing the lives of Yale graduates adorned the six corners of the buttresses, one on each side: Courage and Effort, War and Peace, Generosity and Order, Justice and Truth, Life and Progress, Death and Freedom. At the top were sculptures honoring soldiers and students.

I spent six of the most intense weeks of my life the summer of 1997 at Yale immersed in writing. In the hotel restaurant, I sat with a book propped up on a cup so I could eat and read. Other times I was in my room writing essays. One assignment was to interview a fellow student. I wrote about Jane, a fascinatingly brilliant 16-year-old Chinese American who lived in Chicago. Her dream was to graduate from Yale and go on to be the first Chinese American woman Supreme Court judge. I'm sure she will.

We were a diverse group of students. In our small class there were two young high school students, a former nun, a newspaper journalist, a poet, and myself.

In the American lit class there were 20 or more students. For our last and most important paper, I asked the professor if she had any examples of excellent work from other classes so I could "see" what she wanted. She said they'd just moved her office and everything was still in boxes. I was at a loss. I chose Henry James's *Portrait of a Lady* on which to write a 15-page essay from a close reading of one paragraph, and I didn't know what that meant. I called my sister, whose bachelor's degree was in English, and she went over and over the assignment with me until I began to understand.

The paragraph I chose showed how James used the psychological technique of dream symbolism to demonstrate the inner working of the mind of his main character, Isabel Archer. I applied dream symbolism to the paragraph. It described the house in which Isabel had her happiest childhood memories. I interpreted it as a road map to her state of consciousness throughout the novel and even to the novel itself. Stylizing it, I pointed out how the long paragraph had a dreamlike tone and rhythm like poetry:

> One enters through a door with a closed one next to it
> to numerous rooms with no names, yet in communication.
> All painted alike, a yellow grown sallow
> with arched frames on the first floor and
> arched way on the third.
> Called "tunnel," denoting darkness,
> but, this one well-lighted.
> Yet, always strange and lonely . . .

For my efforts on this paper, I received 4.0. And overall grades of A's in both classes! Plus, I was accepted in the fall to work toward a degree.

I learned three important things that summer at Yale.

One, I'm a writer.

Two, the reason I'd never been a good student is that I don't learn through my ears. I kept asking to see examples of what was wanted. I now understood why I never got around to listening to all those taped courses I'd bought over the years. I also understood my studying problem. I didn't know what to study. I needed someone to show me how to study.

The third important thing I discovered after learning how to get A's at Yale was that yes! I *am* good enough!

I decided to take the two weeks after summer school to finally go and find my cabin in the woods. I wanted to discover the one I had seen in my mind's eye for so long. There I would decide what to do next. Did I need to stop my life and finish college? Or would knowing I could be enough? Was it time to finish my book? Perhaps I was being guided to study left-brained college information and should concentrate on getting a degree.

217

Somehow, though, it seemed like a diversion to keep me from doing the task at hand. I wanted my actual cabin in the woods where I could reflect, meditate, and hear the answers.

First though, I just had to call UMASS and ask if getting A's at a little community college near me named Yale would satisfy their requirements. I know, I know, petty of me—remember, although I'm headed toward enlightenment, I'm not there yet. The man in admissions was turning somersaults trying to figure out how to find space for me in the fall semester. Who says revenge isn't sweet?

I never got to my cabin in the woods. During the two-week break, my friend in Rehoboth had a mastectomy and her son was killed the same day. After returning from the funeral, I received a phone call that my father had died. This happened the same week Princess Di and Mother Teresa died. By the time we buried my father in Texas, it was time to start classes at Yale.

Duane and his sister Mary had packed up what I needed from Nantucket and taken everything to the small apartment I'd found in New Haven. The decision was made. I was back in school with not a day to think, mourn, or meditate about what had happened or on what I should do next.

There I was at Yale with thousands of fresh-faced confident 18-year-olds. Shell-shocked, I stumbled around wondering why I was there and what courses to take. In my daze walking to class through the quad, I bumped into one of the young girls who had been in my English class. She said, "Patricia, I was hoping I'd see you. Did you see the seminar they're offering? It's called Twentieth Century Women's Spiritual Autobiographies."

That had to be the answer to why I was there.

So far the only classes available to me as a "special student" (nice word for older) in which I had even a remote interest were a Chekhov acting class, Italian, and the history of architecture with Vincent Scully presiding. Fortunately, ten days were available to pick and attend classes before payment was nonrefundable.

Yale doesn't cater to "special students." There is no program and virtually no support system, as at Smith or Mount Holyoke with their programs for older women returning to school. I was attending classes, getting A's on my work, and wondering how classes in acting, the history of architecture (no matter how fun Scully was), and elementary Italian would help me write a book on self-healing and heart-centered transformational journeying to higher consciousness. The teacher for my Italian class took me aside and asked why I didn't go to Italy to learn the language. After she said it, I wondered why, too.

The spiritual autobiography seminar had to be the reason I was there. Though it was for upperclassmen only, I wouldn't be deterred. I know it sounds like the beginning of a joke, but a young Jewish woman rabbi, a Catholic nun, and an Episcopal minister were giving the course.

First I tried to talk with the rabbi. She was unavailable because her child was sick. I never did get in touch with the nun. Finally I got an interview with the minister. She told me that although she would love to have me in the class, there was only room for 18 upperclassmen, and 54 had signed up. She gave me the class study plan and a list of all the required reading.

I was back to square one. I went to talk with my counselor, who had also been my creative writing teacher that summer. She looked at me and said, "Patricia, you don't need Yale. Finish your book. After the work you've done here, you'll be welcome at any school in the world if you decide to finish a degree. You're a writer. Go write your book." While I left her office with tears in my eyes, I felt complete. I had achieved my goal and proved to myself it is never, never, too late to fulfill a dream.

A lot changed after Yale. I told you I had been bulimic for 25 years. I used it as a diet aid and a way to salve sagging feelings about myself. It started at 23, when a girlfriend said to me when I was complaining about weight, "Why don't you try 'the stewardess diet?' You know, 'the two-finger diet?'" I tried it. It worked.

I could get emotionally distraught, binge on comforting soft foods like crackers, breads, basically any carbs, and with the addition of ice cream or milk, have an easy mixture to purge. The problem with this great diet was that I was slowly messing up my metabolism. No matter how seldom I did it, it totally screwed up my body's awareness and ability to tell me what it needed and when it needed it. Top that off with never having been aware of my bodily functions anyway, and this distanced me even more.

After accomplishing A's at Yale, my being a "little bit bulimic" disappeared. I never purged again.

Why? Because I'd gotten to the core problem that was causing my bulimia. I was, finally, in my mind, "good enough."

I decided, at the same time I stopped being bulimic, that I wouldn't go back to dieting either. That was how I'd always controlled my weight, bulimia and every new diet or spa. It was time to learn to listen to what my body wanted and eat when it was hungry, not because my emotions or boredom were guiding me.

It hasn't been easy. About the time I gave up purging, I hit menopause. Without my former diet aids of trying every new diet and bulimia, I gained 10 pounds over the extra 20 I already carried. I refused to diet and left the weight alone. I wanted to learn how to eat physically, not emotionally. Or better still, how to feed my spirit, not stuff my emotions. I tried to enjoy being an Earth Mother for two years, with boobs, a big butt, stomach, and hips. The problem with the weight was that I just couldn't live with learning how to dress so I could still think of myself and be thought of as attractive. Another was learning how to act in a way that wasn't seductive. Not that I wanted to give up being a spider woman and seducing everyone I met into my web, but I found with an extra 30 pounds, even at five feet ten inches I couldn't pull it off. I was being taught more lessons. How to be beautiful without using my body.

I learned a lot at Yale.

16

MANIFESTING GREATNESS IN OUR LIVES: Creating and Accepting Abundance and Miracles

Manifesting

When I returned home to Nantucket from Yale in September 1997, I got into the habit of climbing up to the widow's walk on top of my house every morning just before dawn to meditate. I'd wrap up in a comforter, climb up the ladder in the second-floor hall overlooking the open entryway, go into the attic, climb up another ladder, open the skylight hatch, and walk out onto the widow's walk spanning the house. From this bird's-eye vantage point I had a view of the entire island and harbor. I'd sit all bundled up, meditate, and wait for the rising sun.

I surmised that since I'd done well at Yale in a structured and disciplined atmosphere, maybe that was what I needed to help me finish my book, someone to give me structure and discipline. From my perch on top of the world, I kept asking, "What's next? What's next?" until one morning, I heard the answer.

Very clearly in my head, I heard, *Writers on the Net.*

I'd recently hooked up my computer to an online connection. So I crawled back downstairs and punched "Writers on the Net" into Yahoo, and there it was. Voila! A whole school of published authors who tutor or edit people in fiction, nonfiction, autobiography, and poetry. I chose a male editor who, in his biography, said he was offering his editorial services to "give back" since he'd had such rewards writing. When we talked, he told me he had just finished writing a famous woman healer's last book and a TV personality's autobiography. When I looked up the books, I was surprised. There was nothing in them about someone else being the author. I began to realize writing my own book was pretty unique. It seems many "autobiographies" of healers and celebrities are, for the most part, penned by ghostwriters. That didn't seem very spiritual. This was an awakening. I began to wonder why I was putting myself through so much agony to become an author when all I had to do was hire someone to write it for me. Ah, it would have been so easy. But no, I had to become an author.

I picked him as my editor because I thought he would be gentle with a fledgling writer. I sent him my "manuscript." Actually, what I sent him was probably more like 80 pages of what Julia Cameron of *Artist's Way* calls brain drain. She directs a wannabe author to faithfully write three pages every morning to "drain their brain" of extraneous thoughts. This male editor very kindly went over what I sent him and indicated that I shouldn't consider my book a spiritual autobiography. Then he wrote what he thought I needed to do and left me on my own to follow his instructions.

All my red flags went up. I'd had many signs that my book was going to be a spiritual autobiography. At Yale, for instance, when I went running all over the place to get into a spiritual autobiography class because a fellow student recognized my book as such. Another sign was one of my "out-of-the-blue" letters I receive. When my sister and I visited Meditation Mount in Ojai, California, I signed their visitors' list. Months later, I petitioned for information about my book when I went to sleep. The next day, out of 300 affirmations that could have been sent, I received a three-by-five card from Meditation Mount with the words "SPIRITUAL APPROACH" in big, bold letters. I've never had another piece of mail from them.

Why had I manifested an editor who was suggesting one thing, while my inner guidance was saying another?

When I didn't follow through on his suggestions, I lost his interest and felt like a procrastinator who'd lost her only chance at writing a book. Feeling like a slug, I was happy when my friend Jody called and recommended a three-day introductory motivational conference in Dallas she was attending. It was on December 7, 1997, my father's birthday and three months after his death in Dallas.

On the last night of this conference, the motivational guru pumped us up to peak state by playing really loud music and having us jump up and down on our chairs just before we were to go outside to walk across hot coals. He told us to scream out whatever we wanted to manifest. All 2,000 of us at the same time started yelling out our different desires. I yelled out to the universe, *"I WANT A WOMAN EDITOR, I'M TIRED OF AUTHORITATIVE MEN TELLING ME WHAT TO DO!"* Then, letting all the emotional fervor go, I went into a meditative state and calmly went outside to walk across hot fiery coals. At the coals, the speaker's team leaders were shouting at us, "Are you ready?"

From my now peaceful meditative state I quietly replied, "Yes."

My tranquility unnerved the lady team member, who shouted again, "ARE YOU READY?"

Again I serenely stated, "Yes."

Finally I realized she wasn't used to anything but a passionate frenzy before someone walked on burning coals, so to satisfy her third shouted "ARE YOU READY?" I yelled back, "YES!" and went back into my composed, serene space.

Then I walked across 20 feet of burning coals, repeating in my head over and over as instructed, "Cool moss, cool moss, cool moss."

This three-day Dallas motivational conference in December 1997 had a big crew with a high-pressure sales technique, which went something like, "You must sign up for all the different ses-sions at one time. You will save a bundle with this one-day offer."

Sigh. I signed. Unfortunately, the last day of the conference "awakened" me to the fact this man was teaching manifesting without any connection to spirit. Too late. I had already paid a huge amount for more conferences. And, "Oh, we forgot to tell you. No refund." It was either continue or lose all the money I'd paid, so, off I went in February to Hawaii to have A Date with Destiny.

Now, while manifesting without attachment to spirit is entirely possible, my observation is that eventually a feeling that something is missing comes with it. I witnessed this happening to our motivational "guru" at the next conference. For ten to 15 years he, by the force of his will and personality, walked people barefoot across hot coals. He hoped to show them, "If you can do this, you can do anything, get anything."

He personally told us how he'd bought a castle, cars, and planes. All his dreams had been realized, by believing in himself and his motto, "All-I-need-is-within-me-now." He said he was going to be a billionaire by the time he was 40. He also implied he'd be the president of the United States soon after that. He had it all mapped out and was in a motivational upswing.

Apparently, though, not long before this Hawaii conference, his father had died. Even though he was close to his father and it affected him deeply, he took no time off to stop, honor, mourn, or reflect his father's passing. It was business as usual. The guru went on with a scheduled interview on the *Larry King Live* television show, and continued on his breakneck-speed con-ference schedule. Toward the end of our conference, he came back to one of our 18-hour-long sessions after a dinner break and said to us, his 2,000-person audience, "For the first time in 10 years, I'm feeling a little depression today. I don't know why. Does anyone have any thoughts?" He was hurting, and he put it out there to see if anyone had an answer or remedy.

It didn't require psychic ability to see what was going on with him. This motivational guru had pumped himself up to "peak state" and barreled right through losing his father, so he wouldn't miss an opportunity to promote himself on national television. Yet, when his father died, a door opened a crack. He saw a glimpse of something more. With his father's death, he had a glance at a connection greater than anything he could possibly manifest by his will alone. Now, all of a sudden, all the incredible things this man had pulled out of his manifesting hat seemed to pale in comparison, and he didn't know why. He had his whole life mapped out and now it didn't seem to matter. Skipping over deep emotions and repressed feelings no longer worked. What he told other people to do, which was to close their eyes to reality, be in denial of what really is, and barrel on through, wasn't happening for him.

Years later, when I went to what I thought was a speech class at the Learning Annex, I found myself with a woman teacher who had worked with and was promoting this motivational guru's techniques.

During the class, she occasionally would make a loving comment about her husband. Without preparing us in any way, she dropped this bomb, "Let me show you how this technique works (pump-up-to-peak-state and barrel on through). Six months ago my husband was killed in a car crash. I'm using these techniques and here I am tonight, just fine, teaching you." When she revealed the heartbreaking information about her husband, I felt like I'd been hit in the chest. I had a sharp intake of breath and closed my eyes. She noticed my reaction and talked with a lump in her throat the rest of the class.

Later, I told her my concerns about her boss not connecting to spirit. Her reply was a "bottom line" answer. "Oh, he understands, but he tried speaking about God at one of his conventions and some people walked out."

So, why shouldn't he manifest what he wants any way he wants? Isn't doing what he does the best way to reach his goal of becoming a billionaire? Sure, he can do it his way. However, he was already showing signs of unraveling. An unconscious climb to the top just doesn't seem to cut it anymore. We are rapidly moving into a period of spirit first. You can be a billionaire and not deny spirit. Actually, honoring spirit makes it easier to manifest.

I had gone to his Hawaii conference, A Date with Destiny, because it was paid for. I decided while there I'd make it worth my while and swim with dolphins. I wanted an experience that would connect me to spirit. When I arrived in Hawaii, I quickly hooked up with people who guide dolphin adventures. I went out three different times and dolphins never appeared. And I prided myself on already being a good manifester who didn't have anything to learn at this conference? I realized later that if dolphins had appeared, I would have been so excited, I never would have recognized why I really was there.

At the beginning of the conference, we were broken down from 2,000 people into teams of 30 and told to meet with our team leader every morning. My team gathered outside at picnic tables under a lanai that had a view of the bright Kelly green grass that sloped to the ocean.

The morning after I had my last *no*-dolphin experience, I was talking to the woman sitting across from me while we were waiting for our meeting to begin. (From 2,000, to 30, to one.) I was telling my standard story about my favorite teacher, Brugh Joy. "He's a former conventional medical doctor with impeccable credentials—Mayo Clinic, Johns Hopkins, Phi Beta Kappa Southern Cal, blah, blah blah," when for some reason I added, "Actually, Michael Crichton wrote about him in his book, *Travels*. He studied with Brugh and wrote a whole chapter about it. Crichton's such a good writer. You know, he wrote, *Jurassic Park, Andromeda Strain. . . .*"

"Yes, I know," she said. "I was with him for seven books. Actually, I've met Brugh Joy."

It took about two seconds for what she said to sink in. My mouth flew open. I looked at her, pointed my finger at her, and gasped.

"You're a woman!"

She said, "Yes?"

"You're an editor!"

Again she replied, "Yes?"

Waving my finger back and forth from her to me, I blurted out, "We're going to be working together—I conjured you up!!!"

With my ego firmly out of the way because no dolphins had showed, I did have a "Date with Destiny." Halfway around the world, at a conference in Hawaii, there I was sitting across from the woman editor I had asked the universe for in December. Valery, my new editor, and I started work on the book in June of 1998. She taught me how to organize my thoughts, and when she'd challenge me on something, I'd have incredible break-throughs.

Manifesting Greatness

One day when Valery and I were working, she told me she wanted irrefutable proof that I was automatic writing a conversation with Jesus. "Ask him to tell you something about me that is undeniable," she said. I thought, *Well, okay, why not?* I closed my eyes and instantly saw a black-and-white silhouette of her as a little girl with a bird sitting in her hand. I heard Him say, "Tell her I was the bird in her hand."

I didn't know what this was supposed to mean, but I told her what I saw and heard.

She instantly negated it. "No, no, when I was a little girl, I stood outside for hours on end holding out birdseed in my hand and no bird came to feed!"

Now, I don't want to wax religious on you, but it was so clear to me. She wasn't ready to hear what I'd said, or even listen to what she said. She confirmed that something bigger was going on herself. How could I have come up with that image of her on my own? Jesus was telling her through me that He had been with her all those hours when she was a little girl. He saw her. He was, and is, that for which she waits. A return to spirit. He is, and will always be, the bird in her hand.

Manifesting a return to spirit is greatness.

Manifesting "Stuff"

When I married Alfred, he wanted to make sure I liked New York. He asked a friend's wife if she'd take me out and introduce me to some of her women friends. She was delighted and called to say we would be going to her country club luncheon. She told me it was a charity event with door prizes and drawings. I laughed and said, "Oh, I'll embarrass you, I win everything." She laughed.

When we arrived at our table, she presented me to the other six ladies who, like us, were attired in silk dresses, hats, and heels. When she introduced me she said, "Patricia says she wins everything." They all laughed.

By virtue of my seat, I won the prize on our table, a set of pearl-handled steak knives. By virtue of my birthday, I won the centerpiece on the table. And by virtue of the raffle tickets I'd bought, I won first prize, a VCR. I never saw any of those ladies again.

I've always been good at manifesting "stuff." Money, cars, houses, prizes, parking spaces, and first prize at drawings. I love to win, want to win, expect to win, and am grateful when I win. So, win I do. I think anyone can.

It's the Law of Attraction. When we vibrate out to the universe what we want and how happy we'll be when we get it, it appears.

I told Alfred that my son wouldn't play backgammon with me because no matter how far ahead of me he was at the end of the game, I'd roll doubles again and again and again until I won. Alfred's eyes lit up. He tried me out at the craps table in Puerto Rico, and sure enough, I could call the dice. He loved it. Some nights, because he knew how to bet, he'd win up to $12,000. I'd win $2,000 betting the "hard way," which is rolling doubles, my specialty.

Is this telekinesis—the power to move and bend objects at will? Maybe. Raising my energy vibrations to that of the dice? Most probably.

One night in Santo Domingo, the table was four people deep during my 45-minute roll. Someone in the crowd would yell out, "Four! Roll four!" (the number), and I'd say, "No." Then I'd shake, shake, shake, shout out, "Three!" and there it was! I'd say, "Eleven!" Boom! Done! Alfred would say, "Roll five!" and five would show up.

Finally I'd get around to rolling four, the hard way with two twos, and I'd win my doubles bet. On this particular trip, our plane home had to land in Puerto Rico because of bad weather. A big man with a Hawaiian shirt peeking out through his raincoat came down the airplane stairs, saw me, pointed, and shouted, "That's her, that's the woman I won $15,000 on. Hi, little lady!"

I can also help other people win. Alfred became a believer. When we were on vacation, there were times I wouldn't feel like rolling dice. I had to be in the right mood. A "what if I can't do it tonight?" feeling wouldn't work. Which is still the Law of Attraction. You put out a negative "I can't do it," that's what will come back to you, not doing it. On the nights I didn't feel like shooting craps, I enjoyed seeing how long I could make $50 last at the slot machines. Alfred would finish at the craps table and come to see how I was doing. One night I'd told him to put five quarters in the machine next to me. "No, slot machines are a rip-off," he said.

"Oh come on, I've been sitting here for an hour, and I've made a 100 dollars off my 50. It's fun." I gave him five quarters. He put them in the slot machine, saying, "I never win anything on these things." He pulled the handle. *Clang, clang, clang, ding, ding, ding.* Bells and lights were going off all over the machine. He'd just won $750. Either my positive energy and high vibration got his going or it overrode his negative "I never win anything."

Our biggest win was when we bought four tickets for a raffle at Doug's school parents' day weekend. One hundred dollars a ticket, and we won first prize—the $50,000 Mercedes!

Several years after Alfred died, I attended a business conference with a friend in Hawaii and decided to consciously try to see what I do when I help someone win. I was in a small auditorium with seats for 100 waiting for my friend, Richard, to give a speech. When I sat down, the man in front of me, about 40, medium height and wiry, introduced himself. We had a short, pleasant conversation. After Richard's speech, an announcement was given that there would be a drawing in the lobby. As we were walking, I looked up at Richard, grinned, and said, "So, what are we going to win?"

He replied, "No, Patricia, you can't win this one, we're hosting the conference and holding the drawing."

When we walked into the crowded lobby and booth area, I saw the man with whom I'd been chatting. Jerry was standing with his arms folded, looking like he was barely enduring the ordeal of listening to everybody else's number being called. I touched his arm and said, "Jerry, you win anything?"

He replied with a stern-looking face, "No, I never win anything."

I laughed, patted his arm and said, "You will now," then walked on.

As I moved away, I mentally stopped and connected to the universe. I visualized going up, out, and back of myself, connecting to a higher power. I said politely, clearly and directly, "Please make Jerry win." Then I let it all go and went to make a phone call. In doing something else, I let go of my attachment to the outcome and turned it over to the universe to work its magic.

Later when I was sitting in my friend's booth in the lobby, I thought about Jerry and wondered if he'd won anything. All of a sudden the crowd separated like the parting of the seas. Jerry came running through, pointing at me, saying, "She did it, she did it, she made me win first prize!"

Richard, used to my "powers," rolled his eyes as if to say, "Here we go again. . . ."

The universe only says, "Yes!" I've said this before, but it needs emphasizing. Think about it. Whatever we put out is what we get back. If we are scared or negative about something happening? That's what the universe reads we want. That's when the fearful things we were afraid would happen *do* happen. "Yes!" says the universe. Energy out, same energy back. If we really, really want something, think we deserve it, and believe we will have it? It happens. Always, the answer is yes.

Think what would happen if you told an employee you wanted something done, only you weren't sure *when* you wanted it, nor did you know exactly *how* you wanted it, or whether you really *deserved* having it. You would get poor employee performance. The universe/God/Source/Higher Power/Inner Self works the same way.

We are vibrating energy. The universe is vibrating energy. What we get back will be vibrating at the same frequency we projected. Put out negativity and fearful energy, you'll attract the same vibrations—car accidents, illness, rapes, and even murder. All vibrate at the same low energy. Put out joy and unconditional love, you'll get back love, money, abundance, jobs, power, and passionate creativity.

Knowing You've Manifested

I think I've made it clear throughout the book that there are no coincidences and no accidents. If you sincerely ask for something and you've tied up your camel—my favorite Egyptian saying, "Trust in Allah, but tie up your camel"—then you can sit back and let the universe work its magic. However, if you ask for a million dollars and you don't have a job, a rich relative on the brink of death, or a nice house to sell, then you better start buying lottery tickets. Do groundwork on manifestations. Help make it possible.

I kept asking for a million dollars. I'd buy lottery tickets and nothing would happen. Three months later, I sold my house in Nantucket for a million dollars over what I'd paid for it five years before.

I can still be slow in recognizing messages that I've manifested. Sometimes, in spite of everything, it takes three times before I get it. Last summer, Angel, my handyman showed me a diamondback rattler in Quan Yin's Garden off the side of my house. The snake sat nestled about three feet off the rock pathway in a flower bed filled with yellow shrub roses and lots of lavender. He was rattling away, angry at being disturbed. Beautiful as well as deadly, he lay coiled, ready to attack. Angel safely put the small snake in a trash can to await pickup by our resident snake charmer, Jim Sloan, who transports found rattlers to his ranch.

A couple of weeks later, incident forgotten, I was walking out to my sacred garden at dawn. Feeling free and diaphanous in my white cotton nightgown with long lace on the scoop neck and cuffs, I was exuding the glow of life. The sun was just peeking over the horizon and red, pink, and orange filled the sky. My decaf in hand, I'd slipped on my little Sandalz flip-flops and was singing at the top of my lungs, "Oh What a Beautiful Morning" as I glided over to the garden. When I moved the bolt back on the gate, I thought, *Wow, the cicadas must have migrated here last night. What a racket they make. I thought they were only back East. Don't they only come every 17 years? Or is that locusts? Boy, it's loud. Wonder if I should look for it?*

Not particularly appreciative of a big, ugly bug with iridescent wings that sheds his entire outer body, I decided to let it go, realizing I'd probably see his shell later. When I stepped back to open the gate, I looked down and let out a wild scream as I jumped back about four feet off the flagstone. Coiled in the dirt next to the entry within three inches of my left leg was a large four-foot prairie rattler. He was mad. Head up, tongue out, hissing away, and rattling to beat the band. I ran into the house to call Jim. The prairie rattler stayed happily in the same place, guarding the entrance to the sacred garden all day, until Jim came to pick him up.

A couple of mornings later, I once again was on my way to drink my morning decaf in the sacred garden. Now, though I was still diaphanous in another white nightie, I was wearing my combat boots, with my street smarts totally awake and alert. There were no more songs from O-K-L-A-H-O-M-A. I was vigilant in my search for predators. I clomped from the house to the garden, solidly grounding to the earth with each clomp of my boot. Having decided I would never again be caught unawares, once I safely reached the garden, I was still a little shaky about relaxing into my dawn meditation.

I finished the seventh day of my new 30-day discipline in which I individually moved 12 two-inch stones every morning precisely at 7:00 A.M. Walking each one from the east altar to the west altar in the garden, I asked for transformation and grace.

Feeling pretty good about how the morning was going so far, I opened the gate to leave. When I looked down, under my foot overhanging the one-inch lip of the stone that led to the entranceway was a huge, slithering snake crossing the path.

This time as I jumped back screaming, "Aggghh!" I slammed the gate (like that would help). Now I was angry. I stomped over to the other gate muttering, "What the—!" I remember thinking, *So much for the people who tell you to be still and stare the snake down.*

By the time I was coming around the side of the garden stone wall, I was shouting at the heavens at the top of my lungs, "All right, already! I've got it! Snakes are transmutation and transformation. I know that! So, transform me, *just stop sending me snakes!*"

I'd been asking for transformation. Why wasn't I being transformed? Why all the snakes?

I had been totally unconscious of my surroundings, just as I was totally unconscious about my request for transformation. What did I want when I asked for transformation? I didn't know. I figured whoever I was asking would know. What I really wanted was to live a more conscious, graceful, less fearful, and content life.

The snakes were perfect. They transmute from one life to another by shedding their old skin, their old way of protecting themselves. Sams' and Carson's *Medicine Cards* book says that "snake medicine people are rare because their initiation involves experiencing and living through multiple snake bites, transmuting all poisons, be they mental, physical, spiritual, or emotional.

"Snake energy on the material plane creates passion, desire, procreation, and physical vitality.

"On the emotional plane, it becomes ambition, creation, resolution, and dreams.

"Mentally, it becomes intellect, power, charisma, and leadership.

"Spiritually, it is wisdom, understanding, wholeness, and connection to the Great Spirit."

Everything I wanted.

Once again, I'd been expecting divine light to shoot down from the heavens into my little sacred garden where it would transform me in a rainbow of colors. I let it go. I let go of being afraid I might do something wrong. In that state, I wasn't in the present enough to see what was going on around me.

Transformation is going to the left to get to the right. You take in from the left, transmute it, and let it go from the right. Go through the poison, transmute it, to get to the desire. Everything can be transmuted with the right state of mind.

Now, in spite of the fact I seem to live in snake central, I haven't even seen a snake, much less had a close encounter with one. My life *has* become a lot more conscious, more graceful, less fearful, and more content.

Manifesting Miracles

After Alfred died, along with all my other problems surrounding money, I had a terrible problem with the IRS. The IRS couldn't decide whether monies were due them and if so, how much. My lawyers showed them that I had never received the money they wanted to tax and pointed them in the direction of my husband's partner, his brother. My lawyer, the foremost tax attorney in Manhattan, advised me to put the matter out of my head, saying if we forced them into a decision, it might not be what we wanted.

In the seven years the IRS was trying to make up their minds, the amount in question, with penalties and interest, grew to an astounding half million dollars. Having to pay that amount of money would have ruined me financially. Though I didn't want this hanging over me like a big black cloud of financial disaster, I took my lawyer's advice and tried not to focus on it.

I did pretty well, except one day when a physic reader of good repute came to Nantucket. After her reading, I said, "You know, I should have asked if you could give me any information about the IRS." She closed her eyes for a moment, connected back in, opened her eyes, and said, "Pray for a miracle."

Oh, great, I thought, *I'm doomed.*

I had a dilemma about how to handle this advice, since I never admit to myself that I pray. I quickly decided that "petitioning to Source" would be just as effective. Every night, when I'd think about it, in that meditative place between wake and sleep, I'd petition to Source saying, "Please make the IRS go away. Please make me owe nothing."

My statement was almost childlike in its politeness, simplicity, sincerity, and clarity.

A month later, I was up in Vermont when my lawyer tracked me down, "Patricia," he said, "Are you sitting down?"

I replied, "Yes."

He said, "Well, stand up."

"Josh, what *are* you talking about?" I asked.

"In 20 years of practice, Patricia, I've never seen it happen. The IRS wrote the whole thing off."

I jumped up and down, saying, "I did it, I did it, I created a miracle!" and told him what I'd been doing.

He laughed and said, "Well, it worked!"

For the first time, I was traveling with a portable altar. I had set up a candle and incense on a piece of lace with three heart-shaped rocks on a little table. When I hung up the phone, I got on my knees and bowed up and down in front of the altar saying, "Thank you! Thank you! Thank you! I am so very, very grateful!"

Now, you can think what you like. Yes, the IRS was getting a bad rap in the press at the time regarding their appalling treatment of taxpayers. Yes, I was a "helpless" widow going up against the big, bad IRS. True, the IRS knew my lawyer was considered the top tax attorney in New York. Those things might have affected their thinking. But consider this: in seven years, the agents on this case changed many times. Each would extend the statute of limitations so they could have time to study it. Why at that particular time, just when I was petitioning for a miracle, was my case in front of *the* right person? The one who would and could do exactly that for which I was petitioning? "Please make the IRS go away. Please make me owe nothing."

As far as I'm concerned, only divine intervention can make the IRS go away. I accept it,

I created a miracle.

Manifesting Is Easy—It's Knowing What You Want That's Hard

If you don't know what you want? If you don't know how to follow your bliss, because you don't know what your bliss is?

As you go off to sleep, petition for that information. Write it down if you like. Ask, "Please, what's next?" Or, "Please, what do I need now to _____?" Or, "What is my passion, what is my purpose?" Go to sleep and be open to the answer—whether it comes in a dream, a conversation over the next week, through a sudden "knowing." Be aware to whatever way it reveals itself to you. Manifest knowing your bliss.

KNOWING WHAT YOU WANT IS POWERFUL. MANIFESTING IT? EASY. . .

17

AN AMERICAN WALKABOUT: A Quest for Answers in a Cabin in the Woods

In the fall of 1998 I drove down the long, winding, dirt driveway and pulled up alongside what looked to be the cabin in the woods I had envisioned all my life. You remember, the one I dreamed would magically appear and in its very walls would be the answers to everything I've ever wanted to know? A Thoreau-on-Walden-Pond-type problem solver.

My cabin was in the woods 40 miles in the middle of nowhere, near Elliotsville, Maine, on the shore of Big Greenwood Pond. I had picked up a brochure at a bed-and-breakfast in Portland and there it was, the picture of the cabin of my dreams. It had a cedar shake roof sloping down over the porch running the entire front of the house. It was small, about 25 by 30 feet, and there were rustic unfinished pine shutters on all the windows. Stairs off the big front porch led down to a path that the owner had told me on the phone wound down the mountain through oaks and pines to a large, pristine-clean pond. He said I could even drink out of it! I hadn't been able to drink out of a pond or river since my childhood in Alaska. The owner also informed me that while there was one cabin nearby, he felt it would be vacant this time of year.

When I pulled up to my cabin, I was terribly disappointed to see signs of life at the cabin next door. There were no people around, but a truck was parked out front, with a large metal dog cage nearby and a toy dump truck, bulldozer, and other toys scattered about. This would not work. How could I get answers to unformed questions with dogs and kids around?

I quickly unpacked my SUV so I wouldn't have to deal with my neighbors. Actually, "quickly" might not be the word I want. Quickly unpacking anything I ever pack is never an option. This trip, driving instead of flying, I'd outdone myself in the packing department. Unlike an Aborigine's walkabout, in which one treks around naked and barefoot in the outback of Australia for months on end, mine was more of an American Yuppie New England version of a walkabout—Barbie goes to find a cabin in the woods.

My SUV was filled to the bursting point with everything that might ever be needed on a trip of no known duration or destination. The back was filled with three designer suitcases overstuffed with jeans, jogging clothes, tennis outfits, dress clothes, formal wear, and my pink cashmere robe. I had stopped at the farmers market in Portland and filled the front seat with a Styrofoam cooler and two bags of fresh organic products, chicken, fish, meats, fruits, and vegetables. My new massage table was behind the front seats in case I was called upon to do some healing. The backseat was crammed with a large Nantucket basket of meditation tapes, candles, and my favorite pillow. Plus, a box of books, my laptop, and a boom box. I was prepared. I was going to say I was ready for bear, but as I had no gun, unless he was coming to a black tie dinner, that really wouldn't be accurate.

Not wanting to see my neighbors, I carted everything in before I took time to look around inside the cabin. When I opened the old refrigerator's freezer door, there was so much ice, I couldn't have slipped a piece of paper in it, much less all the food I'd purchased. In the refrigerator compartment, it looked like there was dried blood dripping down the walls, and when I pulled out the dirty vegetable drawers, I found that brown-red whatever-it-was had puddled and dried beneath them.

While my hair dryer was melting the ice in the freezer and hot water dissolving the unknown entity in the bottom of the refrigerator, I looked through the rest of the place. The floor was dirty. More than that, it was old linoleum, not the beautiful, sparkling, buffed-to-a-mirror-finish, thick wood floors I'd envisioned in my cabin. I looked for a mop. In the owner's closet I found a mop so dirty, it left more dirt on the floors than on the mop. I started a shopping list and consoled myself with the thought that, after all, I had wanted to rough it. I had just wanted to rough it in a really, really clean-to-the-sparkling-point cabin. Talking myself into a better mood, I said, "Ah, come on, Patricia. This is it. This is your cabin in the woods you've been dreaming about your whole life."

While I felt better after my pep talk, I still only unpacked just what I needed for the night, certain there wouldn't be any drawer or closet clean enough for my standards. Then I went to the bedroom to get my bed ready for later. No blanket on the bed, just a shabby, thin, polyester bedspread covering old, stained, faded flower sheets. All this when the owner assured me a cleaning crew had been there all morning getting it ready for me. Yes, the sheets had been washed. They smelled clean, but, yuck, stains. There was no mattress pad, so the sheets slid all over the cheap mattress. I added 300-count Egyptian cotton sheets, a nice, thick mattress pad, and a cozy warm blanket to my list. Now, just where I thought there'd be a store with such goods in the middle of nowhere, I didn't pursue. I just continued making up a feel-good list. Tonight I decided I'd sleep under my fur coat for warmth.

I took a break from my organizing and walked out on the porch. Outside was beautiful. There was, as advertised, a gently sloping path down the mountain through oaks and pines to the shimmering pristine pond. I'd been told there was a green canoe I could use down by the shore. I decided to forget the cabin, hike down to the pond, paddle out to the middle, and watch the sunset. That was really why I was here, even with all my accoutrements. I wanted to connect to Source through nature.

It was so quiet on the water. The reflection of the tall pines made it seem that there were two dimensions to reality. One that could be viewed from above looking into the trees in the pond's reflection and one that came from below looking up at the pines reaching to the sky. I reached the center of the pond, with my canoe gliding serenely over the top of the water leaving only faint ripples behind. As the canoe stopped, I sat and marveled at how beautiful it all was as the sun began to light up the sky with bright reds and pinks. With the sun sinking below the tree line, in the shadows I felt a chill, shivered, and noticed my feet felt wet. I looked down and wondered how I managed to get so much water in the bottom of the canoe when I'd been careful getting in. I thought about that for a while and slowly came to the realization that I hadn't gotten water in the canoe. The canoe was leaking! I was out in the middle of a huge pond with no one else around for miles and my canoe was bubbling with leaks? Just what else could possibly go wrong during my *On Golden Pond* experience? *No*, I thought, *Cancel that, don't ask.* I paddled back to shore like a woman possessed. When I dragged the canoe back on land, I seriously considered putting my foot through it so the next unsuspecting tenant wouldn't have the same experience.

By now it was getting dark. I went back up to the cabin, fixed dinner, got ready for bed by putting on my nightgown and pink cashmere robe, and settled down on the sofa to read. When I stoked the fire in the potbelly stove, I soon discovered a pink cashmere robe and a black potbelly stove were not particularly compatible. Black soot was all over the arms of my robe.

The next morning, I figured things were picking up when I awakened to sounds of the people next door leaving. Yay! I was convinced that now, alone, I'd be able to hear all the answers to my, as yet, unformed questions. I peered outside to watch and noticed someone walking down to the pond. *Photo op!* went off in my head like a shout. Since I was not a photographer, it never hit me that this was rather strange as I raced around looking for my camera. Not wanting to miss what was happening, I gave up on the camera and walked out on the porch to spy on the unsuspecting person. I knew they were going down to the water one last time to say good-bye.

At first I couldn't tell if it was a man or woman. The distance from me was about 50 yards. I watched as she or he stood down by the lake for a few minutes. On the return trip up the path, I realized it was a woman and felt a tremendous sadness overcome me. I heard myself thinking, *Our lives will never be this happy again. We'll never feel this kind of peace and contentment. It will never be the same. When we leave, it will be over.*

First, I wanted to run over and comfort her by saying, "Don't worry, you can take it with you. All you did was connect to Source through nature. You can take the feeling home." However, since I'd been hiding from them like I was in a witness protection program, I decided busting in on them as they were getting ready to leave probably wasn't a good idea.

Then I stopped and realized what had just happened.

I had just picked up, from half a football field away, the woman's thoughts and sorrow. I was thinking her thoughts and feeling her feelings as if they were my own.

Well, this was more frightening than staying alone in a cabin in the middle of nowhere. Did this mean that I'd not only been a sponge picking up other people's illnesses but that I could do the same with their emotional baggage and thoughts, too? How many times had that happened and I hadn't noticed, thinking what I was feeling was my own stuff? This time it was only because I was out alone in the middle of nowhere that I picked up on the fact that what I was thinking wasn't my own thoughts. I was soon going to find that this happens more often than I could have possibly imagined.

I was beginning to realize that answers to my unformed questions were already coming in loud and clear. Would there be more information that would come from my finally finding my cabin in the woods?

Well, yes, just not this particular cabin.

As I settled in for my second night, all dressed up in the now clean pink cashmere robe that I had hand washed, I basked in the warmth of the fire in the potbelly stove. I sat on the sofa with my laptop and began typing in my journal. Typing away, I suddenly stopped.

Did I just hear a noise inside the house? I listened with all my senses for a long silent moment. *Oh, it's my imagination,* I thought and started typing again. I heard it again. I stopped typing. It stopped. I started. It started. Then the noise kept going when I stopped. *Oh my—there's something huge and live and noisy scurrying around in the open loft above me!!!*

That was it! *Last straw!* No more! Animals in the wilderness were one thing, but critters in the house? Not even . . .

It took me less than ten minutes to throw on my clothes, pack up the entire car that had taken an hour to unpack, and get the heck out of there. Even though I was upset as I drove up the long, one-lane driveway in the dark, I realized how relieved I was to be leaving. Staying in a dirty cabin in the middle of nowhere had been just too unnerving. I wanted answers, sure. But not particularly in a cabin at the end of a long, long one-lane driveway, where, if someone in a truck, like the man with the hook for a hand, decided to visit, I'd be trapped. (You remember when we were in high school the story of the man with the hook for a hand—two teens were parked at a secluded kissing spot when a news bulletin broke in on the radio, "Be on the look out for a vicious killer with a hook for a hand who escaped from our local mental hospital." The kids rammed the car into reverse and tore home to find a hook hanging off the car door handle.)

I continued to drive for about a half hour before I calmed down enough to realize how long a drive it was back to Cape Cod. And after seven hours driving, there wouldn't be a ferry running from Hyannis to Nantucket in the middle of the night, and most of the hotels were closed for the season. Besides, I hate to drive at night.

I turned around and headed for the little town of Moosehead Lake, where I found a hotel on the lake and spent the night. The next morning, I decided to try one more time to find a cabin. The one the realtor came up with didn't look like my dream cabin. This was a new, large modern A-frame in an exclusive development. The realtor assured me that at that time of year, I'd be alone in the neighborhood nestled next to Moosehead Lake.

At least in this cabin I had the polished-to-a-gloss wooden floors and the big stone fireplace I'd always envisioned in my cabin. I also had central heat, huge rooms, a designer tiled kitchen, and a whole glass wall looking out on the lake. Maybe I couldn't drink out of this lake, but the house had nice fresh linens.

I'd brought my boom box so I could listen to meditation tapes. For some reason, that afternoon I wanted really loud music. I hadn't considered that a possibility, since I usually live at home with no sounds. I went out to the car to see if I had any CDs in the CD player. What a smorgasbord, Bob Marley with "I Shot the Sheriff," Beethoven, Paula Abdul (from Dad's CD collection), Bach, and some sacred sounds. I opted for Paula Abdul. After singing away with the first number, I found myself feeling really strung-out and anxious. Now what was happening? I had been fine before I put the music on. Then it hit me. This album had been made during Abdul's frenetic bulimic/anorexic years. Somehow I was taking on *her* feelings and symptoms through her music. I was on uppers! No wonder I'd turned all music off in my house years ago. Not only could it be nostalgic, but it actually connected me into other people's emotions. What did all this mean?

The next day, I settled in and started doing exercises to practice using intuition from the book *Practical Intuition* by Laura Day. The fire in the big stone fireplace had burned down, so I went outside to find more firewood. There was no more firewood. I called the realtor. He didn't know where to get any. I didn't need a fire for heat, but how can one be in a cabin in the woods with a big stone fireplace and no fire?

I was having such an annoying trip. Other than discovering that I pick up other people's feelings and thoughts, I felt I wasn't doing this right. I hadn't even decided what questions I wanted to ask, much less settled in and let the answers flow. It was about then it started raining. I thought, *Good, maybe an exciting storm will wash my annoyances away.* Actually, what it did was exacerbate them by providing another problem. The entire beautiful glass front wall leaked and the storm was blowing the rain right into it. I had pots and pans filling with water everywhere. It was time to abort my mission. Finding answers to unformed questions had to be easier at home.

I called up my friend in Nantucket who always said I'd love Maine and asked him, "Tim, to just what part of Maine were you referring?" He was so excited, he said, "Moosehead? You're in Moosehead? That's it. You must call my friend, John. He's the guy I always go up to visit."

Before I called John, I decided to pack up and check the weather on my computer to make sure I wouldn't run into any snowstorms on the drive home. I needed a local zip code to pull up the weather. Looking around for a magazine or piece of mail with a zip code on it, I once again wondered what in the world I could have been thinking, taking off for no place in particular. If anyone knew answers didn't come from a place, it was I. I knew they came from inside. I knew that. It had been dumb to come. Finally I found a flyer with an address on it. The zip code for Moosehead, Maine? 04441.

0**444**1.

I heard the message. "Patricia, you are here for a reason. Get your big elephant ears up and pay attention. You will become more conscious through this experience."

My attitude changed. I left to visit John and went on the rest of my trip with an open mind. I ended up staying with John a few days and had another experience like my cave dive in which I couldn't bring myself to dive into unknown waters. We had taken a sauna (a real outdoor wood-burning sauna) and John plunged into the quarry next to it. I don't know if you know how black the water is in a quarry, but this was black. There was no way I was ready to make the dive into seeming nothingness.

I left John's and decided to head for Canyon Ranch Spa in the Berkshires. I know, not quite the quiet roughing-it style of a cabin in the woods, but I decided I'd make do. Once again, as I drove up to the big baronial estate, it was like a haven. Everything was ready for me. A lovely clean room, meals prepared and creatively presented, beautiful views, and people all around who were there only to care about my welfare.

At lunch the following day, I walked to the salad bar and noticed a lady eating alone. Many people ate alone, I just happened to catch her eye when she looked up. We nodded and I went on to get my salad. After she finished eating, I noticed her again as she passed by me. I read her thoughts as though she were speaking to me. First I felt lonely and thought, *Why isn't he here with me? It's not fair that I have to be here alone.* Then I felt angry, sad, and sorry for myself.

This was her stuff, not mine. Alfred had been dead for six years at this point. I'd been feeling great.

This was why I'd come on my circuitous American walkabout. I needed to be away from my familiar environment to be shown just how connected we are. How many times does this happen—that we take on other people's moods and think their thoughts? Maybe it happens all the time. Would we notice if our mood made an almost imperceptible shift and then went back? It was the same lesson I'd been learning in different ways all along. This time it had to become apparent that my cabins didn't hold the answers. I did.

I had another realization at Canyon Ranch. I wrote in my journal about the similarity between my aborted cave dive in Kauai and my not being able to dive into the blackness of the quarry in Maine. I realized what my fear was. I wasn't afraid of diving into the blackness or the unknown. I was afraid of going into the blackness and never wanting to come out. One time in a dream, I went into a black hole. I had no fear. Once in the black hole, I realized all it was was black. There was nothing scary. It was just black and peaceful. It was nothing. Once I had no fear, little pinpricks of light started to seep through the blackness.

In my dives, I was afraid of the blackness and what could be around me. I would have had to stay a long time to feel the peaceful, restful, connected-to-all-that-is-place I found in my dream. My former illnesses all pointed to my fears of the unknown. Chronic Fatigue? Not wanting to be here, yet not wanting to die and leave—asleep on the horns of a dilemma. Allergies to the world? Again, allergic to being alive, sleeping away, yet not ill enough to get sick and die. Sleeping Beauty. The weight I'd gain and lose? Same thing, slim and trim, I had to accept my own sexuality and attractiveness. Heavy, I had a self-imposed boundary, so I didn't feel attractive enough to have to seduce man or mankind into my web.

My walkabout showed me life is a paradox. Wellness/Illness. Light/Dark. Awake/Asleep. Individuals with separate bodies and personalities, but also indivisible parts of the Whole.

The way out of the paradox?

Surrender, as I did in the black hole.

All is perfect.

All is one.

Consider. Each of us, as a separate entity, is a wave that is part of a vast ocean.

A wave is aware of, but doesn't worry about, being the ocean.

It just is.

18

SPONTANEOUS hEALING:
Accepting Our Dark Side

I have mentioned the dark side before, but I think it deserves another short look because of an incident that happened to me late in the writing of this book.

Norman Cousins.

One day, for no apparent reason, this man's name went off in my head like a shot, just as I was reaching for the chrome handle of a glass door to the office building I was entering. I'd been at the building earlier that morning to schedule a meeting and noticed a small library in the lobby filled with self-help, metaphysical, and self-healing books. I remembered Norman Cousins from his 1979 book, *Anatomy of an Illness*. I decided, while I was waiting for my appointment, to see if there was a copy of his book. Of course, there was. You'd think I'd be used to universal guidance by now.

I glanced through the book and confirmed that Cousins was considered the man who "laughed his way to health." Diagnosed in the mid-1960s with ankylosing spondylitis, a degenerative disease that causes the breakdown of collagen, he, almost completely paralyzed, was given only a few months to live. Cousins checked himself out of the hospital and with his doctor's support, moved into a hotel room and began taking extremely high doses of vitamin C. The rest of his therapy was equally high doses of humor and laughter from watching films of the slapstick comedy of the Three Stooges, the Marx Brothers, and *Candid Camera.*

Norman Cousins laughed his way to health and professed that this was *the* way to heal.

I recognized anger, let it go, and thought I'd found *the* way to heal.

There was a piece missing.

A few days later, back in Nantucket, I was driving my friend Kay home from our tennis game. I mentioned my experience with Norman Cousins. This is another perfect example of the "fluidity zone"—a time when the universe provides everything you need because you're in the "zone." Out of six billion people in the world, I'm in a car next to a woman in her tennis clothes who says, "Oh, I met Norman Cousins."

"You what?" I asked with my jaw dropping.

"Years ago," she continued, "I was a nurse for Doctor Hitzik, Cousin's doctor. When the doctor had a heart attack, I lived in his home and took care of him. He invited me to attend his soirées. I sat next to Cousins three or four times at dinner parties."

Before I could ask, Kay volunteered more information. She told me exactly what I needed to know but had no way to find out. She described Cousins as "rather formal, a man who measured every word."

That was it! That was the missing piece!

Cousins was a journalist geared to look at life from the gritty reality of daily headline news. Of course he measured his words. They could have a global effect. Humor and laughter? The comedic fantasies he watched were what Cousins repressed. Watching happy, funny films was engaging his dark side.

Growing up, I got kudos for being quick-witted and funny, not for measuring words. In my family, if you took time to think about what you said, you lost the limelight. Grim reality had no place in my fantasy life of joy and light. For me, my dark side was repressing anger and fear, something Cousins dealt with daily on a global scale.

If I, like Cousins, had holed up in a hotel with slapstick films, the men in the white coats would have had to have come and taken me away. Being funny and making everyone happy hit too close to home for me. That was how I lived my daily life. To engage my dark side and get well, I would have to watch realistic, angry movies like Oliver Stone's *Platoon* and *Fourth of July* and fearful movies like Stephen King's *The Shining* or Ken Russell's movie *The Devils* with Oliver Reed and Vanessa Redgrave. I've always had an involuntary scream that comes out in scary movies. I clear theaters with it.

So, were Cousins and I both right?

Yes.

To heal, each individual has to engage their own dark side.

In Cousin's case, joy and the light side of things were what he repressed.

In my case, it was fear and anger that I had to face to heal.

For Harvey, the man I met at the Dark Side Conference, his shadow was passion and joy.

Whatever emotion is repressed stresses the immune system— and the way it is manifest depends on the emotion repressed.

Back to the circle.

Stressed, the immune system sends out a signal to the body for help. Then the body gets sick with the exact illness that can bring us the message of what we are repressing.

When we shed light on our dark side, as Cousins did, as I did, as Harvey did, whatever emotions we were denying or repressing can be recognized, accepted, released, and let go.

That's spontaneous healing.

Of course both Cousins and I had to heal our bodies, bring them back from the brink, but the click that made that possible was stumbling into and acknowledging our own individual dark sides.

19

WALK LIKE AN EGYPTIAN:
Pilgrimages to Our Higher Self

For thousands of years on starry, starry nights the Great Sphinx has sat ruling majestically over all the land. Unspoken words in the crisp night air whirl, whisper, and ride on the winds gently blowing the Sahara sands.

> You want knowledge?
> Come to me.
> You want secrets of the Universe?
> Listen carefully.
> You want gratitude and unconditional love?
> Rest in my embrace . . .
> I am the guardian of truth.
> The mother, the journey's face.
> Come to me, pilgrim,
> Here you'll find grace.

For years, I had felt compelled to spend a night alone in the Great Pyramid of Giza. People I met who had had this experience told of profound spiritual growth. One person told me this was to be done in awe and reverence, as an initiation into higher consciousness.

Knowing this desire was unlikely to be sanctioned by Egyptian authorities, I made discreet inquiries and found various guided tours to Egypt, but none that I trusted to guide me on my specific quest. Waiting for the tour in which I'd feel safe took two years. Finally in September 1998, a friend introduced me to a psychic reader she liked in Cape Cod. The reader, Salina, is Egyptian and owns a tour company that hosts sacred journeys to Egypt. She told me about a 10-day trip to Cairo and temples along the Nile planned for February. John Anthony West, a world-renowned Egyptologist and author of *Serpent in the Sky* and *The Travelers Key to Ancient Egypt*, was to be their American guide.

Then she told me it was a closed, private tour for members of a spiritual foundation connected to an investment firm. I drove an hour to the offices of the foundation in Marion, Massachusetts, introduced myself to the founder and president, and was invited to join the tour.

I flew to Egypt a week earlier than the rest of the group with the other owner of the tour company, Rasheed, so we'd have time to arrange my stay in the Great Pyramid. After 18 hours of aircraft delays in Zurich, I finally arrived in Cairo. Any irritation and fatigue disappeared the moment I walked out on my balcony.

I, Patricia Heller, was looking out over riverboats going up and down the Nile. The same Nile Cleopatra sailed on her golden barge to reach Mark Anthony. I couldn't believe it. I was in Cairo! Yet there it was, stretched out before me as far as the eye could see—a most ancient of ancient cities with age-old domed mosques with their minarets reaching up to the sky between modern, new buildings. Five times a day, I heard the summons to prayer cried by the muezzin from the balconies of the minarets. While I didn't drop to my knees on a prayer rug, I liked being reminded to connect to Source five times every day.

The first night, Rasheed arranged for an English-speaking

guide to take me to see the Sound and Light Show at the pyramids. I intentionally had not read up on Egypt before going there. I'd wanted the freedom of beginner's mind to experience all the wonders. However, walking into the area where we were to sit, I realized I had had huge misconceptions. I was expecting to see two large matching sphinxes guarding the pyramids. Of course, there was only the one huge sculpture gazing down the pyramid mesa in Giza. Also, while I knew the pyramid complex wasn't alone in the middle of the Sahara Desert, I was still a little disappointed to see that the town of Giza had grown to right behind the chairs set up for the show. It took me awhile to adjust to this romance of old and new.

The show began in the dark with a booming Richard Burton-type voice giving me much-needed facts. Then a laser show extraordinaire commenced. To show the incredible size of the Great Pyramid of Cheops, the silhouette of the Vatican, Madison Square Garden, and another large building were superimposed on it with laser lights. The narrator's voice thundered on, telling us the three Pyramids were built over a span of three generations by Pharaohs Khufu, his second-reigning son, Khafre, and Menkaure, and laid out with such breathtaking accuracy, scholars were inspired to look to the stars for answers to the Pyramids' placement. They found that three of the major stars in Orion's Belt precisely matched their alignment.

The Great Sphinx was built by slaves quarrying a U-shaped ditch in bedrock. A lion's body, a solar symbol and an archetype of royalty, was sculpted from the reserved stone block. The royal human head symbolized power and might. A scarf folded in a manner exclusive to Egyptian kings replaced the lion's mane.

While unanswered questions floated on the air like fine perfume wafting on a breeze, all mystery was kept secret. Nothing was revealed except the facts, just the facts. The majestic Sphinx sat in her royal splendor, quietly dominating all.

When the light and laser show ended, my guide, Mohammed, and our driver introduced me to a man they met who could make arrangements for me to spend the night alone in the Great Pyramid. Improbably, the man's name was Sam and he said his relative was captain of the guards at the mesa complex. Sam said it would take some time to arrange a night because the Great Pyramid was being restored and would be closed the entire time I'd be in Cairo. It seemed that salt from the breath and sweat of tourists was ruining the plaster covering the Grand Gallery that had held the King's Tomb.

Knowing the Great Pyramid had been rented the last night of our tour to allow us a private entrance for a four-hour group meditation, I said nothing, thinking I might work something out myself.

Sam offered an alternative. "Would you like to spend tonight alone in the Great Sphinx? Sleep over the Hall of Records?" he asked in broken English. "Edgar Cayce?" The date was Saturday, February 13, 1999. Before leaving for Egypt, I had been told it was a powerful astrological day with a solar eclipse and a unique alignment of planets.

I knew I couldn't pass this up. Too many things had fallen into place to make this extraordinary event come together. Still, I wasn't going unless I felt safe. At dinner, Rasheed, who had flown over with me so he could visit his family, begged off going with me because he was too tired. His employee, Mohammed, was nervous about being caught doing something illegal. However, I think he was more concerned about the possibility of awakening universal information from the Hall of Records.

I later learned that Edgar Cayce, the Nostradamus of the twentieth-century, prophesied from a trance that there were hidden areas below the Sphinx and that the Hall of Records would be discovered near the end of the twentieth century. Cayce relayed that the survivors of the lost civilization of Atlantis had built the Sphinx in 10,500 B.C. and concealed beneath it a Hall of Records containing all the wisdom of their lost civilization and the true history of the human race. Seismographs proved the prophecy might be true. Tests reveal several underground cavities or voids in the immediate area of the Sphinx, including a large rectangular space some 12 by 15 meters in area, and five meters below the surface, right between the paws of the Sphinx. Exactly as Cayce predicted.

No wonder Mohammed was nervous. Me nervous? No. This was what I'd come seeking.

After much pleading on our part, Mohammed agreed to go to "protect" me. Rasheed warned me against wearing my expensive watch, which I locked in a hotel safety deposit box, and I took the precaution of covering my long blond hair with a scarf in the Muslim tradition. Egyptians had already made it known to me that a tall blonde who treated everyone as if "we are all one" with a big happy smile on her face was regarded as a goddess. While I lapped up the attention, I didn't need catcalls of "Ooh la la, I can't believe my eyes," while trying to clandestinely enter a closed area at night.

We met Sam at the stroke of midnight near the entrance to the pyramid mesa and, after Rasheed queried him a bit more, Mohammed and I were off. We followed him through one back alley after another, came to the side of the pyramid mesa, and began to climb up a path along its side. It hit me that the sand shifting beneath our feet was the Sahara Desert! I was in Egypt walking on the Sahara Desert! About halfway up, we met a guard in Arab garb who was waiting to sneak us past the other guards. When we reached the top, we were told to crouch down and scurry across the plateau. Feeling like a scampering crab, all I wanted to do was stop, stand, and reflect. There, in front of me, were the pyramids shining in the moonlight with big bright stars everywhere!

We made a hurried descent down a hill and were told to hide behind a guardhouse until the guard in the flowing Arab robes checked to make sure it was safe for us to cross over to the Sphinx's legs. As we were hurried across the wooden walk over to the Sphinx, I got my first close look. Here I had to stop for a moment, even if I got caught. I hadn't expected to feel such allure. Nothing had prepared me for the experience of meeting the Great Sphinx face-to-face. I was transported to another time, another place. She was by far the most remarkable work of art I'd ever seen—a relic of an ancient culture that possessed knowledge far greater than ours. Older than historical Egypt, her gods, and the pyramids.

With the guard shooing me on, I quickly followed the others around the Sphinx's right leg. After a boost up the inside of the leg at the corner of the body, I turned, walked under the Sphinx's head, and crawled down where Sam directed me into a dark excavated hole. I wiggled through a side opening about two feet by four feet into a tiny four-by-four-by-four-foot area covered with a metal lid. This was to be my home for the night.

Sam who, for the Egyptian pounds I'd given him, would have probably told me anything, said that archeologists had been excavating this site and were digging two small tunnels about eight inches wide for a robot fiber-optic camera. As far as I knew, I spent the night with my left foot in the small tunnel leading to the Hall of Records and my right foot in a small tunnel leading to the Hall of Tombs. I was instructed not to make any noise or use my flashlight and was told that they would check on me occasionally.

Alone in my little space in the Great Sphinx, I immediately went against my guide's wishes and beamed my flashlight into the two tunnels to see if I would be sharing my space with any spiders, scorpions, or furry critters. Satisfied I was alone, I turned off my light, settled back, placed my hands over my heart, and closed my eyes to meditate.

What happened next is almost beyond words.

Instantly behind my closed eyes a white light appeared.

At first, I thought it was an aftereffect from the flashlight beam, but it grew larger and larger until brilliant white light filled my vision. The light became so pure, I thought it must have been happening outside me as well. I raised my eyelid a fraction and peeked out. Nothing. It was black inside my hiding place. I closed my eyes, knowing from past experience that this was no time to think. It was either stay in the moment or become fearful and yank myself out.

As the white light continued to grow, I was thinking to myself, *Oh my God, I am alone and am spending the night in the Great Sphinx. I am so unbelievably blessed.* There I was, sitting in the bedrock, breathing in the aura of 10,000 years of history and mystery. My heart was so filled with gratitude that it radiated out into my body until it overflowed as tears.

Waves of peace and contentment reverberated through me as I gently began swaying back and forth with feelings of such unconditional, blissful love. My heart was full of familiar feelings I'd never felt before and familiar places I'd never been. And love, such embracing, loving love—much, much bigger than love between man, this was love with no strings, enveloping me with wave upon wave upon wave.

Was this Nirvana? I'd always thought Nirvana was a place Buddhists only tried to obtain in this lifetime. Yet here I was, nowhere and everywhere in a dimension transcending time and space. Not only was I one with Source, I was Source. I was there. I was in the highest happiness.

I have no idea how long this lasted. Time lost all meaning.

Whatever the time, it was long enough. As I slowly returned to an awareness of where I was sitting in my cubicle in the Great Sphinx, I sat stunned and basked in the afterglow of such incredible peace. I'd heard of people having a "white light experience." Apparently I now had, too.

Now that I was fully back and conscious, my thoughts became distracted by a scratching noise on the metal lid above me. At first I thought it might have been one of the nine wild dogs I'd seen following one after another on the mesa in front of the pyramids. When I focused my attention, I realized it was pieces of trash I'd seen on my way in. As I popped my head and shoulders out of the side to gather up the candy wrappers and potato chip bags, I noticed green lights flashing and reflecting off the sphinx and heard loud laughing and talking.

I wasn't scared, I was annoyed, thinking, "Boy, I'm glad I paid to spend the night alone in the Great Sphinx. It sounds as if everybody and his brother are out front having a party."

Didn't take me long to get out of a state of grace.

Later, Mohammed informed me that Prime Minister Tony Blair of England, his entourage, and about 20 military guards with machine guns had come to view the Sphinx by moonlight. Mohammed, scared to death we'd be discovered, was quaking in the guardhouse bathroom. As fearless as I felt the entire night, Mohammed was just as fearful. He said he hadn't been as scared the night he was mugged in the United States. What a balance we were—I opening to unconditional love and he to abject fear.

Back inside my cubbyhole, quiet again prevailing after everyone left, I heard someone coming to check on me. I'd never seen the face of the guard who had met us on the mesa. Suddenly the metal lid covering my cubicle opened and a strange Egyptian face peered in. Not sure whether he was friend or foe, I looked up, took my hand, and circling it said, "Hi," in as happy a voice as I could muster. He grinned a toothless grin and lit a couple of matches to see what I looked like, closed the lid, and came around to the side where I'd crawled in. He offered me a cigarette and made what looked like an attempt to join me in my small resting place. I said, "No, no, I have to be alone. I'm fine, thank you. Bye, bye." It worked. He left, and once again I was blessedly alone.

Listening to his footsteps crunch away in the distance, I realized I would hear anyone coming long before they reached me. I decided to crawl partially out of my hole and brave sitting halfway out of my hiding place. Still guarded from view, I spent the rest of the night cradled in the Sphinx's arms with my back against a stone slab, not knowing until later that this "slab" was the "Tablet of Dreams" placed there by Tuthmosis IV about 1400 B.C. From my new vantage point, I could gaze up at the beautiful face of the Sphinx surrounded by bright shining stars. I knew I was the luckiest girl in the world.

After a while, Sam returned to check on me. He said nothing about me being partially out of my hiding place. When he left he said, "Pray for Egypt." It seemed all the guards and guides thought I could conjure up anything, including world peace.

Instead of accepting this role with grace, I again lapsed out of my unconditional-love-we-are-all-oneness, and flipped back into aggravation. *This is my night, I don't want to be told what to do,* I thought.

Pulling my blanket up under my chin to stave off the chill, I didn't realize at the time that desert nights could get unbearably cold in February. I had brought extra clothes for my guide that he didn't use, so I put them on and wrapped myself in a blanket I'd brought to sit on. Warm enough, I leaned back against the Tablet of Dreams, and fell off to sleep for a short while and had a vision.

As in many of my dreams, I was an observer. From the rear of a room I saw the backs of Egyptian soldiers dressed in brown uniforms and brown helmets sitting in metal folding chairs in a lecture or ready room. Their commander stood on a dais at the front of the room. Behind him was a large map of the world. Instead of a helmet, he wore a brown beret with an emblem. In his right hand, he held a pointer with a five-point star on its end. I remember thinking during the vision, *Oh no, it's the Star of David. This is showing me there will be a war between Egypt and Israel.* Then the vision changed to two missiles firing off to the right with a silhouette of Cairo in the background with domes, praying towers, and scaffolding.

When I awoke, I immediately began to analyze these images. I was concerned I'd seen Egypt and Israel going to war. Then it dawned on me that the Star of David is a six-point star. The star at the end of the pointer had very clearly been five-pointed. The five-point star is a very powerful symbol employed by the ancient secret alchemists to call on higher energies, keep evil and imbalance away, and protect those turning metals into gold.

The next day, I consulted the runes to gain more information about my vision. The rune I pulled for the present situation was the "Spiritual Warrior." For the action rune, "Harvest" or one year. The rune "A Journey, Communication, Union, Reunion" represented the new situation. At the end of its description was a simple prayer, "I will to will Thy will."

I worked on the vision from a personal standpoint of having two aspects of my personality being represented. One was the warrior and the other the victim. I considered what part of me was a spiritual warrior gearing up for battle, personal growth, or mounting a campaign. Easy; it was the part of me that would be going out into the world with my missive or missile. The victim? The aspect of me that feared the future.

The Sphinx was preparing me to surrender feelings of entitlement and to have faith that I was being protected by a will higher than my own.

The next four days after my night with the Sphinx, I was violently ill with chills, fever, aches and pains, and a terrible cough. On a psychic level, I'd been opened and healed by divine presence and been given a big "Go" sign. On a physical level, I was putting on the brakes. I could not yet stop and fully surrender to that which I'd come seeking.

I have learned the hard way after incredible experiences like this that I have to stop, process, and take care of myself, so my body doesn't have to do it for me by becoming ill. Retraining myself from a lifetime habit of retreating into illness when overloaded, hurt, or scared takes time. After all, I'd successfully used it as my survival tool since I was a child.

I recovered just in time to begin the tour with the rest of the group.

We flew south from Cairo down through Egypt to Luxor, where we boarded the deluxe riverboat, the MS *Liberty*, so it could travel north with the currents and allow us a shorter journey on the water. This was the first time I'd experienced a river running south to north.

The first morning, we awoke at sunrise and went to the Temple of Isis, one of the gems of ancient Egypt. Situated on a beautiful tropical island surrounded on all sides by the gently flowing Nile, it looked as though it had been there for all time. It was hard to believe that the entire complex had been moved to a higher site when the British built the Aswan High Dam. The temple is an exquisitely sensual and serene, feminine healing sanctuary.

We started with a powerful group toning meditation at the altar with all 40 of us chanting "om," the most sacred symbol in Hinduism. Afterwards, I wandered alone, lay down on a stone wall in the front of the temple, and fell asleep in the warm morning sun.

I awakened slowly. With my eyes still closed, I noticed a buzzing sensation at my regenerative, or second chakra, located at the womb area of the female body. Curious, I decided to lie there with my eyes closed and observe what was happening. I felt a vibration like a hum without the sound, almost as if I had internalized our chanted tone at the altar and the sound was reverberating in my uterus. Behind my closed eyes I saw bright orange, the color of this regenerative chakra.

I smiled inwardly. This area of the body is the creative space, both literally and figuratively, for women. Babies are produced there, as are all creative endeavors. I'd asked for higher consciousness and healing at Isis's altar and it was already happening. I wondered if the fibroid tumor I'd had for years was healed. When I returned home I found out, that indeed, it was gone.

Later that day we visited the Temple of Horus, located midway between Luxor and Aswan in Edfu. It is the best-preserved temple of the ancient world. The god Horus is commonly depicted as a falcon-headed male divinity and symbolizes a return to the Source. As I walked through the temple, I gazed at the huge columns that rose up to the black, smoke-covered ceiling and visualized the cooking fires lit thousands of years ago by those who came inside to shelter themselves from the cold desert nights.

Nothing has to be left to the imagination in this temple. It is completely intact. From the moment you step on the sacred ground of the site, you feel a pull to walk straight through until you reach the Holy of Holies. I placed both hands on the altar and asked, in a deeply meditative state, *Please, allow me to open to higher consciousness so that I might help others do the same.* Immediately I had a vision of a huge, gold falcon mask set on stilts, placed on the shoulders of a priest. Long robes covered the framework, making the priest look larger than life.

My third chakra initiation occurred after a night visit to the Temple in Luxor. Our guide, John Anthony West, suggested that we not look directly at the temple when we first arrived. Rather, proceed to the left up the long walk flanked on both sides by dozens of large sphinxes. I did as advised and when I turned back to look at the temple, I thought my heart would burst. Completely floodlit, the temple, the obelisk in front of the temple, and the long row of sphinxes on either side of the walk were spectacular.

After I drank in all that my eyes could hold, I walked the entire processional with my right hand over my heart and left hand over my right, past the lighted sphinxes to the luminous obelisk. I passed a huge statue of Ramses II on my way into the Colonnade, where once again I was awestruck at the magnificence and grandeur. How could this be? These ancient blocks of stone weighed hundreds of tons and were thousands of years old. The beauty of this man-made creation brought me close to tears.

Many times during the trip, I'd wander away from the group, who were bunched together to hear the "facts" about these incredible monuments from John Anthony West. I was more interested in the history stored in the stone and the energy surrounding us. I sat in a quiet spot in Amenhotep's Court for two hours with all the attributes of the heart chakra—compassion, innate harmony, healing presence, and unconditional love circling around, bouncing off one column to another and back to me in this immense sacred space. I felt part of the universal plan and wanted to applaud its beauty.

On our way back to the boat, John Anthony West's girlfriend told me that the courtyard where I had sat for my two-hour heart meditation was the temple's solar plexus. Apparently, ancient architects often designed temples to coordinate with the human skeleton, and Amenhotep's Courtyard corresponded to the solar plexus area when a drawing of the human skeleton was overlaid on the plan of the Temple of Luxor.

The next morning, I once again became violently ill with vomiting, stomach cramps, and diarrhea. I had requested at the altar of this temple, like all the others, that I be allowed to open to higher consciousness so that I might help others do the same. I sat for two hours heart-centering in the temple's solar plexus and now I had "mummy's tummy." Once again, I had to get out my detective's hat and open my awareness, so I could understand why I was ill. What this violent retching illness showed me was that the time had come to finally and, violently if necessary, purge whatever I was repressing. Withheld emotions of fear, anger, jealousy, envy, scarcity, love, and even joy and laughter were holding me back and wouldn't allow me to make the transformation that was already in motion.

I began to understand what had happened. I had gone through a three-part initiation into higher consciousness brought about by the petition I continued to make to the universe at each site on this trip. "Please allow me to open to higher consciousness so that I might help others do the same." The first part was my initiation into the heart chakra at the Great Sphinx. The experience was almost beyond words. It was there that I'd been opened to the bliss of unconditional love, gratitude, reverence, and oneness.

The second part was the initiation of the creative chakra at the feminine healing Temple of Isis. The resistance I had to allowing my creativity to be birthed was exorcised. A vibrational energy set the tone to allow this chakra to open to its full potential.

The only obstacle left in the way of making my request of opening to higher consciousness complete was the solar plexus chakra. Removing its obstacle was the key that would make this chakra triad work. In Anodea Judith's *Wheels of Life*, the solar plexus chakra is explained this way, "The solar plexus chakra or third chakra's purpose is transformation—it transforms inertia into action, energy, and power. Once we overcome inertia to the point where energy is easily produced, the third chakra 'kicks in' and begins producing the power with which it is associated." That was what was left, transformation out of inertia into action and acceptance of what is. What was the obstacle in the way of my letting go of the inertia that was keeping the other two chakras from starting into motion?

Fear.

The day following my solar plexus chakra initiation, I was vomiting up the powerful obstacles that I'd allowed to be placed in my way of transformation. I was letting go of all the things in the past that I attracted to myself that took me out of my birthright of being heart-centered, intuitive, and balanced.

Since my body had, once again, given me an opportunity to stop and think, I spent the day contemplating my experiences thus far. One thing just beginning to dawn on me was that I had no idea, when asking the universe for help, that it would be so instantaneous. I thought I'd have time to grow into the higher consciousness I was asking for. Where was the lag time? Receiving unconditional support from the universe was literally turning me inside out.

I had gone from temple to temple reverently, but blithely, asking that I might be allowed to open to higher consciousness so that I might help others do the same, and *whack!* there was what I asked for, and *wham!* I was brought to my knees by illness so I'd have to take time to process what I'd learned.

Later, when I mentioned my confusion at having instantaneous answers to my questions to a friend, he explained it this way. He said once you get tuned into Source, it's like radio waves. Radio waves are always in the air. All you need to do is turn on the radio and the connection is made without delay. I simply turned on the connection at these sacred places and instantaneously began receiving my requests whether I was ready or not.

The day after I was so ill the second time, the tour group was going to Hatshepsut's Temple. This was where the 51 tourists had been violently gunned down in their bus in November 1998. Still dervishly intent on picking up all the information I could while in Egypt, I was terribly unhappy to miss this particular temple. A wise friend told me to be sure to visit Hatshepsut because this first woman pharaoh would have a powerful message for me.

The morning after the others went to Hatshepsut's, I felt shaky but much better. I awakened and left at 6 A.M. with the early group to go to the Temple of Karnak for a sunrise meditation. Karnak, unlike other temples or tombs where work stopped when the pharaoh died, had always been in a perpetual state of construction. From the Middle Kingdom's Eleventh Dynasty (2125–1991 B.C.) to the Seventeenth Dynasty (1650–1550 B.C.) onward, almost every king left some mark of his presence at Karnak.

As everyone settled in to meditate, the guards appeared and shooed us off the temple stones where we sat to await the sun. I wandered back to the altar and stood with my hands outstretched on it. My eyes closed, I felt the sun rise through a small window as it lighted the room and warmed me.

After a long meditation, once again asking that any blocks to higher consciousness be removed, a guard appeared saying, "Hatshepsut? Hatshepsut?" and pointed to the right. I followed him around the corner, under some scaffolding that was in an area closed to the public. A little nervous about following a man I didn't know, who was leading me I knew not where, I was almost ready to turn back and join my group when he pointed into a room with no door. There was Hatshepsut. The actual carving of her on the wall had been hacked at by a frightened priest trying to obliterate it, but her image was still quite clear. She was suspended on a scale, balanced and held by the Sun god Horus on the left and the god Anubis on the right. Horus with the head of a falcon symbolizes the return to divinity. Anubis has the head of a jackal and is the protector and judge of the dead.

I hadn't been able to visit Hatshepsut's temple the day before, so she had come to visit me. A large beetle scarab was carved beneath her. The guard kept placing my hand over it, rubbing it and placing my hand on my third eye, my heart, and my knees. He indicated it brought good health, luck, or whatever I wished to evoke. Two more Egyptians in uniform arrived and each placed my hand on other sacred images carved on the walls. Once again, I was being helped to a message three times.

So what was Hatshepsut's message to me? Later when I quieted myself, I began to gather information. Hatshepsut was being balanced between gods of light and dark. Balance between here/now and there/after. Balance. I pulled a tarot card from the William Blake deck to give me more information. The card was "Woman of Music." Its explanation was, "In balance vibrate in tune with life's energy to become a conduit for creativity and inspiration to others." Balance in all things was my message.

When we returned to Cairo, we spent our last day back at the pyramid complex. The Valley Temple of Chephren is off to the left of the Sphinx. It is believed this temple was used for purification rites. Elaborate rituals were performed on the body of the dead king before he was carried to his actual tomb.

This temple was the perfect place to view and consider the mystery of "how." Thousands of years ago, how were these perfectly carved blocks of limestone weighing over a 100 tons each placed so intricately together that even a piece of paper can't fit between them? The joints of these huge, chiseled blocks were precisely cut in a curious jigsaw pattern. How? How were they moved to the site? Lifted into place? No one has arrived at an irrefutable answer.

While I found those questions fascinating, I kept wondering why I really didn't care that there were no answers. Our guide, John Anthony West, had dedicated many years of his life to dating the Sphinx and trying to discover the secret to her mysteries. Famous historian Graham Hancock, who was also to have been on our trip, spent even more years uncovering the "truth" about this history. To me it all seemed inconsequential.

My curiosity was directed to what I kept feeling was my own participation in building the ancient temples, Pyramids, and the Sphinx. No, I wasn't doing some past-life regression thing. It was more along the lines that if we truly are all one, which is the message I keep getting, then we can connect into this ancient wisdom. We already have all the answers. We need only to open the connection. The radio waves are there. We only need to turn the radio on and tune it in.

In this ancient temple, I once again placed my forehead, or "third eye," and hands on one of the massive stone block columns to "feel" the vibrational energy from the structure. I felt a surge and instantly experienced a vision. I saw the temple enclosed with a roof made of the same huge stone slabs only a foot and a half thick. I was viewing the room in which I was standing. It was bustling with activity and was steaming hot from the heat of huge pots of oil bubbling over fires and the many oil lamps hanging off the walls. I saw many priests and men, going quietly and reverently about their work. They were dressed in white Egyptian costumes and preparing bodies for mummification. Some overseers were adorned in gold head-dresses and large gold necklace collars. Various parts of the bodies to be mummified were being drenched in different oils, to dehydrate fluids from them. The place had an acrid smell. I heard the words "grape seed oil."

The final night of our tour, we went to the Great Pyramid for a group meditation. As we toned, each of us had an opportunity to climb into the sarcophagus. While being allowed to climb into the sarcophagus was interesting, I felt nothing. However, when the guards turned off all the lights in the Pyramid for our group meditation in the King's Chamber, I was amazed how light the dark was. The entrance to this chamber from the outside is down one long small corridor and up another long one. It was night outside. No light could possibly bleed in. This was possibly the darkest dark one could experience. Yet, I saw light. I wondered if I was picking up other people's auras.

I could have easily stayed on after the others left, hidden from the guards, and spent the night alone in the Great Pyramid and explored this phenomenon. Yet, I felt no need to do so. My body, still recuperating from the latest bout of "mummy's tummy," was screaming at me to go home, heal, process, and grow. A peacefulness of knowing my inner self was beginning its ascent upon me. Fear was being replaced with trust. And ego was beginning to be set aside for heart.

I was called to Egypt, Muslims are called to Mecca, the Hindus to Ganges, the Jews and Christians to Jerusalem, and the Catholics to Rome. The pilgrimage traveler learns an ancient secret. Take sacred space, add pure intention, and connect to extraordinary healing energies and age-old wisdom.

20

IS THERE A GOD? *Connecting to Source*

I am six years old. I'm short because I'm a child. I have medium-length semi-curly blond hair. It's curly because Mom rolls it up in spoolies every night. I'm dressed in my favorite out-fit: cowgirl boots, jeans, and short-sleeve shirt, with my cowgirl hat hanging down my back. My little friends and I have just spent the morning playing in the mounds of dirt in the field across the road from my house in Kodiak. Tuckered out from our rousing games of tag and hide-and-seek, we all flop down on the grass to catch our breath. Lying on our backs, we gaze up at the bright blue sky and the immense fluffy white cumulus clouds from which my friends start picking out shapes of animals. Trying as hard as I can to see a bunny, a dog, or a bird, I'm embarrassed because I see nothing.

Just as I'm straining my brain one more time to turn a cloud into an animate object, my perspective shifts and I look beyond what my eyes can see, past the clouds, past the sky, to all that is.

The enormity of it scares me.

At that moment I know there is way more to life than I can see, and I'm afraid.

Four years later when I was stomping around in the woods, looked up and had my God smiling down on me experience, I wasn't afraid. By then I'd forgotten all about my fear during my "all that is" experience. The God who was looking down on me seemed quite wonderful and someone I would have liked to get to know. However, when my parents didn't acknowledge this amazing occurrence and even shushed and shooed me away, I decided this seeing God thing was not going to improve my status around the house and forgot about it, too.

It took me 40-some years to fill these original experiences with knowledge about the truth. The truth of who I am and the truth about all that is.

In 1993, during my initiation into heart-center at the first conference I attended on consciousness, I had a vision that combined both of these childhood experiences and unfolded yet another part of the mystery.

The large, round conference room was set up with four waist-high platforms draped with warm, comfortable afghans. Any objects we, the four initiates, wanted to bring were lovingly placed around our area. Someone brought a small Buddha; I, the cross necklace I wear; another person, a picture of her son.

The rest of the conferees were sitting around the room in the large circle we normally sat in for our sessions. Soft music, Bach or Mozart, filled the air as the four of us entered dressed in white for ritual. We proceeded to our platforms that were set up in the four directions. Mine was to the west, which represents ancestors and reflection. As we lay down, the conference teacher and an assistant stood at the head of two of us. Dividing into two groups, everyone else joined them in a circle around us. Each person put one hand softly on our bodies, sending unconditional love and healing energies.

In a resonant voice that seemed to be speaking new words for the first time, the conference teacher led us through a beautiful ritual into heart-center. His powerful words took us to a sacred temple, which I envisioned as the Acropolis in Greece. There I saw our four platforms. When he spoke of a cave and a bubbling artesian well, I saw my white gown drop away as I walked through the sand into the warm water. It was as if I had a baptism that I, alone, gave to myself. Renewed and refreshed, I saw my white garment float back around me as I stepped from the water and left the cave, once again in love with the mystery. Coming back to the present, I could feel the radiant energy of people's hands upon me. It filled me with a love and gratitude for my fellow man that seemed to spill over into the room, filling it with contentment.

As the ritual drew to a close, I was lovingly covered with an afghan and left alone with my meditative blissful feelings. When I heard the teacher beginning the two others' ritual with the same new words, my mind began to drift. As my euphoric feelings waned because they were too much to maintain, I almost laughed at my irreverent thoughts. I found myself contemplating the effect the energy my healing hands might have on a certain part of my friend Bill's anatomy at his initiation.

And then, just as quickly, my attention was again diverted.

Behind my closed eyes, I was being shown a big arch filled with sky blue light. Immediately a face on a card the size of a poster appeared in front of it. My mind became riveted. The face started changing and two faces on large poster cards appeared side by side. My thought about the first face was, "Oh, my God, it's God." I wanted to go back for another look, but the faces began changing too fast. It was like two sets of flash cards flashing so rapidly that it was hard to catch the faces, all set against the background of the big blue arch. Wise men, all ethnicities, Gandhi, Buddha, Muhammed, Allah, Indian gurus, Mother Teresa, holy men, Jesus; all fast, beautiful, handsome, radiant faces flashing before me. Some I could name. Others I recognized but couldn't name, and some I'd never seen, but knew that they, too, were higher evolved human beings.

When this ended, I lay in awe for many minutes, then sat up and, without speaking, immediately wrote it all in my journal. I had never spoken of it until this moment.

Now nine years later, my life has filled this experience with enough knowledge and truth so I understand what I was shown.

The sky blue light was the same beautiful bright blue sky I looked into as a child when I saw the enormity of all that is.

Next I was shown one being, as I had in my childhood—my version of God.

The new information followed immediately, showing there was little or no delineation between the God I'd seen and the hundreds of faces of evolved holy men and women.

Buddha, Allah, and Muhammad.
Brahma, Vishnu, Shiva, and Shakti.
Krishna and Jesus.
On and on, on and on.

This was the culmination of my 40-year puzzle.
I'd been shown the order of the universe.
From all that is,
To my version of God,
To all who have walked the Earth living their godlike energy.

Where do we fit in?

After a few months of trying to figure it out with my logical left brain, I decided to bypass it and meditate for the answer.

Arriving at my inner teacher, I asked, *Okay, a while ago when I was automatic writing I was told we (mankind) were gathering more knowledge for the Big Bang. What is the Big Bang?*

Inner teacher: *The Big Bang is where all consciousnesses collide—physical, emotional, mental, and spiritual.*

Patricia: *And how will that happen?*

Inner teacher: *Without too much fanfare, you are getting ready for it now. It will affect most peoples. The ones it does not affect will pass on, just as you've seen happen already. Those are people who die because they can't face being conscious about the who, what, where, when, and how in their lives.*

Patricia: *I do understand that. I've seen a young healthy man die of a heart attack because he couldn't change his relationship to money—so his wife's spending killed him. Do you mean the Big Bang will be when our godlike consciousness and awareness become the dominant reality in our makeup or being?*

Inner Teacher: *Yes.*

Patricia: *So, what you are saying is that the Big Bang will be internal and individual?*

Inner Teacher: *Always.*

Patricia: *And what about all the big bangs we've been having around the world? The wars, the Twin Towers, the mayhem?*

Inner Teacher: *They are pushing you to make the change. You saw it in New York after the collapse of the World Trade Center. People were living their spirit/godlike self first and foremost. Once everyone brings these traits to the forefront—compassion, innate harmony, healing presence, and unconditional love—on a forever, daily basis without having to point a finger at a "bad guy," all else will change.*

Patricia: *When with this all happen?*

Inner Teacher: *It's happening now, its been building for 2,000 years. The physical, mental, and emotional, and the ego have to get to the point where there is nothing else to do but surrender to spirit. Once you (mankind) surrender to your spiritual side, everything will change. You will be living your godlike self as much as humanly possible, continuing to enjoy all the sensate, taste, sight, smell, and tactile gifts your wonderful lush wet human bodies brings to this spiritual, emotional, mental, and physical experiment.*

It all comes back to love, yourself and one another, because

we are all one.

As you, my reader, and I say good-bye, I'd like for you to imagine we are standing in front of one another.

We do not say good-bye by shaking hands or kissing cheeks.

Instead, we stand with our hands in prayer position in front of our hearts, look deeply into each other's eyes, bow our heads and shoulders, and softly say, "Namaste."

In that departing gesture we are quietly saying in our small inner voice,

I see the Deity in both of us, and bow before him or her.
I acknowledge the holiness of even this mundane meeting
For I cannot separate that which is spiritual in us from
That which is human and ordinary.

Namaste

APPENDIX

Meditations

The following are three meditations I mention in the book. The first is the Heart-center Meditation, which I consider the cornerstone of this work.

Second is what I call the Spirit Meditation that can take you back to Source and Spirit and introduce you to the aspect of yourself that can be a dispassionate but loving observer or witness.

And the third is what I call my Smorgasbord Meditation, where you can decide when to pause, whether it be in the place you feel most safe, or perhaps in the purple flame of transmutation, or by staying to comfort your own inner child.

Find a comfortable, quiet place, and sit in any position you like. If you lie down, you might fall asleep, so sitting is preferable. You may read these meditations into a tape recorder so you could listen to them. For now, you can prop the book on a table, so you can gently open and close your eyes and read along while meditating.

Please know that whatever way this is done and whatever comes up for you is "right." Guided meditations are just that, guides. There is no right or wrong way to experience meditation. A sincere intention is more important than how one physically goes about the process. Ask for whatever is needed for your highest and greatest good and prepare to have it happen.

Heart-center Meditation[1]

Starting where all human life begins—with the breath.

Breathe in through the nose deeply and slowly to the count of four.

Hold for four.

Slowly, with the tip of your tongue gently touching the roof of your mouth behind the front teeth, exhale out the mouth for four.

And hold for four.

In through the nose, one, two, three, four.
Hold, one, two, three, four.
Out through the mouth, one, two, three, four.
Hold, one, two, three, four.

Once again, in through the nose, one, two, three, four
Hold, one, two, three, four.
Out through the mouth, one, two, three, four.
Hold, one, two, three, four.

Going to a place of inner calm, gently and tenderly, place your right hand over your heart-center (in the middle of your chest) and your left hand over your right, thumbs touching at the top. Touch your heart-center with the same energy and awareness you would give when compassionately comforting a child or someone who needs love. With eyes closed, breathe in deeply through the heart. Feel the flow of energy and warmth coming from your hands to your heart and your heart to your hands. You might at this point feel your hands becoming energized. Envision someone or something that brings you great joy or happiness. Bring the warm feelings your image evokes into your heart.

Now with your focus concentrated on your heart area, begin opening to the four main attributes of the heart-center:

---

[1]Based upon a heart-center meditation by W. Brugh Joy.

Compassion
Innate harmony
Healing presence, and
Unconditional love.

Imagine *compassion* pouring into your heart from a Higher Source. Let the feelings of compassion embrace you. Sense it swirling down from the universe. Feel the wonderment of being touched by something that brings you into a larger consciousness. Compassion from a higher source to you—from you to yourself—and then from yourself to others. Feel arms with which you'd envelop someone who needs comforting now enveloping and comforting you. Experience your heart filling with soothing compassion and giving you peace.

Deeply, breathe in compassion. . . .

Now sense *innate harmony* flowing into your heart from the universe. Peace beyond all understanding, the calm in the midst of chaos, the center of a spinning wheel. It is innate harmony that makes the heart lighter than the feather. That in which we, through its force, may explore any range including the deepest and most profound mysteries of life. This is the same harmonious emotion felt when listening to a great piece of music at the moment the heavens and Earth and all people come together as one. Know this innate harmony is your birthright and feel it sending balance and calm throughout your body.

Deeply, breathe in innate harmony. . . .

Feel the *healing presence* of your Higher Self swirling around you, entering your body through your heart, restoring, renewing, and regenerating to make whole. Graced by healing presence, feel it in full, and open to it, for it is the force that the healer utilizes. See it flooding your heart, sending well-being and wholeness to every cell, every thought, every breath you take. Purifying, vivifying. The same healing presence you give when stroking a cool hand over a loved one's feverish brow, feel now for yourself.

276

Deeply, breathe in healing presence. . . .

Open your heart to the *unconditional love* of your Higher Power. Without strings or conditions—let this most profound mystery of the heart-center flood your being with ecstasy. Unconditional love causes us to fall in love with the mystery itself. It unites all things in wonderment. Feel now the same rush and welling up of your heart as when you come upon your first panoramic view of an ocean, the inside of a great cathedral, or the simple view of a patient child tentatively offering unconditional love to a new pet. Become the up-surging feeling that fills your heart, making you a part of a larger and grander consciousness.

Deeply, breathe in unconditional love. . . .

See, feel, and *be* compassion, innate harmony, healing presence, and unconditional love from the universe. When united, these are the experiences that bring forth heart-centeredness. As you feel these words filling your heart, sense these feelings overflow from your heart into your body. Sense them replenishing your body until it, too, overflows, wrapping you in the white, protective light of compassion, innate harmony, healing presence, and unconditional love from Source. Be it. Feel it. See it.

Sit with these feelings, breathe them in . . .

And when you are ready, envision yourself coming back to your body. Move your fingers and toes and slowly open your eyes. . . .

Spirit Meditation: Observer or Witness[2]

First sit comfortably with arms and legs uncrossed, unless you prefer the lotus position. Spine straight creating a line from the earth through you to the universe.

Lower your eyelids and breathe in deeply through your nose to the count of four.
Let out all the air through your mouth to the count of four.
Again, in through your nose for four and
out your mouth for four.
Once again in for four and
out for four.

Now visualize breathing in through your third-eye chakra (middle of forehead)
And out through your solar plexus (right below rib cage),
In for four through your third eye and
out for four through your solar plexus.
Once more in for four, and
out for four.

Now breathe in higher, through your crown chakra (at the top of your head) for four,
and out through kundalini chakra at the bottom of your spine for four.
In through the crown for four,
out through the base of your spine for four.
In for four, and
out for four.

Now take your breath even higher this time—in from the heavens for four,
and out to the center of the Earth for four.
Universal energy in from the heavens for four,
and out for four, grounding you firmly to the center of the Earth.

---

[2]Based on a meditation by Bernard Gunther

278

One last time, in for four, and
out for four.

Allow your breath to return to normal as you mentally scan
your physical body.
From your head to your toes.
Notice any sensations.
Don't dwell, quickly check letting your mind's eye travel
down,
head, neck, shoulders, arms, hands, chest, waist, hips, thighs,
calves, feet
Just observe.
And now—
Let it go—
You are not your physical body.

Now visualize your mental body,
If you need to visualize a container for it,
visualize a room or box and look inside.
Notice any colors, sensations, thoughts.
Now, let it all go—
You are not your mental body.

Next visualize your emotional body,
Again, if you need a container
visualize a room or a box and look inside.
Notice any colors, sensations, and feelings.
See whatever is there, be with it a moment,
and then let it all go—
You are not your emotional body, either.

Be in this place for a moment.
Think of a word that would describe what you feel now that
you have let go of your physical, mental, and emotional bodies.
Freedom?
Comfort?
Peace?

Love?
Nothing?

Whatever the word is, just be it for a moment and know this is who you truly are.

This is who you were before your body, your mind, your emotions, and who you will always be. Welcome to the real you. You as essence. You as spirit. You as authentic self. You as soul. You as your godlike self.

This you is always available. You can come here in this simple way any time you want to remember.

Now, from this place visualize yourself going even further.
Go up, out, and back and connect with the universe.
Stay there for a while in universal energy.
Light, free, patient, loving.
Drift around getting acquainted, once again, with *All That Is.*
Enjoy the comfort of being cradled in the lap of the universe.
Rest here as your true self.

Do you have questions only the universe can answer? Ask them now.
Be open to hear, see, or feel the answers.
Pause for as long as you like. . . .

Then,
when you are ready,
bring your spirit back into your body,
wiggle your fingers and toes,
and open your eyes.
Welcome back.

A Meditation of a Heterogeneous Mixture Consisting of Dissimilar or Diverse Ingredients (or My Smorgasbord Meditation)[3]

Have a pad of paper and pen with you in case you want to take notes during this meditation that you can work with later.

Do three-part breathing by breathing into your lower stomach, then up to your solar plexus, and last fill your chest. As you breathe out, feel your stomach contract as you push out all the air.

Again, into your lower stomach, your solar plexus, and your chest. Breathe out.

Last time, in your lower stomach, fill your solar plexus and your chest, and release.

I want you to go to the place you feel most safe. Wherever it is, a garden, your grandmother's house, go there and experience how safe and secure you feel.

When you are filled with a sense of peace, leave on a path that leads to the right. Follow the path through a lovely woods with light shining down through the tall trees. See and hear the birds calling one another and bees buzzing. Feel well-being.

You see an inviting, warm house. Go inside. Notice there are doors that lead out of the large round room you entered. Behind each door are rooms with different aspects of yourself.

In one room you can meet your masculine consciousness.

In another your feminine consciousness.

In an additional room your wise man or wise woman awaits.

Behind another is your spiritual warrior.

And, in one is your child within.

Choose whichever door you wish, open it, and see who is there to greet you, knowing this is the aspect you need to meet and address now.

When you open the door, introduce yourself to the consciousness that resides there. Look at them, and if you like, stop for a moment and write down what they look like, act like, and

---

[3]Based upon many, many different meditations by Barbara Biziou.

sound like. Ask questions, what do they need from you? What do you need from them? Write down the answers to work with later.

When you are satisfied, say good-bye and tell them you'll be back.

With the child within, as with all children, tell him or her when you'll be back and don't forget to follow through.

Leave the building and continue on the path. As the path turns, it begins a gentle ascent up a slight hill. You look up to see a beautiful temple at the top. As you climb the seven stairs, feel yourself going deeper into meditation with each step.

One, Two, deeper.

Three, Four, deeper still.

Five, Six, Seven, relaxed and deep into meditation.

As you reach the top, turn and look out at the view, say good-bye to whatever doesn't serve you.

Turn back and take a moment to gaze at the massive doors that lead into the temple. If you wish, write down what you see. This is the threshold to being all you want to be.

When you are ready, enter the temple.

The room you've entered is filled with riches, jewels, gold, silks. In the center what you see transfixes you. There, burning bright, is the purple flame of transformation. In this flame, anything in your life you wish to transform will happen. Walk into the cool, refreshing purple flame and feel everything that is not necessary for your highest and greatest good floating off you. Feel your clothes, resistance, and all that doesn't serve you slip away.

Now fill yourself with the potential of what can be.

Pause, visualizing the new you.

When you are ready, leave this miraculous flame. You have a choice between a robe of gossamer white soft linen or a kimono of dark rich silks that magically wraps around you.

You turn and see a beautiful bed in a jeweled-studded room. As you lie on the large four-poster bed, covered with multicolored silks, satins, and soft down pillows, shafts of rainbow light pour in on you from the universe above. Blues, yellows, reds, oranges, pinks, purples, and greens stream down, gently caressing your body as their light revivifies and rejuvenates every cell of your body, filling it with the glory of unconditional love and innate healing. Rainbow healing energy.

Stay as long as you need.

When you are satiated, leave the bed, replace your clothes, and go out through the temple doors. Leave a gift of gratitude in whatever way you wish.

As you walk down the stairs and the path, come back to yourself.

When you are ready, wiggle your fingers and toes and open your eyes.

There are many meditations within this meditation. Next time, you might want to pause and do a whole meditation on one of the aspects of your consciousness. Another time, you might just stay with the purple flame or in the healing rainbow light. Before you go into the meditation, ask what you need to do for your highest and greatest good.

About the Author

In her forties and fifties Patricia Heller briefly studied voice at Julliard and writing at Yale. She feels her most valuable education, though, came from being forced by an incurable illness into studying psychic energy and spiritual healing. Heller, now gloriously healthy, lives her passion and purpose, helping everyone she meets the way she's helped herself—opening their eyes to resources considered by many to be mystical and magical. While Heller still has a home in The Land of Enchantment, New Mexico, she spends most of her time in New York, the Land of Reality. She is working on a novel, *Rise From Generation Free*, that explores how secrecy surrounding the scandalous murder of her grandfather affected future generations. Another book, *The Procrastinator's Guide to Writing a Book*, may be out first.

Hampton Roads Publishing Company

... for the evolving human spirit

Hampton Roads Publishing Company
publishes books on a variety of subjects,
including metaphysics, health,
visionary fiction, and other related topics.

For a copy of our latest catalog, call toll-free
(800) 766-8009, or send your name and address to:

Hampton Roads Publishing Company, Inc.
1125 Stoney Ridge Road
Charlottesville, VA 22902

e-mail: hrpc@hrpub.com
www.hrpub.com